ISBN 978-1-331-69548-6
PIBN 10222627

THE MAQÁMÁT OF BADÍ' AL-ZAMÁN AL-HAMADHÁNÍ

THE

MAQÁMÁT OF BADÍ' AL-ZAMÁN AL-HAMADHÁNÍ

TRANSLATED FROM THE ARABIC

WITH AN INTRODUCTION

AND

NOTES

HISTORICAL AND GRAMMATICAL

BY

W. J. PRENDERGAST, B.LITT. (OXON.)

DEGREE OF HONOUR ARABIC AND PERSIAN; M.R.A.S.; FELLOW OF THE UNIVERSITY OF MADRAS; DIRECTOR OF ORIENTAL LANGUAGES, NIZAM COLLEGE, HYDERABAD, DECCAN

LONDON: LUZAC & Co.
MADRAS: S. P. C. K. DEPOSITORY
1915

PRINTED AT THE
S. P. C. K. PRESS, VEPERY, MADRAS
1915

TO

HIS HIGHNESS

ASAF JAH MUZAFFAR-UL-MÚLK WAL MUMÁLIK,

NIZÁM-ÚL-MÚLK, NIZÁM-ÚD-DAULA NAWAB MIR

SIR OSMAN ALI KHAN, BAHADUR, FATEḤ JUNG, G.C.S.I.,

NIZAM OF HYDERABAD

THE TRANSLATOR DEDICATES WITH PROFOUND RESPECT AND DEEP GRATITUDE THIS WORK WHICH OWES ITS INCEPTION AND COMPLETION TO THE GENEROUS ENCOURAGEMENT AND GRACIOUS APPRECIATION OF ORIENTAL STUDIES ALWAYS SHOWN BY HIS HIGHNESS AND HIS HIGHNESS' GOVERNMENT

نْ تَرَ مَا يَشِينُ فَوَارِهِ * كَرَمًا وَإِنْ تَرَ مَا يَزِينُ فَأَفْشِهِ

(Harírí)

PREFACE

THIS Translation of the Maqámát of Badi' al-Zamán al-Hamadhání from the original Arabic with an Introduction and Notes was prepared as my thesis for the Research Degree of Bachelor of Letters, Oxford University, during the years 1913–14, and I now publish it as it was then written.

The original being largely in rhymed prose to which sense is sometimes subordinated to sound, there will necessarily be much in the rendering that will appear insipid and uninteresting to the English reader unacquainted with Arabic; but, as the Maqámát gave the first impulse to a species of composition which has for centuries been regarded as an important branch of *belles lettres*, it is hoped that this first translation of the work into English will be favourably received by Arabic scholars and that students will find it an aid to the understanding of this famous classic.

In the Notes I refer to the following by the names of their respective authors:—

Ibn Khallikan's *Biographical Dictionary* (London, 1841).

Ibn Khaldún's *Prolegomena* (Paris, 1878). Translated by M. G. de Slane.

Nicholson's *Literary History of the Arabs* (London, 1907).

For typographical reasons 'q' instead of 'ḳ' has been used throughout to represent the Arabic ق in transliteration.

My respectful thanks are due to His Highness the Nizam, G.C.S.I., for graciously permitting me to dedicate the book to him. My acknowledgements are also due to His Highness' Government and the Madras School Book and Literary Society for generous grants towards the cost of publication. I also desire to acknowledge my indebtedness to the Rev. Canon E. Sell, D.D., for much valuable advice and help in regard to the arrangement of the Notes and to the Rev. J. Passmore for kindly assisting me in seeing the work through the press.

W. J. P.

September, 1915

ERRATA

Page	13,	note	4,	*for*	Lyden	*read*	Leyden.
,,	14,	line	15	,,	الكَدْيَةُ	,	الكُدْيَةُ.
,,	26,	note	2	,,	ḥamúthá	,,	hánúthá.
,,	30	,,	5	,,	illusion	,,	allusion.
,,	33	,,	4	,,	الرِّفَدِينِ	,,	الرَّافَدِينِ.
,,	47	,,	2	,,	reported	,,	retorted.
,,	,,	,,	3	,,	satire	,,	satirize.
,,	48,	line	9	,,	of	,,	off.
,,	51	,,	19	,,	دَلِيَةٌ		دَنِيَةٌ.
,,	52,	note	1	,,	illusion	,,	allusion.
,,	82,	line	7	,,	course	,,	coarse.
,,	90,	note	2	,,	الجِرقَةُ		الخِرقَةُ.
,,	131,	line	14	,,	chose	,,	choose.
,,	137,	note	2	,,	dates	,,	figs.

CONTENTS

The Maqámát of Badí‘ al-Zamán al-Hamadhání

INTRODUCTION

I. LIFE OF THE AUTHOR

THE Ḥáfiz Aḥmad ibn al-Ḥusain ibn Yaḥya ibn Ṣa‘id ibn Bashar Abú’l-Faḍl al-Hamadhání, surnamed Badí‘ al-Zamán (the Wonder of the Age), was born at Hamadhán on the 13th of Jumádí al-Ákhir A.H. 358 (A.D. 967) and, therefore, like many other eminent Arabic writers, lived far from Arabia and may have even been of Persian origin.[1] He himself claimed to be descended from the tribes of Taghlib and Muḍar.[2]

Unlike Ḥariri, his great imitator, he had not the advantage of being born and bred in the atmosphere and amid the inspiring associations of a great seat of learning, and he himself appears to have shared the popular opinion as to the stupidity and churlishness of the people of Hamadhán.

He is said to have satirized his native place in the well-known lines :—

هَمَذَانُ لِي بَلَدٌ أَقُولُ بِفَضْلِهِ * لَكِنَّهُ مِنْ أَقْبَحِ الْبُلْدَانِ[3]

صِبْيَانُهُ فِي الْقُبْحِ مِثْلُ شُيُوخِهِ * وَشُيُوخُهُ فِي الْعَقْلِ كَالصِّبْيَانِ

Hamadhán is my native town, I must allow it that honour, but it is the vilest of cities.

In ugliness its children are like its old men, and, in reason, its old men are like its children.

[1] See Letters of the author, p. 47, line 1.

[2] Ibid., pp. 8 and 9.

[3] Abú’l-‘Alá Muḥammad ibn Ḥusul, a native of Hamadhán, is the reputed author of these lines.

On page 419 of the Letters he quotes the verse of another poet :—

لَا تَلُمْنِي عَلَى رَكَاكَةِ عَقْلِي * ان تَيَقَّنْتَ أَنَّنِي هَمَذَانِي

Thou wilt not blame me for the weakness of my intellect,
If thou art assured I am a man of Hamadhán.

Ibn Fáris, Hamadhání's instructor, ironically hints that the ignorance of the people of Hamadhán was contagious. ‘Why should I not’, says he, ‘offer a sincere prayer for that city where I had the good fortune of forgetting all I ever learned?’[1] In spite of the uninspiring character of his immediate surroundings, ‘Aufi tells us he gave, at a very early age, evidence of those great gifts which eventually made him famous.

That great patron of letters, the Sáḥib ibn ‘Abbád, the famous Buwayhid minister, tested his skill in *ex tempore* translation at the age of twelve by giving the young scholar Persian verse to render into metrical Arabic, a feat which he accomplished on the spot, the Ṣáḥib himself, at the instance of the youthful poet, suggesting the metre and the rhyme.[2]

It must, however, be borne in mind that he had the good fortune of sitting at the feet of learned men like Abú'l-Husain ibn Fáris (ob. A.H. 390), the philologist and author of the *Mujmil fi'l-Lughát*, or *Collection of Philological Observations*[3] and ‘Ísá ibn Hishám the traditionalist. It is not improbable that in the latter we have the original of the name of the Ráwi or narrator of the Maqámát. The relater of tradition might by an easy transition become the narrator of the story or adventure. Each maqáma begins with حَدَّثَنَا which, being literally rendered, signifies ‘he related news, or traditions to us’. It should also be remembered that, notwithstanding internal dissensions, internecine strife and the frequent wars with the Greeks, he lived in an age of great intellectual activity. The literary renaissance, which began in the reign of Saif al-Daula,[4] was still making itself felt.

Mutanabbí, considered by his countrymen to be the greatest of Islámic poets, had just completed his great work. Two years before Hamadhání was born Abú ‘Ali al-Qáli had finished in Cordova his excellent work on philology, the *Book of Dictations*,

[1] Ibn Khallikan, De Slane's Translation, i, 101.
[2] *Lubáb al-Albáb*, p. 17.
[3] Ibn Khallikan, De Slane's Translation, i, 101.
[4] See *Yatíma*, i, 9.

and Abú'l-Faraj al-Isfaháni had completed one of the most important and useful works in the Arabic language, that rich mine of poetry, history, antiquities and legend, the *Kitáb al-Aghání*, on which he had spent fifty years of his life. In A.H. 360, or two years after the birth of the author, the Brethren of Purity were endeavouring by means of their teachings, set forth in fifty treatises, to reconcile science and religion and to harmonize the law of Islám with the philosophy of the Greeks.

Among other prominent men of his day were Abú Firás, the famous poet prince, regarding whom the Ṣáḥib used to say, 'Poetry began with a prince—Imr al-Qais—and ended with one—Abú'l-Firás.'[1] There were also Abú'l-Alá al-Ma'ari, the poet, philosopher and free-thinker; al-Babbghá, the poet and Ibn Nubáta, the fiery preacher. To be called the Wonder of such an age was indeed a proud distinction. And here one is led to enquire as to what were the system of education and the method of study that could produce such a prodigy.

In Hamadhání's time, education, in addition to the study of the Qur'án and the commentaries thereon, consisted of the study of Traditions of the Prophet, jurisprudence, legendary lore concerning the pagan times of the Arabs, their days or battles, *ex tempore* recitations, philosophy, philology, poetics, grammar, the art of writing ornate prose, and travel.[2]

In his reflections on knowledge, the course to be pursued in the acquisition thereof and the essential qualifications of the seeker after knowledge, the author gives us an insight into his own methods of study. These comprised self-denial, dogged perseverance, much reading, patient investigation and deep meditation joined to extensive travel. He makes it clear that he knew of no royal road to learning and that he had learned 'to scorn delights and live laborious days'.[3] In the Maqámát he shows how thorough had been his education and how deeply he was imbued with the culture of his age.

In the year A.H. 380 at the age of twenty-two he left his little-loved native place and proceeded to the court of the Ṣáḥib. There is no evidence as to the precise duration of his stay there, but, in the society of the litterati that had gathered round the

[1] Ibn Khallikan, De Slane's Translation, i, 366.
[2] See De Slane's Introduction to Ibn Khallikan, pp. xxxi and xxxii.
[3] Text, pp. 202-4 and Letters, pp. 165-8.

great Wazir and with, doubtless, free access to a library so vast that the Ṣáḥib is reported to have said that it would require 400 camels to transport it,[1] it must have been for the young aspirant to literary fame a period rich in opportunity and experience. A breach of good manners on his part in the presence of the Wazir is said to have brought his sojourn at Arraján to an abrupt termination. Thence he journeyed to Jurján where, according to Tha'álibí (A.H. 350–429) he frequented the society of the Ismá'ili heretics, from whom he acquired a great deal of knowledge and received much enlightenment.[2] In A.H. 382 (A.D. 992–3) at the age of twenty-four he reached Nishapur where he composed the work upon which his fame rests, the Maqámát. On his way to this city he appears to have fallen among thieves who robbed him and stripped him of everything he possessed.[3]

If we accept the dates given by Tha'álibí in the *Yatíma*,[4] of Hamadhání's arrival at Nishapur (A.H. 382) and [5] of al-Khwárazmí's death (A.H. 383), the Maqámát were the work of a very young man, completed within the short space of two years. If such was the case there must have been a great deal of scholarly preparation during the author's stay at the court of the Ṣáḥib and his sojourn among the Ismá'ili heretics at Jurján. The evidence in favour of this view is supplied by Hamadhání himself. In replying to al-Khwárazmí's criticism of his work he tauntingly remarks that, while he had dictated four hundred maqámát, his detractor was unable to compose a tenth part of one.[6]

There is, however, reason to suppose that the work was begun before the author left his native city. For example, the scene of the maqáma of Maḍirah is laid in Baṣra while the concluding appeal is made to an audience in Hamadhán.[7] The inference is, therefore, that the Maqámát were begun in Hamadhán and completed in Nishapur, probably some time after the death of al-Khwárazmí in A.H. 383.

While in this city a great literary duel took place between Hamadhání and Abú Bakr al-Khwárazmí (A.H. 323–83), a nephew of Ṭabari, the well-known historian. Al-Khwárazmí was a poet of the first rank, a master of the art of official writing,

[1] Ibn Khallikan, De Slane's Translation, i, 215.
[2] *Yatíma*, iv, 168.
[3] Letters, pp. 104–5.
[4] *Yatíma*, iv, 168.
[5] Letters, pp. 104–5.
[6] Ibid., p. 390.
[7] Text, pp. 110–15.

a renowned authority on philology and genealogy and noted for his sententious sayings. In addition to all this he was endowed with a marvellous memory.

It is related of him that having gone to see the Ṣáḥib ibn 'Abbád, who was then holding court at Arraján, he requested a chamberlain to announce to him that a literary man desired permission to see him, and his master replied: 'Tell him I have bound myself not to receive any literary man, unless he know by heart twenty thousand verses composed by Arabs of the desert'. The chamberlain returned with the answer, and Abú Bakr said: 'Go back and ask him if he means twenty thousand composed by men or twenty thousand composed by women?' This question was repeated and the Ṣáhib exclaimed: 'That must be Abú Bakr al-Khwárazmí: let him come in!'[1] Such was the intellectual giant, now about sixty years of age, whom the youthful scholar of twenty-five essayed to challenge to literary combat.

Hamadhání opened the discussion. Addressing al-Khwárazmí he said: 'We have cited thee in order that thou mayest fill this assembly[2] with benefits and quote unfamiliar verses and rare proverbs. We will discuss with thee and profit by that which thou hast, and do thou question us that thou mayest benefit by what we have. Now we will begin with the arts of which thou art master and which have made thee famous. They are memory, if thou wilt, poetry, if thou desirest, prose, if thou choosest, or improvisation, if thou please, for these are the subjects of the boast with which thou dost fill thy mouth.'[3] Al-Khwárazmí chose improvisation and the result was his complete discomfiture.[4]

We are afraid the decision in favour of the author was not altogether free from bias. Al-Khwárazmí was supported by his students while the leading men of Nishapur, who had a grudge against him, sided with Hamadhání.[5] The verdict must have been a foregone conclusion.

Hamadhání does not appear, however, to have cherished any

[1] Ibn Khallikan, De Slane's Translation, iii, 108. *Yatima*, iv, 114.

[2] The author uses the word *Majlis* (مَجْلِس). Letters, p. 41, line 5.

[3] Ibid., pp. 41-2.

[4] Letters, pp. 80 and 83 and Yakút's *Dictionary of Learned Men*, i, 101.

[5] *Yatima*, iv, 137.

ill-will against his vanquished rival. In his reply to some one, who subsequently was uncharitable enough to write and felicitate him upon al-Khwárazmí's illness, he administered a sharp rebuke to the writer and told him that in the time of trouble all resentment disappears, that he entertained the deepest affection for the great scholar and sincerely prayed for his recovery.[1]

As no one had imagined there was a scholar who, under any circumstances, had the temerity to enter the lists with al-Khwárazmí, Hamadhání's success in vanquishing the great man caused his fame to spread far and wide and secured him the patronage of the great and the powerful. In the course of his subsequent travels there was not a prince, governor or chief whose bounty he did not enjoy, and whose largess he did not receive.[2]

On the death of al-Khwárazmí in A.H. 383 (according to Ibn al-Athír in A.H. 393) Hamadhání found himself without a rival. How long he remained at Nishapur is not known, but writing to Shaikh Abú 'Ali for a letter to the Amir he complains that his sojourn there had been long, that he was suffering from insomnia and, if there should be any delay in sending the letter, he would be obliged to leave without it.[3] After leaving this city he visited every important town in Khurásán, Sijistán (Seistan) and the kingdom of Ghazna, probably reciting his maqámát to admiring audiences wherever he went. He finally settled in Herat[4] where he greatly improved his position and circumstances by marrying the daughter of a rich man named Abú 'Ali Husain al-Khushnámí. By this marriage he had an only daughter to whom he refers in the most affectionate terms. He writes: 'I am as devoted to her as a father to an only son and I would not exchange her for ten sons.'[5]

He appears to have carried on an extensive correspondence with a large number of distinguished personages, the chief among whom were: Shaikh Abú 'Abbás, first minister of Sulṭán Maḥmúd of Ghazna, Adnán ibn Muhammad, the governor of

[1] Letters, p. 187.

[2] *Yatima*, iv, 169. The only one deemed worthy of praise in the Maqámát was Khalaf ibn Aḥmad, the Amir of Sijistán.

[3] Letters, p. 189.

[4] See Letters, p. 337 for the motives which prompted him to settle there.

[5] Letters, p. 398.

Herat, Abú Ja'far al-Míkálí, Muhammad ibn Zuheir, the governor of Balkh, the Wazir of Rayy and others.

Proficiency in the epistolary art, such as Hamadhání could boast of, was a sure passport to preferment in the author's time, but he does not appear to have held any official position and the allusions to his being appointed governor of Baṣra[1] and administrator of a province in Syria[2] are, in all probability, a fiction.[3] He died at Herat on Friday, the 11th Jumádi'l 'Ulá A.H. 398 (February, 1008)[4] at the comparatively early age of forty lunar years, or eight years younger than Hariri was when he began to compose his Maqámát.[5]

According to Abú Sa'id 'Abd al-Raḥmán ibn Muhammad, 'He fell into a lethargy and was buried with precipitation. He recovered when shut up in the tomb, and his cries having been heard in the night his grave was opened and he was found dead grasping his beard'.[6] It is also said he was poisoned.

Judged by his Letters[7] he was a man to whom family ties strongly appealed. His advice to his sister's son manifests a commendable concern for the boy's education. He writes: 'Thou art my son as long as learning is thy business, the school thy place, the ink-flask thy ally, and a book thy friend, but, if thou come short, but methinks thou wilt not do so, then let another be thy uncle.'[8]

Tha'álibí, his acquaintance and biographer, sums up his ability and character as follows: 'He was remarkable for his choice and correct Arabic, the elegance of his epistles and the beauty of his poetry. He was of pleasing appearance, cheerful, sociable, modest, large-hearted, high-souled, a man of his word, sincere in his social relations, a true friend, but a bitter enemy.[9]

His death, according to the same authority, was a great blow to learning, and he was universally lamented and regretted; 'but', adds Tha'álibí, 'he is not dead whose fame liveth'.[10] These words were written a short time after the death of Hamadhání; and the succeeding nine centuries, during which his influence

[1] Text, p. 196. [2] Ibid., p. 233. [3] See Letters, pp. 266–7.
[4] Letters, p. 295. [5] De Sacy's Introduction to Ḥarírí, p. 50.
[6] Ibn Khallikan, De Slane's Translation, i, 114. [7] Letters, pp. 245–9.
[8] Ibid., p. 523. [9] *Yatíma*, iv, 168; also Letters, pp. 253–5.
[10] *Yatíma*, iv, 169.

has penetrated the vast realm of Islámic literature, have prove that they were not inappropriately applied to the author o the Maqámát.

II. RHYMED PROSE

RHYMED prose called saj' (سَجْع) because of its evenness or monotony, or from a fancied resemblance between its rhythm and the cooing of a dove, is a highly artificial style of prose, characterized by a kind of rhythm as well as rhyme. It is a species of diction to which the Arabic language, because of its structure, the mathematical precision of its manifold formations and the essential assonance of numerous derivatives from the same root supplying the connexion between the sound and signification of words, peculiarly lends itself.[1]

According to Jáḥiz (ob. A.H. 255) the advantages of rhymed prose are twofold; it is pleasing to the ear and easy to remember. He says the Arabs have uttered a far greater quantity of simple than of rhymed prose, and yet not a tenth of the former has been retained while not a tenth of the latter has been lost.[2]

In pagan times it is supposed to have been the mode of expression in dignified discourses, challenges, harangues and orations.[3] It was also the form in which the oracular sayings and decisions of the *kahana*, the soothsayers or diviners, each of whom was supposed to have a familiar spirit, were expressed.[4]

Because of its association with these pagan practices[5] its use 'in commands and prohibitions' in the early days of Islám is said to have been forbidden.[6] The Prophet is reported to have said: إِيَّاكُمْ وَسَجْعَ الْكُهَّانِ 'Avoid ye the rhyming prose of the soothsayers or diviners.'

On the high authority of Aḥmad ibn Ḥanbal (ob. A.H. 258), the founder of one of the four Schools of Law, we have it that the Prophet had a rooted repugnance to this kind of composition. In an incident related by him the Prophet is reported to have

[1] See Chenery's Introduction to Ḥarírí, pp. 50–51.
[2] *Kitáb al-Bayán wa'l-Tabyín*, i, 112.
[3] Ibid., p. 119 (oration of Koss ibn Sa'ida).
[4] Ibid., p. 113; Qur'án lii, 29.
[5] *Life of Muḥammad*, Wüsṭenfeld, Band I, pp. 171, 191.
[6] *Kitáb al-Bayán wa'l-Tabyín*, p. 113.

indignantly exclaimed, 'What! rhymed prose after the manner of the Arabs of the Days of the Ignorance?'[1]

There is, therefore, naturally, no trace of it in the sermon of the Prophet after the capture of Mecca, nor is it to be found in his farewell address and final charge on the occasion of the last pilgrimage.[2] Nor is it used by the Khalifa Mu'áwiya in his last khutba.[3]

In spite of the ban, however, it appears there were orators who spoke in rhymed prose, and one of the earliest specimens of a khutba in rhymed prose is by the celebrated preacher and orator, contemporary with Muhammad, Sahbán Wá'il (ob. A.H. 54).[4] On the other hand he did not use it in his reply to Talha al-Ṭalḥáṭ the governor of Sijistán.[5]

With the spread of Islám the reason for the prohibition disappears and rhymed prose reasserts itself in some of the speeches made by Muslim orators in the presence of the first Khalifas and no objection appears to have been raised.[6]

In early Islámic times it seems to belong to repartee, sententious sayings, the epigram, solemn utterances such as paternal advice,[7] religious formulae, prayers, elogia addressed to princes and governors. Jáḥiz cites several specimens of these[8] and the author of the Agháni quotes a eulogy in rhymed prose[9] by al-Nabigha al-Ja'adí, one of the most celebrated of the poets contemporary with Muḥammad.[10]

During the first century of the Hijra it appears to have been regarded as the symbol of an elevated style peculiar to the orator.[11]

In the earlier specimens of female eloquence compiled by Abú'l-Faḍl Aḥmad ibn Tahir (A.H. 204–80) there is, however, very little trace of this species of composition.[12] In fact it was regarded as a rare accomplishment if not a lost art. But a few sentences of this form of composition by the wife of Abú'l-Aswad

[1] *Musnad* of Ibn Ḥanbal, iv, 245.

[2] *Kitáb al-Bayán wa'l-Tabyin*, ii, 163–4 and *Life of Muhammad* (Wüstenfeld) Band iv, 968.

[3] *Kitáb al-Amáli*, ii, 313.

[4] Chenery's Translation of Ḥaríri, p. 309.

[5] Ḥaríri, p. 49.

[6] *Kitáb al-Bayán wa'l-Tabyin*, i, 113.

[7] *Agháni*, iii, 6.

[8] *Kitáb al-Bayán wa'l-Tabyin*, i, 111.

[9] *Agháni*, xiv, 3.

[10] Ibn Khallikan, i, 456.

[11] *Kitáb al-Amáli*, ii, 73.

[12] See *Balághat al-Nisá*, pp. 15 and 16.

al-Du'li sufficed to draw from the Khalifa Mu'áwiya the exclamation, 'Good gracious! What rhymed prose the woman speaks!'[1]

The institution of the weekly address (khuṭba) by the Khalifa, led no doubt to careful preparation and thus paved the way for pulpit oratory which found its loftiest expression in rhymed prose. It is not, however, until the beginning of the third century of the Hijra that it reappears in the khutba and becomes the conventional style of the professional preacher. An excellent specimen of a khutba in rhymed prose on death, resurrection and judgement is that by Ibn Nubata (A.H. 335-74) entitled 'the sermon of the vision.'[2] The language is dignified and solemn, but perfectly plain and intelligible. A vast empire with its numerous provincial governments and political and commercial relations with neighbouring states required that its edicts, foreign despatches, and official correspondence should be expressed in language at once dignified and forceful.

Out of the necessity of this situation arose the study of the epistolary art and towards the beginning of the second century of the Hijra official letter writers had developed that florid style which has ever since been the distinguishing feature of such compositions. Nevertheless there were writers who eschewed this ornateness and wrote in language easy to be understood.

A notable example of this natural and simple style is Jáhiz whose diction Hamadhání, writing a century later, condemns as wanting in artifice, adornment, and ornateness.[3]

With such assiduity was the art of official writing cultivated, so great was the importance attached to it and so highly did it come to be appreciated, that the Kátib, or secretary, not infrequently rose to the highest position in the state, that of Wazir, or chief minister. Tha'álibí throws considerable light upon the rise and development of this official correspondence. He says that epistolary writing began with 'Abd al-Hamid (ob. A.H. 133), Kátib, or secretary, to Marwán the last of the Omayyad Khalifas, and ended with Ibn al-Amid (ob. A.H. 359 or 360), the Wazir of Rukn al-Daula, the Buwayhid prince.[4]

[1] See *Balághat al-Nisá*, p. 54.
[2] *Journal Asiatique*, January, 1840.
[3] Text, p. 72.
[4] *Yatíma*, iii, 3.

In this striving after an ornate and elevated style the adoption of a species of composition, that had raised pulpit oratory above the language of every-day life, seems to be a natural result, and thus rhymed prose became the essential feature not only of official writing, but also of the private correspondence of the learned and the cultured.

It will be sufficient to mention three collections of such Epistles: those of Abú'l 'Alá al-Mu'arrí (A.H. 363–449), edited and translated into English by Professor D. S. Margoliouth; extracts from those of Abú Bakr al-Khwárazmí cited by Tha'álibí;[1] and those of al-Hamadhání himself, edited and published with notes by Ibráhim Ibn 'Ali al-Ahdab (Beyrút).

It was Hamadhání, however, a master of the epistolary art himself, who conceived the idea of demonstrating in a series of dramatic discourses, known to us as the Maqámát, how the use of this mode of composition might be extended to literature so as to include the entire range of the life and language of the Arabian people. He was, therefore, the popularizer of rhymed prose, in a class of compositions with which his name was first associated, and which have not only penetrated all Islámic literature as well as that of the Syrian Christians, and the Spanish Jews, but have served as models of style for more than nine hundred years.

III. THE WORD MAQAMA (مَقَامَةٌ)

MAQAMA, plural Maqámát, from قَامَ he stood, primarily signifies an occasion of standing, or a place where one stands upright. Standing appears to have been not only the natural, but the conventional position of the speaker, e.g.

(1) قَامَ النَّاسُ يَخْطُبُونَ

The people stood up to speak.[2]

(2) I have heard that 'Alí ibn al-Ḥusain was standing admonishing the people.[3]

(3) Come near and eat, or, if thou wilt, stand and speak.[4]

1 *Yatíma*, iv, 114–23.
2 *Kitáb al-Amáli*, ii, 73.
3 *Maqámát* of al-Hamadhání, p. 130.
4 *Maqámát* of al-Ḥarírí, p. 21.

The practice of standing to speak goes back to Homeric times :—

> O Damaan, friends and heroes, men of Arie's company,
> seemly it is to listen to him who standeth to speak.[1]

According to Ibn Qutaiba (A. H. 276) reports of the literary discussions held in the assemblies of men of learning and culture received, early in the ‘Abbásid period (A. H. 132–656), the name Maqáma.[2]

These literary reunions appear to have been a recognized institution. Saif al-Daula used to hold an assembly every night to which men of learning came and conversed in his presence;[3] and Tha‘álibí, in referring to the literary splendour of Bukhára in Hamadhání's time, mentions a remarkable gathering of the chief scholars of the day at the Court of that State.[4]

Maqáma probably acquired the more restricted meaning of a discourse, exhortation or oration, between the time of Jáḥiz (ob. A.H. 255) and that of Hamadhání (ob. A.H. 398).

The extracts given below illustrate the various uses of the word from the time of the pre-Islámic poet Zuheir (end of the sixth century A.D.) to that of the author (end of the eleventh century A.D.) It is thus used by early writers :—

(1) By Zuheir and quoted by Hamadhání :—

وَفِيهِم مَقَامَاتٌ حِسَانٌ وُجُوهُهُم * وَأَنْدِيَةٌ يَنْتَابُهَا الْقَوْلُ وَالْفِعْلُ

> And among them are *maqámát*—champions and the like—
> whose faces are fair,
>
> And councils where words are followed by deeds.[5]

(2) By Abú Tammám (ob. A.H. 190) :—

وفي كلّ مُعتَرِكٍ وكُلّ مَقامةٍ * يَاخُذنَ منه ذمّةً وعهودا

> Concerning every battlefield and in every *maqáma*
> (situation) :
>
> Which obtain from poetry covenants and contracts.[6]

[1] *Iliad*, Book xix, line 79.

[2] Brockelman, *Gesch. der Arab Litteratur*, i, 94.

[3] Ibn Khallikan, i, 105.

[4] *Yatima*, iv, 33.

[5] *Shu‘ará al-Nasrániah*, p. 573.

[6] Abú Tammám (Beyrút edition), p. 82, last line.

وَمَقَامَةٍ تَبَلَ ٱلْكَلَامَ سِلَاحُهَا * لِلْقَوْلِ فِيهَا غَمْرَةٌ لَا تَنْجَلِي

فَرَّجْتَ ظُلْمَتَهَا بِخُطْبَةٍ فَيْصَلٍ * مِثْلُ لَهَا فِي ٱلرَّوْعِ ضَرْبَةُ فَيْصَلِ

Of many a *maqáma*—speech—whose weapons have rendered other people's talk weak, wherein there are waves of language which cannot be cleared away,

Hast thou dispelled the darkness with a decisive speech like unto a determining blow in the time of peril.[1]

فَإِنْ شَهِدَ ٱلْمَقَامَةَ يَوْمَ فَصْلٍ * رَأَيْتَ نَظِيرَ لُقْمَانَ ٱلْحَكِيمِ

And if he is present in the *maqáma*—assembly or council—on the day of final decision,

Thou wilt see the equal of Luqmán the sage.[2]

(3) By al-Qattál :—

نَشَدْتُ زِيَادًا وَٱلْمَقَامَةُ بَيْنَنَا * وَذَكَّرْتُهُ أَرْحَامَ سَعْرٍ وَهَيْثَمِ

In the presence of the *maqáma*—a company of people—I adjured Zíád to desist,

And I reminded him of the ties of relationship of Sa'r and Haitham that bound us together.[3]

(4) By Jáhiz (ob. A. H. 255) :—

(i) وَجَلَسَ وَٱلْقَوْمُ عَرَبٌ وَكَانُوا يُفِيضُونَ فِي الحَدِيثِ وَيَذْكُرُونَ مِنَ ٱلشِّعْرِ ٱلشَّاهِدِ وَٱلْمَثَلِ وَمِنَ ٱلْخَبَرِ ٱلأَيَّامَ وَٱلْمَقَامَاتِ

And he sat down and the company were Arabs who were discussing tradition and citing proof passages and proverbs, and from history, battles and *maqámát*—speeches or orations.[4]

(ii) عَوَازِبُ لَمْ تَسْمَعْ نُبُوحَ مَقَامَةٍ

Solitary ones who have not heard the barking of the dogs of *maqáma*—a company of Bedawín.[5]

(5) By Abú 'Ali al-Qálí (ob. 356) :—

ٱلْمَقَامَةُ ٱلْمَجْلِسُ [6]

Maqáma = Majlis, a company of people.

[1] Abú Tammám (Beyrút edition), p. 211, line 4. [2] Ibid., p. 256, line 4 from the end.
[3] *Hamasa*, p. 95. [4] *Book of Misers* (Lyden edition), p. 218, line 23.
[5] *Haywán*, part iv, 154. [6] *Kitáb al-Amáli*, i, 95.

(6) By Hamadhání :—

(i) وَكَانَ يَبْلُغُنِي مِنْ مَقَامَاتِ الْأَسْكَنْدَرِي وَمَقَالَاتِه

There used to reach me of the *maqámát*—discourses and
the like—and sayings of al-Iskanderí.[1]

(ii) فَاصْبِرْ عَلَيْهِ إِلَى آخِرِ مَقَامِهِ

So wait for the end of his *maqáma*—a discourse. The
word here refers to a stirring sermon which 'Isá ibn
Hishám had been listening to.[2]

(iii) وَمَنْ يَأْتِي الْمَقَامَاتِ

And him who enters the *maqámát*—companies or assemblies of respectable people.[3]

(iv) وَمِنْ عَلَامَاتِهِمْ قُبْحُ مَقَامَاتِهِمْ

And of their distinguishing marks is the vileness of their
maqámát—assemblies of chief men, or speeches.[4]

(v) إِنَّ مِنْ أَمْلَى مِنْ مَقَامَاتِ الْكُدْيَةِ أَرْبَعَمِائَةِ مُقَامَةٍ

Verily he who has dictated four hundred *maqámát* on
mendicity.[5]

Although the maqámát were composed chiefly for assemblies
of the learned and for the entertainment of the great, the word
maqáma is applied by Hamadhání himself to the species of composition first associated with his name, and not to the people
who assembled to listen to his discourses.   It is in this restricted
sense that it has come down to us.

As the extracts from different authors do, however, show that
the word has the triple signification of an oratorical address or
harangue, a collection of champions, or a company of people,
I have preferred a transliteration to the rendering by the familiar,
but unsatisfactory, term assembly.

IV.   ORIGIN AND CHARACTER OF THE MAQAMAT

IN the first century of Islám there were scarcely any books and
knowledge was handed down orally.   In fact there was, till well

---

[1] Text, p. 25.   [2] Ibid., p. 135.   [3] Ibid., p. 160.   [4] Letters, p. 106.
[5] Ibid., p. 390.

within the second century of the Hijra, a decided antipathy towards the written word [1] and those who desired to learn the traditions of the Prophet were obliged to travel.[2] Indeed the only way knowledge could be had was by travelling.

Those who wished to study Arabic philosophy, poetry, legend and the idiom of the desert were obliged to pursue their researches and investigations among the Bedawín tribes.[3]

Travel in search of knowledge thus rendered necessary at first by circumstance became the fashion not only for the acquisition of knowledge, but also for the dissemination and display thereof. It thus led to the evolution of the vagabond scholar, a kind of knight-errant of literature and the prototype of the medieval wandering man of learning.

Inspired by such examples of peripatetic scholars as well as by his own wanderings and varied experience,[4] Hamadhání imagined a profoundly clever and witty but unscrupulous improvisor wandering from place to place, appearing in a variety of disguises unexpectedly, but always opportunely, in the gatherings of the great and the literary assemblies of the learned and living on the rich presents,[5] the display of his erudition rarely failed to produce from the generous and the cultured, and a ráwí, or narrator, a man of means of mature age, of a grave and generous disposition with a penchant for learning who should continually meet him and relate his learned compositions.

Abú'l-Fatḥ, therefore, represents the vagabond scholar of Hamadhání's own day, and, one is inclined to believe, occasionally the author himself relating his own experiences or personal adventures.[6]

The conception was an advance to the dramatic style which, on account of the religious objection to the portrayal or realistic representation of life or the human form, had hitherto been wanting in Arabic literature [7]

[1] De Slane's Introduction to Ibn Kallikan, p. xxiii.
[3] Ibid., p. xxxi.
[2] See Ibn Khallikan, i, 102.
[4] See Letters, pp. 101-2.
[5] Numerous examples of these rich rewards, out of all proportion to the performance, might be quoted, e.g. Abú'l-'Anbas, the hero of the forty-second maqáma, received from the Khalifa Mutúwakkil 10,000 dirhems for a few verses. (See Yaqút, *Dictionary of Learned Men*, vi, 406). Several instances are mentioned by Ibn Khallikan in his life of *Saif al-Daula*, ii, 334-7.
[6] See Letters, pp. 104-5 and Text, pp. 187-8.
[7] See Qur'án, v. 92 and Hermann Reich, *Der Mimus*, p. 80.

According to the Zahr al-Adáb the occasion of the composing of the Maqámát was as follows: Abú Isḥáq,[1] surnamed al-Huṣri, or the maker or seller of mats (ob. at Qairawán A.H. 413). contemporary with Hamadhání, after referring in the most flattering terms to the unique appropriateness of the author's name and appellation, Abú'l Faḍl and Badi' al-Zamán, the 'Father of Excellence' and the 'Wonder of the Age' respectively, writes: 'When al-Hamadhání observed that Abú Bakr ibn Duraid the Azdite (A.H. 223–321) had composed forty rare stories on a variety of subjects expressed in strange sounding speech and obsolete and incongruous words, such as men's natures would shrink from and their ears be closed against, which he said he had produced from the springs of his breast, extracted from the mines of his thought and exposed to public view and perception, Hamadhání met him with four hundred Maqámát on mendicity.'[2] These are instinct with interest and beauty and between no two of them is there the slightest resemblance, either as regards words or ideas. He attributes the composition and narration of them to two persons.[3] One of them he called 'Isá ibn Hishám and the other he named Abú'l-Fath al-Iskanderí. These two he made to exchange pearls of thought and to give expression to bewitching language such as would cause the sorrowful to laugh and the staid to become excited. 'In these compositions he acquaints us with every kind of pleasantry and informs us of every species of subtlety. Generally, one of the characters is made the author of the story and the other the narrator of it.'[4]

Ibn Khallikan makes no mention of these stories in the list of works ascribed to Ibn Duraid[5] nor is there any reference to them in that cited by Yaqút.[6] The nearest approach to a work of this kind by that author is the *Kitáb al-Lughát* on the dialects or idiomatic expressions of the Arabs.[7]

[1] Ibn Khallikan, i, 34.

[2] On p. 49 of the Letters, Hamadhání taunts Abú Bakr al-Khwárazmí with having persistently practised mendicity and condemns the practice as a degrading one!

[3] Ḥarirí says: 'Both these are obscure persons not known.' Harírí, p. 6.

[4] *Zahr al-Adáb*, i, pp. 254-5.

[5] Men of learning said of Ibn Duraid that he was the most learned among the poets and ablest poet among the learned. Ibn Khallikan, iii, 38.

[6] *Dictionary of Learned Men*, vi, 489.

[7] Ibn Khallikan, iii, 38.

If, therefore, the stories were what they were represented to be by al-Ḥuṣri they were probably written in a dialect which had become obsolescent.

It is interesting to observe that Hamadhání's compositions had reached and were known in Qairawán, the sacred city of Islám in Tunisia, at this early date, and that we have from the pen of another contemporary a criticism, which probably expressed the opinion of the learned world as to the literary merits of the Maqámát.

The triple aim of Hamadhání appears to have been to amuse, to interest and to instruct; and this explains why, in spite of the inherent difficulty of a work of this kind composed primarily with a view to rhetorical effect upon the learned and the great, there is scarcely a dull chapter in the fifty-one maqámát. There is little evidence that the story or the adventure is subordinated to the style.

When the author essayed, in the course of these dramatic discourses, to illustrate the life and language both of the denizens of the desert and of the dwellers in towns, to give examples of the jargon and slang of thieves and robbers as well as of the lucubrations of the learned and the conversations of the cultured, and to show the use of strange and obsolete words and phrases, such as are found in the proverbs—probably the oldest forms of the Arabic language and the earliest utterances of the Arabian people—difficult and obscure passages were inevitable. On page 10 of the text the author asserts that one of his objects was to capture these rare words and strange sayings. In fact the collection of nawádir, or recondite expressions, was a favourite pursuit.[1]

In electing to do this in rhymed prose he imposed upon himself all the limitations of a style which, in any but the hand of a master, tends to become oppressively monotonous and depressingly dull.[2]

In pleasing contrast, however, to the numerous obscurities, intentional and otherwise, the hypocritical and dishonest Qádi, the Bedawin robber, the simple rustic, the eloquent and fearless

[1] See collection of nawádir in *Mabadi al-Lughat* by Shaikh 'Abdulláh (ob. A. H. 421) pub. A. H. 1325.

[2] See Ibn 'Arabsháh, *Life of Tímúr*.

preacher, the garrulous trader, the miserly merchant, and the loquacious barber with his amazing malapropisms containing cleverly concealed allusions, are portrayed with all the graphic skill of a master of the art of description.

The commentator in referring to the author's descriptive power says: ‘He combines the accuracy of the idiom of the dwellers of the desert with the refinement and taste of the people of the towns, so that the reader imagines himself to be now among the hair tents of a Bedawin encampment and anon amidst the stately buildings of a city.’[1]

The second point of importance in this extract from the *Zahr al-Adáb* is the reference to the number of the compositions. Al-Husri must have had the Maqámát and the Letters before him, because he gives copious extracts from both in the work above mentioned, and if there had not been four hundred he would, in all probability, have alluded to the fact when mentioning their number. We have, therefore, in the printed text about one-eighth of the original work.

The question, as to whether the maqámát are impromptu compositions, as they were represented to be, may be disposed of by a consideration of the maqámát themselves. They bear evident trace of scholarly preparation and literary finish, and I think the author himself, unconsciously, furnishes the explanation. In the fortieth maqáma he says: ‘I wrote elegantly by virtue of much reading. I passed on from reading to investigation and from investigation to composition.’[2]

Again, on page 389 of the Letters, in replying to certain strictures passed on the maqámát and to the taunt by his great rival, Abú Bakr al-Khwárazmí, that he was unable to produce any more, he writes: ‘Now if that savant were just he would have endeavoured to produce five maqámát, or ten original compositions, and submitted them to the judgement of the cultured and then, if they approved and did not reject them, he might have adversely criticized us. Now let him understand that, while I have dictated four hundred maqámát on mendicity, between no two of which is there any resemblance, either as regards words or ideas, he is unable to produce a tenth of a maqáma, and, therefore, he deserves to have his faults exposed.’

[1] Introduction to the Text, p. 1.

[2] Text, pp. 203–4.

It seems reasonable to suppose that his *modus operandi* was the plan which he suggested that al-Khwárazmí should have adopted, namely, to first submit a few maqámát to the learned for their opinion.

The author's boast that 'between no two maqámát is there any similarity, either as regards words or ideas,' is not consistent with fact, and if the entire work had been known to al-Khwárazmí in A. H. 383, it is very doubtful if such a statement would have been made. Al-Huṣri reproduces the assertion without comment.

There are several cases of resemblance and not a few of repetition, both in regard to words and ideas.

For example, the line on page 13, 'In the evening they are Arabs, in the morning Nabateans', reappears, with a very slight variation, on page 88 of the text. The themes of the twenty-fifth and the thirty-fourth maqámát are identical. The fourth and the thirty-seventh have much in common.

The fifteenth and the fortieth have similar concluding verses. The forty-fourth is a variation and largely a reproduction of the twenty-eighth. Other instances of resemblance are recorded in the notes.

Each maqáma is complete in itself and generally consists of a *mélange* of prose and verse.[1] It usually concludes with some clever verses in which the improvisor administers a sharp rebuke, or explains, or justifies his conduct to the narrator.

The maqámát vary in length. Some of them extending over several pages [2] while others are limited to a few lines.[3] In some both persons of the drama are not introduced, and the narrator, who is, of course, the author himself, speaks in his own character.[4] In others one is left to conjecture as to the identity of the improvisor.[5]

As regards the style of the work, its distinctive feature is parallelism, which consists in making the second part of a

[1] There are more than a hundred pieces of poetry distributed throughout the Text.

[2] The Maqámát of Maḍirah, pp. 101–15 and Saimara, pp. 207–16.

[3] The Maqámát of Knowledge, p. 202 and Advice, p. 204 and the Yellow, p. 229.

[4] The Maqámát of Baghdad, Saimara and Bishr.

[5] The Maqáma of the Nájim.

sentence balance with the first, either by way of antithesis, or by expressing the same idea in different words, thus producing, as it were, a rhyme of the sense as well as of the sound.[1]

The Maqámát did much to fix a style of composition in which Persian and Greek ideas could make little inroads. Still there is more of the foreign element than the purist would approve. More than sixty such words have been collected and traced, as far as possible, to original sources.

The copious notes and numerous references essential to the elucidation of the text afford in themselves abundant evidence of the difficult nature and comprehensive character of the Maqámát. The sources the author has drawn upon for his materials are, as might be expected, exclusively Muslim. They consist of the comparison of the poets, an important branch of *belles-lettres* (أَدَب), the relative merits of Jarir and Farazdaq, a question the Arabs never seemed able to decide; incidents from the lives of Dhúr'l-Rumma and Farazdaq; tests of acquaintance with the principal poets and their poetry;[2] polemical questions such as the Mu'tazilite heresy, the doctrine of free will and the dogmas of predestination and the uncreate Qur'án.

There are examples of the proverbial generosity of the Hamdánid prince Saif al-Daula and the Arab's knowledge of the points of the horse, popular superstitions such as the belief in charms, pulpit oratory, the dangers of the desert, apt quotations from the Qur'án, popular sayings and customs illustrative of Bedawin life, insolence of the servants of the great, flattering and faithless friends and their treatment,[3] eulogy of the patron, satirizing of the Qáḍi and the convivial assembly. Others might be mentioned, but these are sufficient to show the subjects Hamadhání laid under contribution, and the versatile character of the Maqámát.

The question as to whether Hamadhání owed anything, directly or indirectly, to Greek scholarship or Byzantine models is an extremely difficult one upon which to venture an opinion.

In the matter of the lavish display of erudition, intentional obscurities, and the use of words of doubtful meaning, the

1 See Chenery's Introduction to Ḥaríri, p. 45.

2 The *Kitab al-Aghání*, which the author was able to consult, contains numerous references to these four themes.

3 Taken from Abu'l-'Anbas.

Maqámát may be compared with the Cassandra, or Alexandra of Lycophron (285–247 B.C.).

It is highly improbable, however, that the author derived any inspiration from this product of antiquity. But the similarity suggests that the same demons of difficulty, obscurity, and pedantry, entered the orators and poets of both nations at different periods.

For instance, Hamadhání boasts of his ability to employ no less than four hundred artifices in writing and composition,[1] such as the writing of a letter which, if read backwards, furnishes the required reply, or an epistle containing no dotted letters, or without using the letters (ا) or (ل), or a letter which if read one way constitutes a eulogy, and, if taken in another, is a satire; feats which, when they were proposed to Abú Bakr al-Khwárazmí as literary tests, he denounced as the tricks of a juggler.[2]

He shows little disposition, however, to make use of such artifices in the Maqámát, but the suggestion was not lost upon Ḥariri, who frequently employed them for the display of his superior skill and learning.[3]

In point of literary style and in regard to the manner of describing in an amusing way the occurrences of everyday life there is a closer resemblance between the Maqámát and the Satires of Horace (65–8 B.C.). Here again the resemblance is accidental rather than essential.

There is, however, a far closer resemblance between the Maqámát and the Greek Mimes. The similarity is indeed so striking that one is almost forced into the belief, either that they must have had a common origin or that the same informing spirit speaks to the nations irrespective of race, time, or place.

So far as we know the Mime commences seriously with Sophron (about 430 B.C.), whose Mimes, unlike those of Herondas, which we have, were in prose. 'These dialogues contained both male and female characters. Some were serious and some were humorous in style. They portrayed the daily life of the Sicilian Greeks, and were written in pithy, popular language full of proverbs and colloquialisms.'[4]

[1] Letters, p. 74. [2] Ibid., p. 76.
[3] See Ḥarirí, vi, xv, xvi, xviii, xxix, xliv, etc.
[4] *Encyclopædia Britannica*, xxv, 429.

Almost every word of this description of the Mimes might, *mutatis mutandis*, be applied to the Maqámát. According to Reich the Mime influenced the thought of early ecclesiastical writers, and was a subject of considerable concern and controversy with the Christian Fathers.[1] It found its way to India and flourished in Syria, Palestine, Alexandria, Antioch and Constantinople.[2] It would be strange indeed if the Arabs alone remained ignorant of its existence. That the term Mime was known to them appears from the word مُومِسَةٌ and it is conceivable that the practice of composing humorous or entertaining dialogues passed from Greek to Syriac and from Syrian to Arabic.

Once having received the impulse or inspiration the Arabs would, in accordance with their national genius, develop the idea on their own lines, as they did in the case of law and grammar. This is, of course, mere conjecture, but the outstanding fact of the striking resemblance remains a problem upon which investigation and research may some day shed new light.

Finally, the practice of making one person the hero of a series of adventures has been tried by some modern writers. In Grant Allen's *An African Millionaire* Colonel Clay has much in common with Abú'l-Fath al-Iskanderí, the hero of the Maqámát.

V. HAMADHANI AND HARIRI COMPARED

WHEN Ḥariri undertook to compose his Maqámát ‘following the method of Badi‘’ a close imitation was inevitable. A comparison of the two works reveals how closely he followed his model and how largely he drew upon the original source, not only for ideas but also frequently for themes and, occasionally, for the language in which to express them.

For example, in maqáma xiii, 147 Ḥariri, in imitation of Hamadhání, p. 61, introduces the names of colours in an artificial manner. Ḥaríri's poem, p. 159 closely resembles Hamadhání's verses on p. 90. Ḥariri v, 49 and Hamadhání v, 20 are identical in title and theme. Ḥariri xviii, 199 is a very close imitation and, in parts, a literal copy of Hamadhání xxii, 101

The themes of Hariri xii and xxxix and Hamadhání xxiii are the same. Ḥariri xxx is a variation of Hamadhání xxx. In the

[1] *Der Mimus*, pp. 154–5. [2] Ibid., pp. 699–700.

former we have the cant of beggars, mountebanks, and the like, and in the latter an enumeration of the methods pursued by the fraternity of burglars, cutpurses, thieves, and the like. The themes of Hariri viii and Hamadhání xxxi are similar. Ḥariri iii and xlvii have much in common with Hamadhání xvi and xliii.

In Hariri xlix and Hamadhání xli the improvisors are each made to give his son advice as to his future career. In the former Abú Zeid advises his son to follow what he had found to be the freest and most lucrative of all pursuits, that of mendicancy. In the latter Abú'l-Fatḥ al-Iskanderí, influenced perhaps by the consideration that he had derived little personal advantage from the life of the vagabond scholar,[1] takes a different view and lays down the rules his son should observe in pursuing a commercial career. Other points of resemblance will be found mentioned in the notes.

Allusions to popular sayings and customs, history and legend, theology and jurisprudence, specimens of eloquence and pulpit oratory, apt quotations from the Qur'án and the citing of proverbs, the use of the rare and the recondite, constitute the groundwork common to both books. The maqámát of Hamadhání are, therefore, an excellent introduction to the ampler, more elaborate and comprehensive work of his great imitator.

In a comparison of the works of these two masters of the art of maqámát writing regard should be had to the fact that the maqámát of Hamadhání are the work of a young man, completed in all probability before he had attained his thirtieth year, whereas those of Hariri were begun when the author had reached the mature age of forty-eight, and occupied the last twenty years of his life.[2]

As regards their relative merits Hamadhání is much more natural than Hariri. He has more of art and less of artificiality than his imitator. There is less disposition on his part to indulge in grammatical riddles and linguistic puzzles, or to ransack the rich resources of the Arabic language for rare words. The subject is less subordinated to the style, or the sense to the sound than is the case with Ḥariri.

And yet the work of Hamadhání, which in his own day made him famous from Herat to Northern Africa and earned for him

[1] Letters, p. 161. [2] De Sacy's Introduction to Ḥarírí, p. 50.

the proud appellation, 'The wonder of the Age', is little known, while that of Ḥariri has been for centuries one of the best-studied books in Arabic literature and, next to the Qur'án, has engaged the attention of the largest number of scholarly commentators.

In spite of one's disposition to accord the palm to originality and art rather than to imitation and artificiality, an author's countrymen are the best judges of the merits of his literary productions, and therefore the verdict of posterity in favour of Ḥarirí must be accepted. 'The lame horse' has indeed 'outrun the sturdy steed'.[1] Ḥariri, writing nearly a century later, about A.H. 496, deplores the decadence of learning. 'Whose breeze has stilled and whose lights have well-nigh gone out.'[2] Here then is probably the first cause of the neglect of Hamadhání. As far as we know no carefully collated and vocalized text of the Maqámát was in circulation before that edited and annotated by the late Shaikh Muhammad 'Abdú[3] in A.H. 1306, or more than nine hundred years after the author's death. On the other hand, the work of teaching and explaining the Maqámát of Hariri was continued by his sons[4] and the first commentary was written within fifty years of the demise of the author.

Muṭarrízí, the earliest scholiast, was born in A.H. 458, or only twenty-two years after the death of Ḥariri, and even then he asserts that he found it necessary to consult practically the entire range of Arabic literature, and to refer to the principal Shaikhs of the time before he commenced his commentary on the Maqámát.[5]

In the case of the Maqámát of Hamadhání there was probably no vocalized text in circulation, and there certainly was no commentary for more than nine centuries. Without such aids a literary work of this kind, covering so wide a field and written in an original and ornate style, would present considerable difficulty even to the ripe scholar, while to the struggling student it was doomed to be what it actually became, virtually a sealed book. These circumstances and facts account, to some extent at least, for the long neglect of this classic in Arabic literature.

[1] Ḥarírí, p. 6. [2] Ibid., p. 6.

[3] For a character sketch of the commentator, see Blunt, *Secret History of the British Occupation of Egypt*, p. 105.

[4] Ibn Khallikan, ii, 493 and 496.

[5] De Sacy's Introduction to Ḥarírí, p. 58.

If this translation of the text and the efforts to elucidate it but result in making the author known, as he certainly deserves to be, to a wider circle of readers, the labours of the translator will not have been in vain.

THE MAQÁMÁT

I. THE MAQAMA OF POESIE

'ÍSÁ IBN HISHÁM related to us and said: Separation once hurled me hither and thither until I reached the utmost confines of Jurján.'[1] Here, to fortify myself against the days, I took some arable land which I proceeded to cultivate. I invested in some goods as my stock-in-trade, settled upon a shop as my place of business, and selected some friends whom I made my companions. I stayed at home in the morning and in the evening, and, between these times, I was at the shop.[2]

Now one day, when we were seated together discussing poetry[3] and poets, there was sitting, but a short distance off, a youth listening as if he understood, and remaining silent as though he did not know, until we were carried away by our discussion and lengthy disputation, when he said: 'Ye have found the little palm tree loaded with fruit,[4] and got the little rubbing-post. If I so desired, I could talk and that eloquently, and, were I to speak, I should quench their thirst for knowledge.[5] Yea, I would

[1] *Jurján:* A well-known town between Tabaristán and Khurásán, said to have been founded by Yazid ibn Muhalleb. It was once noted for its silk fabrics which were sent to all parts of the world. Yaqút (Wüstenfeld), ii, 48.

[2] حَانُوت *The shop:* arabicized from the Syriac ḥamúthá, a room or cell. It has frequently in Arabic the more restricted meaning of 'wineshop'. For words of this type, see Fleischer, *Kleinere Schriften*, i, 172.

[3] ٱلقَرِيض *Poetry:* probably connected with قرظ to praise. See *Aḍ-ḍád* (Houtsma), p. 252 and the well-known proverb: حَالَ الجَرِيضُ دُونَ ٱلقَرِيضِ 'Choking stops the way of the verse' Freytag, *Arab Proverbs*, i, 340.

[4] *Ye have found the little palm tree loaded with fruit, etc.* Freytag, *Arab Proverbs*, i, 47. The meaning is 'I am one of those by means of whose counsel people seek relief.'

[5] *I should quench their thirst for knowledge:* Literally, I would bring camels up from the watering quenched and take others down.

make the truth clear in the arena of eloquence so as to cause the deaf to hear and draw down the white-footed goats from their mountain haunts.' So I said: 'O learned one! Come near, for thou hast inspired us with the feeling that we shall derive much benefit from thee. Speak, for thou hast cut thy wisdom tooth.' He then approached and said: 'Question me, and I will answer you. Listen, and I will delight you.' So we asked him: 'What dost thou say regarding Imr al-Qais?'[1] He said: 'He was the first to stand lamenting[2] over the encampments and their areas, who set out early while the birds were still in their nests,[3] and described the points of the horse.[4] He did not compose poetry for gain, nor speak eloquently from covetousness and, therefore, he was superior to him whose tongue was loosened designingly and whose fingers were foraging for a prize.'[5] We next asked: 'What dost thou say to Nabigah?'[6] He answered: 'He is as ready to revile, when he is angry, as he is to eulogize when he is pleased; he makes excuses when he is frightened and he shoots not but he hits.' We asked: 'What sayest thou to Zuheir?' He answered: 'Zuheir[7] melts poetry and poetry melts him. He summons words and enchantment answers him.'

[1] *Imr al-Qais:* Prince of the Banú Kindeh, the well-known author of the most celebrated of the *Mu'allaqát*, flourished about the middle of the sixth century A.D. *Aghání*, vii, 60.

[2] *He was the first to stand lamenting:* i.e. he was the first to introduce the prelude in the form of a lament or erotic prologue over the deserted encampment with which almost every subsequent *qaṣida* begins. But, according to Ibn Qutaiba (*Kitáb al-Sh'ir wa'l-Shu'ará*, p. 52), the first to make this prelude fashionable was a certain Ibn al-Humam or Ibn Khedhám. See also *Aghání*, iv, 114 and 149.

[3] *Set out early while the birds were still in their nests: Qaṣida* of Imr al-Kais, v. 53. (Lyall.)

[4] *Described the points of the horse:* ibid., vv. 53-70.

[5] *Were foraging for a prize:* i.e. were writing for gain.

[6] *Al-Nabigah al-Dhubyani:* Proper name Ziád ibn Mu'awiya, a well-known poet, who lived at the courts of Ghassan and al-Ḥira during the latter half of the century before Islám. He is classed with the authors of the *Mu'allaqát* (see ed. by Lyall, p. 152) and is said to have had a close acquaintance with Christianity. For a fuller notice of this poet, see Nicholson, p. 121 and *Aghání*, ix, 154.

[7] *Zuheir* ibn Abi Sulma of the tribe of Muzaina, the author of the third *Mu'allaqa*, flourished about the end of the eigth century A.D. He is remarkable for his wise sayings and moral reflections. It is said of him he only praised a man for what was in him. Hamadhání's opinion of him—Zuheir melts poetry and poetry melts him—is no exaggerated estimate of his poetic genius. He was one of the triad of pre-Islámic poets, the other two being Imr al-Qais and Nabigah. *Shu'ará* al-*Naṣraniah*, p. 510.

We said: 'What dost thou say to Ṭarafa?'[1] He replied: 'He is the very water and clay of poetry, the treasure-house and metropolis of its rhymes. He died[2] before his secret treasures came to light, or the locks of his store-houses were opened.' We said: 'What sayest thou to Jarir and Farazdaq, and which of them is superior?' He answered: 'Jarír's[3] poetry is sweeter and more copious, but Farazdaq's[4] is more vigorous and more brilliant. Again Jarir is a more caustic satirist and can tell of more celebrated battles,[5] whereas al-Farazdaq is more ambitious and belongs to the nobler clan.[6] Jarir, when he sings the praises of the fair, draws tears. When he vituperates,[7] he destroys, but, when he eulogizes, he exalts. And al-Farazdaq[8] in

[1] *Ṭarafa* ibn al-'Abd was a member of the tribe of Bakr. He flourished about the middle of the eigth century A.D. and was the author of a *Mu'allaqa*, No. 2 in Lyall's edition. He early developed a talent for satire which cost him his life at the early age of twenty, so that he is generally called the 'youth of twenty'. Nicholson, p. 107 and Ibn Qutayba, *Sh'ir wa'l-Shu'ará*, p. 88.

[2] *He died:* a reference to Ṭarafa's untimely end.

[3] *Jarír* ibn 'Atiyyah (ob. A.H. 110—A.D. 728-9), of the tribe of Kulayb was court poet of Ḥajjáj ibn Yúsuf, the governor of 'Iráq. He was famous for his satire. He survived al-Farazdaq, his lifelong rival, but a short time—either thirty or forty days. Nicholson, p. 244 and *Aghání*, vii, 35.

[4] *Al-Farazdaq:* Hammám ibn Ghálib, generally known as al-Farazdaq, belonged to the tribe of Tamím and was born at Baṣra towards theend of 'Umar's Khalífate. He was one of the triad of early Islámic poets, the other two being Akhtal and Jarír. He died in 110 A.H.—A.D. 728-9), at the great age of a hundred. *Aghání*, viii, 180.

[5] أهرف يوماً *more celebrated battles:* The Days, i.e. the great battles of the Arabs. For a list of the Days of the Arabs see the *Majma al-Baḥrein*, p. 150.

[6] *Nobler clan:* Al-Farazdaq belonged to the tribe of Tamím and Jarír to the Kulayb, a branch of the Tamim.

[7] *When he vituperates he destroys:* For an example of this, see *Kitáb al-Aghání*, vii, 46 and Nicholson, p. 245.

[8] Farazdaq and Jarir are connected by a strange rivalry. For years they were engaged in a public scolding competition in which they roundly abused each other, and exhibited their marvellous skill in manipulating the vast resources of vituperation of the Arabic language. See *The Naka'iḍ* or *Flytings* of Jarír and Farazdaq in three volumes edited by Professor A. A. Bevan (Leyden, 1905-12). The relative merits of Jarír and Farazdaq were a favourite subject for discussion. See *Aghání*, vii, 37 and Nicholson, p 239.

It is difficult to gather from Hamadhání's comparison of these two poets as to which of them he accords the palm. Probably he intended the question to remain undecided. Yúnas says: 'I have never been in an assembly where the company was unanimous as to which of the two was the better poet.' The Arabs, while they considered Jarír, al-Farazdaq and al-Akhtal to be the three greatest Islámic poets, differed in the matter of assigning precedence to them. *Kitáb al-Aghání*, vii, 36. Comparison of poets formed a branch of *belles lettres* (أدَب). See *Aghání*, iii, 101 and viii, 75.

glorying is all-sufficient. When he scorns he degrades, but, when he praises, he renders the full meed.' We said: 'What is thy opinion of the modern and the ancient poets?'[1] He answered: 'The language of the ancients is nobler and their themes more delightful, whereas the conceits of the moderns are more refined and their style more elegant.' We then said: 'If thou wouldst only exhibit some of thy poetry and tell us something about thyself.' He replied: 'Here are answers to both questions in one essay:—

'Do you not see I am wearing a thread-bare cloak,[2]
Borne along in misfortune, by a bitter lot,
Cherishing hatred for the nights,
From which I meet with red ruin,[3]
My utmost hope is for the rising of Sirius,[4]
But long have we been tormented by vain hopes.
Now this noble personage was of higher degree
And his honour[5] was of greater price,
For my enjoyment, I pitched my green tents
In the mansion of Dara,[6] and in the Hall[7] of Kisra,

[1] *What is thy opinion of the modern and the ancient poets?:* This was another favourite topic for discussion. The opinion of scholars in the time of the author was that the pre-Islámic poets had been excelled by their successors and both had been surpassed by the poets of the day of whom the famous Mutanabbí was chief.

[2] *Do you not see I am wearing a thread-bare cloak?:* The metre of these verses is *rejez.* طمرًا a thread-bare cloak. This word, which is met with so frequently in the Maqámát, is used to denominate an exceedingly old and shabby dress.

[3] *Red ruin*: Literally, red vicissitudes.

[4] *The rising of Sirius*: The greater dog-star. This star rises (aurorally) in the time of intense heat, and this he ardently desires because of the insufficiency of his clothing to protect him from the cold. Certain of the Arab tribes worshipped this star. See Qur'án, liii, 50.

[5] *His honour*: Literally, the water of this face. The ingenuous blush of an honest man is called by the Arabs 'water of the face', hence modesty, self-respect. It also means lustre.

[6] *The mansion of Dara*: Built by Darius I, or the Great, son of Hystaspes, in 521 B.C.

[7] *The Hall* (إيوان) or Palace of Kisra: The Aiwan, or the immense hall of the palace built by al-Núshirwan, in the sixth century A.D., twenty-five miles from Baghdad. Ibn al-Ḥájib writing on the Aiwan says: 'O thou who didst build it a lofty structure and, through the Aiwan relegated the skill of time to oblivion, these palaces, pleasure houses, buildings, and castles of our Kisra al-Núshirwan. See Yaqút, i, 425.

But fortune reversed my circumstances,[1]
And pleasure, my familiar friend, became a stranger to me.
Of my wealth nought remained but a memory,
And so on until to-day.
But for the old dame at Surra-Manra[2]
And the babes on this side of the hills of Baṣra,
Upon whom fate has brought affliction,
I would, O masters, destroy myself deliberately.'[3]

'Ísá ibn Hishám said: I gave him what I had to hand and then he turned away from us and departed. Now I began to deny and then to assert him, I failed to recognize him, and yet I seemed to know him, when his front teeth directed me to him. Then I said: 'Al-Iskanderí by Heavens', for he had left us young[4] and had now returned full grown. So I followed in his track, seized him by the waist and said: 'Art thou not Abú'l-Fath? Did we not rear thee as a child and didst[5] thou not pass years of thy life with us? What old dame hast thou then at Surra-Manra?'

He laughed and recited:—

'Sirrah the times are false,[6]
Let not deception beguile thee.
Cleave not to one character, but,
As the nights change, do thou change too.'

1 *Reversed my circumstances:* Literally turned the back of the shield to me: figuratively, for became hostile.

2 *Surra-man ra'a* (Sámarrá): The Khalifa Mu'taṣim (A.D. 833–42) removed his court from Baghdad, sixty miles further up the Tigris to Sámarrá the official spelling of which was Surra-man ra'a, a contraction of Surur-man ra'a, 'the beholder's joy, which suddenly grew into a superb city of palaces and barracks. For an account of recent excavations at Sámarrá, revealing examples of art and architecture of the 'Abbásid period, see *Lughat El-Arab* No. XI, May, 1913, pp. 515–20.

3 *I would deliberately destroy myself:* قُتِلَ صَبْراً means he was confined alive and then shot at or cast at until he was killed, or he was slain deliberately, not in the field of battle, nor by mistake.

4 خِشْفاً *young*: Literally, a fawn.

5 *Did we not rear thee?:* An illusion to Qur'án, xxvi, 17.

6 *Sirrah! the times are false:* The metre of these lines is *basít*. The author appears to have drawn his inspiration for this maqáma from *Aghání*, vii, 56.

II. THE MAQAMA OF THE DATE

'ÍSÁ IBN HISHÁM related to us and said: I was in Baghdad at the time of the azaz date harvest, so I went out to select and buy some of the different kinds of it. I proceeded a short distance to a man who had got a stock of various sorts of fruit which he had arranged in order. He had collected and placed in rows a variety of fresh dates and I took some of the best of everything and picked [1] some of the finest of every species. Now just as I had gathered up my skirts and placed my load in them, my eyes fell upon a man who had modestly covered his face with a veil [2] and was standing still with outstretched hand. He had his little ones by his side and bore his babes on his hip, while he recited in a voice so loud that it weakened his chest and produced feebleness in his spine:—

'Alas! I have neither two handfuls of Sawíq, [3]
Nor melted fat mixed with flour,
Nor spacious bowl filled with Khirdíq, [4]
To soothe our palate, [5]
And to remove us from the path of beggary.
O Giver of plenty after poverty!
Make it easy for some brave and liberal man
Of pedigree and hereditary glory,
To guide to us the feet of fortune
And release my life from the grip of trouble.'

'Ísá ibn Hishám said: I took from my purse a handful and gave it to him. Then he said:—

'O the one who hath bestowed [6] upon me his excellent kindness!
To God do I communicate his glorious secret,
And I pray God to keep him well-guarded,

[1] قَرَضْتُ *I picked:* Literally, I bit, or gnawed.

[2] بُرْقُعٌ *a veil:* a thing with which a woman veils her face, having in it two holes for the eyes, but here used as synonymous with lithám (لِثَامٌ)

[3] *Alas! I have neither two handfuls:* Sawíq is a kind of gruel made mostly of parched barley. Metre, *rejez.*

[4] *Khirdiq:* a kind of broth in which bread is crumbled.

[5] *To soothe our palate:* Literally, to check the onslaughts of saliva.

[6] *O the one who hath bestowed:* Metre, *rejez.*

If I have not the ability to thank him,
Then God, my Lord, will surely recompense him.'[1]

'Ísá ibn Hishám said: So I said to him, 'There is something left in the purse, therefore disclose thy hidden condition and I will give thee all.' Then he removed his veil,[2] and lo by Heavens! it was our Shaikh, Abú'l-Fath al-Iskánderí! So I exclaimed · ' Mercy on thee, how astute thou art!' Then he recited ·—

'Spend thy life in deceiving[3]
Men and throwing dust in their eyes.
I observe the days continue not
In one state and therefore I imitate them.
One day I feel their mischief,
And another they feel mine.'

III. THE MAQAMA OF BALKH

'ÍSÁ IBN HISHÁM related to us and said: Trade in cotton stuffs took me to Balkh[4] and I arrived there when I was in the first flush[5] of youth, with a mind free from care and a body decked with the ornaments of affluence. My only aim was to subdue to my use the unbroken colt of the mind, or to capture a few stray

[1] *Then God my Lord will surely recompense:* Literally, God my Lord is behind his reward.

[2] *Lithám* (لِثَامٌ) *a veil:* a kind of muffler for covering the lower part of the face. Cf. the term mulaththamun applied to the Berber tribes of the Ṣaḥará.

[3] *Spend thy life in deceiving:* تَمْوِيهًا *in deceiving:* Literally, gilding copper or silver to palm it off for gold. The Constantinople edition has these additional lines:—

' O thou who art greedy for gain, lying in ambush for it,
Thou wilt not remain for ever in this world of thine:
Therefore let a little of it suffice thee, or thou wilt be a toiler for a sitter.'
From the saying attributed to al-Nabigah:—
'There is many a toiler for a sitter', Freytag, *Arab. Proverbs*, i, 544.
Metre, *hezej*.

[4] *Balkh*: The ancient Bactria or Zariaspa, and formerly called Alexandria, was once a great city, but is now, for the most part, a mass of ruins which occupy a space of about twenty miles in circuit. It was at one time the granary of Khurásán. Captured by the Arabs in the Khalífate of 'Uthmán (A.D. 644–56). Yaqút, i, 713.

[5] عُذْرَة *First flush*: Literally, virginity.

sayings [1]. But, during my entire stay, nought more eloquent than my own words sought admission to my ear. Now when separation bent, or was about to bend, its bow at us, there came into my presence a youth in an attractive [2] dress with a beard that extended so far as to pierce the two arteries attached to the jugular vein, and with eyes which had absorbed the waters [3] of the two rivers [4]. He met me with such benefaction that I proportionately increased my praise of it. Then he asked me: 'Dost thou intend to go on a journey?' I replied: 'Yes, indeed.' He said, 'May thy scout find good pasture and thy guide not lose his way! When dost thou intend to start?' I answered, 'Early to-morrow morning.' Then he indited the following:—

'May it be a morn divine and not a morn of departure,
The bird auguring union, [5]
'And not the bird of separation.' [6]

Whither art thou going? I replied: 'To my own country.' He said, 'Mayest thou reach thy native land and accomplish thy business; but when dost thou return? I answered, 'Next year.' [7] He then said: 'Mayest thou fold the robes and roll up the thread? [8] Where art thou in regard to generosity?' I answered, 'Where thou desirest.' He said, 'If God bring thee back in safety

1 شَرُودٌ *Stray sayings:* from شَارِدٌ و شَرُودٌ applied to a runaway and refractory camel, hence strange and unfamiliar words.

2 ملءالعَين *Attractive:* Literally, full of eye.

3 *Had absorbed the waters:* They were so liquid and limpid.

4 الرَّافِدَين *The two rivers:* an appellation applied to the Euphrates and the Tigris. From رَافِدٌ a giver or tributary, e.g. نَهرٌ لَهُ رَافِدَينِ a river that has two other rivers flowing into it.

5 *The bird of union:* The hoopoo هدهد being suggestive of هَدَاهُ he guided him. See Meidání, i, 337 (Bulak-edition) and also Professor Margoliouth's 'Letters of Abú'l 'Alá al-Ma'arrí,' p. 42.

6 *The bird of separation:* The raven which is called غُرَابُ البين the raven of separation and whose appearance or croak is ominous of separation. See Meidání, i, 337 (Bulak edition.) Metre, *wafir.*

7 *Next year:* Literally, the coming (year).

8 *Mayest thou fold the robes and roll up the thread.* A figure used by the author to express the idea of traversing safely the intervening stages to one's destination. Cf. p. 230 of the Text.

from this road, bring with thee for me an enemy in the guise of a friend, in golden vein that invites to infidelity, spins on the finger, round as the disc of the sun, that lightens the burden of debt and plays the rôle of the two-faced.'[1] Said 'Ísá ibn Hishám: 'Then I knew it was a dinar that he demanded. So I said to him, Thou canst have one down and the promise of another one like it.' He then recited and said:—

'Thy plan is better than what I asked for,[2]
Mayest thou continue to be the worthy doer of generous deeds,[3]
Thy branches overspreading and thy root be healthy.
I cannot endure the burden of gifts,
Nor bear the weight of mendicity.
My imagination fell short of the extent of thy generosity
And thy doing has exceeded my fancy.
O prop of fortune and greatness
May time never be bereft of thee!'

Said 'Ísá ibn Hishám: Then I gave him the dinar and said to him: Where is the native soil of this excellence? He answered: I was reared by the Quraish, and in its oases nobility was prepared for me. One of those present asked: Art thou not Abú'l-Fath al-Iskanderí and did I not see thee in 'Iráq going about the streets begging[4] with letters?[5] Then he recited, saying:—

'Verily, God has servants[6]
Who have adopted a manifold[7] existence,

[1] *The two-faced:* Cf. De Sacy, *Hariri*, i, 36.

[2] *Thy plan is better than what I asked for:* Metre, *basit*.

[3] *Mayest thou continue to be:* Literally, May thy wood be sound and thy generosity enduring: figure for strength of character.

[4] مُتَكَدِّيًا *Begging:* from كَدَّى to beg. De Sacy says the word is arabicized from the Persian گدا a beggar and گدائی beggary. (*Chrestomathie Arabe*, iii, 250.) The fact that both Badi' al-Zamán and Ḥarirí regarded the profession of begging as one of Persian origin—see note on the Sons of Sásán, (Text p. 89)—supports this derivation. For an earlier use of the word كُدْيَةٌ beggary, see Dieterici's edition of *Philosophie der Araber*, Thier und Mensch, p. 32, lines 10 seq.

[5] *With letters:* Cf. De Sacy, *Ḥariri*, p. 76.

[6] *Verily God has servants:* Metre, *ramal*.

[7] خَلِيطًا *Manifold:* Literally, mixed or mingled, e.g. لَبَنٌ خَلِيطٌ sweet milk mixed with sour.

In the evening they are Arabs,
In the morning Nabaṭeans.'[1]

IV. THE MAQAMA OF SIJISTAN

'ÍSÁ IBN HISHÁM related to us and said: A pressing need impelled me to go to Sijistán.[2] So I put my resolution into effect[3] and mounted the necessary camel. I sought God's blessing upon my determination which I set before me, while I made prudence my guide until it directed me thither. Now I arrived at the gates of the city after sunset and was, therefore, obliged to pass the night on the spot.[4]

Now, when the blade of dawn was drawn, and the host of the sun sallied forth, I went to the business quarter to select a lodging. And when I had gone from the circumference[5] of the city to its centre, and walked along the circle of shops

[1] *Nabateans:* A well-known Arabian people. In the time of Josephus their settlements gave the name Nabatene to the borderland between Syria and Arabia from the Euphrates to the Red Sea. Before their appearance in history, about 312 B.C., they had already some tinge of civilization. Though true Arabs they came under the influence of Aramean culture, and Syriac was the language of their coins and inscriptions when the tribe grew into a kingdom and profited by the decay of the Selucids to extend itself over the country east of the Jordan. As allies of the Romans they continued to flourish throughout the first Christian century. About A.D. 105, Trajan most unwisely broke up the Nabatean nationality. *Encl. Bib.*, iii, 3254-5.

[2] *Sijistán:* originally Sagistan, the land of the Sakas, Arabicized to Sijistan, the ancient Sacastane and the modern Seistan, the name of a district of Persia and of its chief town. The capital was formerly called Zaranj. It formed a part of the empire of the Khalifa and was a great Khárijite centre. About A.D. 860, when it had undergone many changes of Government under lieutenants of the Baghdad Khalifa, or bold adventurers acting on their own account, Yaqût ibn Laith al-Saffar, made it the seat of his power. In A.D. 901, it fell under the power of the Sámanids and towards the end of the century into that of the Ghaznavids. In Hamadhání's time Khalaf ibn Aḥmad was the Amir of Sijistán (A.H. 354-93). Yaqût says that when the inhabitants submitted to their Arab conquerors they stipulated that no hedgehog was to be killed. The reason assigned for this being that the country was infested with snakes and that the hedgehogs kept the number down. Every house had its hedgehog! Yaqût, iii, 41. *Encyclopædia Britannica*, xxiv, 592.

[3] *I put my resolution into effect:* Literally, I mounted the intention thereof. Cf. De Sacy, *Ḥariri*, i, 14.

[4] *I was obliged to pass the night on the spot:* Literally, the passing of the night chanced where I reached.

[5] قِلَادَة *circumference:* Literally, a necklace.

till I reached the chief one,[1] a loud-toned[2] voice penetrated my ear. I went towards the speaker until I stood near him, and behold it was a man mounted on his horse and panting for breath.[3] He had turned the back of his head towards me and was saying: He who knows me, knows me well, and he, who does not know me, I will make myself known to him. I am the first-fruits of Yemen,[4] the much-talked-of of the age, the enigma of men and the puzzle of the ladies of the harem.[5] Ask of me concerning countries and their fortresses, mountains and their heights, valleys and their watercourses, seas and their springs, horses and their backs. Who has captured their walls, discovered the mysteries of their heights, explored their paths and penetrated into their lava hills? Ask of kings and their treasures, precious stones and their mines,[6] affairs and their inwardness,[7] sciences and their centres, weighty matters and their obscurities, wars and their difficult situations. Who has seized their hoards without paying the price? Who has got possessions of their keys[8] and known the way to victory? By Heavens! it is I who have achieved all that. I have made

1 وَاسِطَةٌ *The chief one:* Literally, the jewel in the middle of a necklace and which is the best thereof.

مِن كُلِّ عِرقٍ مَعْنًى *Loud-toned:* Literally, with something from every root, and therefore well nourished and strong.

3 *Panting for breath:* Literally, choking himself.

4 *The first-fruits of Yemen:* Here Abú'l-Fatḥ begins to enigmatically refer to his name. The fruit of the tree نَبْعٌ *nab'a* resembling that of the *pistachia terebinthus*, except that it is red, sweet and round, is called فَتْحٌ *Fath.* It is also an allusion to the early conversion to Islám of the people of Yemen. The name of the first envoy that came from Yemen to visit the Prophet is said to have been Abú'l-Fatḥ. Al-Fatḥ means the opening, beginning, victory.

5 رَبَّاتُ الحِجَالِ *Ladies of the harem:* حِجَال pl. of حَجَلَةٌ a kind of curtained canopy, or tent, or chamber for a bride.

For courteous phrases for ladies, see Jáḥız, *Ḥaywán*, v. 103–110.

6 *Precious stones and their mines:* I have read أعلاقٌ instead of أغلاق as the former gives the required sense.

7 بَوَاطِن *Inwardness:* From بَطْنٌ the abdomen. Hence the interior of anything. e. g., لِكُلِّ آيَةٍ مِنهَا ظَهرٌ وَ بَطْنٌ To every verse thereof is an apparent ظَهرٌ (lit. back) sense and a sense requiring development. (بَطْن)

8 *Their keys:* i.e. the keys of the positions.

peace between powerful kings[1] and disclosed the mysteries of dark difficulties. By Heavens! I have been even in the place where lovers are overthrown. I have even been afflicted with sickness, even the sickness caused by the languishing eye.[2] I have embraced supple forms,[3] and plucked the rose from the crimson cheeks. Yet, with all this, I have fled from the world as a generous nature flees from the faces of the base. I have recoiled from despicable things as a noble ear recoils from obscene language. But, now that the morn of hoariness has dawned, and the dignity of old age has come upon me, I have resolved to make wise provision for my journey to the next world and I have not perceived any way better to right guidance, than that which I am treading. One of you will observe me riding a horse and speaking at random[4] and say, 'this is the Father of Wonder',[5] nay, but I am indeed the Father of Wonders, which I have both seen and experienced, and the Mother of Enormities which I have estimated and endured. I have with difficulty obtained the keys of treasures[6] and then have lightly cast them aside. I have bought dear and sold cheap. I have, by Heavens! joined their pageants and jostled against shoulders. I have watched the stars[7] and ridden the flesh off my mounts, I have been obliged to engage in dangerous enterprises vowing not to withhold from the Muslims the benefits accruing therefrom. Now I must transfer the cord of this trust from my neck to yours and offer for sale in your streets this medicine of mine. Let him buy from me who shrinks not from the place

[1] ٱلْمُلُوكُ ٱلصِّيدُ *Powerful kings:* ٱلصِّيدُ pl. of أَصْيَدُ a man unable to look aside by reason of disease, probably a crick in the neck, and hence a king, who by reason of pride, does not turn his head to the right or left. But more probably أَصْيَدُ = greatest hunter = lion = strong. Cf. *Arab Proverbs*, i, 748. See also Buḥturí, i, 224.

[2] أَحْدَاقٌ *Eyes:* pl. of حَدَقَةٌ Literally, the black of the eye and then the eye absolutely.

[3] *Supple forms:* Literally, pliant branches; a very common figure for a flexible form.

[4] نَاثِرُ هَوَسٍ *Speaking at random:* نَثَرَ opposed to نَظَمَ in all senses.

[5] *The Father of Wonder:* Cf. H. De Sacy, *Ḥariri*, ii, 571.

[6] For ٱلْأَغْلَاقَ again read ٱلْإِعْلَاقَ precious things, or treasures.

[7] *I have watched the stars:* waited for their disappearance at dawn.

where God's servants stand, nor from the formula of unity. And let him who is of proud pedigree [1] and good breeding [2] preserve the remedy. Said 'Ísá ibn Hishám: I went round in front of him that I might learn who he was, and by Heavens! it was our Shaikh Abú'l-Fatḥ al-Iskanderí. So I waited for the crowd to disperse [3] from before him, and then addressing him I asked: 'How big an opening will this nostrum of thine want?' He answered, 'Thy purse will open as much as thou desirest.' I then left him and departed. [4]

V. THE MAQAMA OF KÚFA

'ÍSÁ IBN HISHÁM related to us and said: When I was in my young days, I rode my mount into every species of blind folly and urged my courser into every kind of error until I had drunk of life a delicious draft and had donned the flowing robes of fortune. But when the day brightened [5] my night and I gathered up my skirts [6] and prepared for the final judgement, I mounted a tame steed [7] in order to discharge a bounden duty.[8] There accompanied me on the road a friend in whom I saw nothing wrong to make me repudiate him. Now, when we had exchanged confessions and confidences, the story revealed that he was a Kúfan by principle and a Ṣúfi by persuasion, [9] and so we travelled on.

Now, when we alighted at Kúfa, [10] we went to his house and

1 *Of proud pedigree:* Literally, whose grandfathers are noble.

2 سُقِىَ بِٱلْمَاءِ ٱلطَّاهِرِ عُودُهُ *Good breeding:* Literally, whose wood has been irrigated with pure water.

3 اجتال ٱلنَّعَامَة *The crowd to disperse:* Literally, until the ostrich fled. The Paris MS. has عَامَةٌ which yields a better sense. Cf. De Sacy, *Hariri*, ii, 431 هَالَتْ نَعَامَتُهُ 'He finished his work.'

4 This maqáma lacks the usual concluding lines of poetry and ends very abruptly.

5 *Day brightened:* Fig. for had turned grey.

6 *I gathered up my skirts:* Fig. for preparing to do something. Cf. Eng. to take off one's coat, or to tuck up one's sleeves.

7 A *tame steed:* Literally, broken in.

8 A *bounden duty:* i.e. the Pilgrimage. See Qur'án, iii, 91.

9 A *Ṣúfi by persuasion:* A Ṣúfi is naturally known by his dress.

10 *Kúfa:* Founded by the Arabs in A.H. 17 or 18 in the Khalifate of 'Umar. It was one of the chief seats of Arabian learning and was long the rival of the great grammatical school of Baṣra.

entered it, when the face of day had become sombre [1] and its
cheeks darkened.[2]   Then, when the eye of the night had drooped,
and the dawn on its lip had sprouted, there was a knock at the
door.[3]   We asked, ' What wanderer is knocking ? '   He answered :
' The envoy of night and its messenger, the defeated and hunted
of hunger, a well-bred personage in the leash of misfortune and
bad times ; a guest, whose tread is light [4] and whose stray [5] is
a loaf ; a neighbour who asks aid against hunger and a patched
smock ; an exile after whose departure the fire of banishment [6]
was kindled, in whose wake the howling dogs have barked, after
whom pebbles were cast and the areas swept.[7]   His jaded camel
is fatigue ; his pleasure is affliction, and between him and his
two chicks is a vast desert.'   Said 'Ísá ibn Hishám ; I took from
my purse the lion's share, [8] passed it to him and said, ' Increase
thy demands and we will increase our gifts to thee.'   He replied,
' No fire so hot to cause aloeswood to diffuse its fragrance as
that of generosity, and the envoy of benevolence is met by no
one better than the messenger of gratitude.   Therefore, whoever
possesses plenty, let him do good, for generosity will not pass
unrewarded [9] by God and man.   But as for thee, may God cause

Kúfa and Baṣra were the resort of the pious and of the adventurer, the centres
of religious and political movements.

'Alí is said to have called the former, the treasure-house of the Faith and the
proof of Islám.

[1] *The face of day had become sombre :* Literally, the face of day was covered
with vegetation. بَقَلَ.

[2] *Darkened :* Literally became green, both of these and the succeeding expressions are figures for the growing of a beard and here, metaphorically, signify it became dark.

[3] *There was a knock at the door:* Cf. De Sacy, *Ḥarírí,* i. 50.

[4] *Whose tread is light :* i.e. one who will cause little inconvenience.

[5] ضَالَّتُهُ *whose stray :* Literally, a stray camel.

[6] *The fire of banishment :* (نَارُ ٱلطَّرْدِ) (Cf. Hamadhání's Letters, No. 128, p.
352), or the fire of departure was a solemn cursing of a man by his enemy when he
set out on a journey.   The fire was lighted, and the ill-wisher exclaimed 'Away !
begone ! '   For the names of the various fires of the Arabs, see Jáḥiz, *Ḥaywán*
Part v.

And the areas were swept : As is done after a death has occurred.

[8] *The lion's share :* Literally, the grasp of the lion.

[9] *Generosity will not pass unrewarded, etc.*   This is a quotation from the
lines of Ḥuṭai'ah who was a contemporary of the Prophet :

مَّن يَصَنع العُرَف لاَ يَعدم جَوَازِيهِ * لَن يَذهَبَ ٱلعُرفُ بَينَ ٱللهِ وٱلنَّاسِ

thee to realise thy hopes and give thee the supreme hand.'[1] Said 'Ísá ibn Hishám: Then we opened the door for him and said 'Enter' and lo! by Heavens, it was our Shaikh Abú'l-Fatḥ al-Iskanderí! So I said: ' 'Distressing is the extreme poverty which thou hast reached and this aspect especially.' Then he smiled, and indited, saying:—

'Let not my demanding deceive thee,
I am in a state of affluence[2] so great that the pocket of joy would tear,
I could, if I wished, have ceilings of gold.'[3]

VI. THE MAQAMA OF THE LION

'ÍSÁ IBN HISHÁM related to us and said: There used to reach me of the maqámát and sayings of al-Iskanderí[4] such as would arrest the fugitive and agitate the sparrow. Poems of his have been recited to us whose refinement pervades the soul in all its parts, and whose subtlety is hidden from the imaginations of the wizards.[5] And I pray God to spare him so that I may meet him and marvel at his indifference[6] to his condition in spite of his art

'Whosoever doeth good will not lose his reward. For generosity will not go unrewarded by God and man.' That is to say, if man does not reward, God will. The Arabs believed this to be a quotation from the Taurát. *Aghání*, ii, 48 and Goldziher's edition of Hutai'ah's poems.

1 يَدَ ٱلْعُلْيَا *The supreme hand:* Here used in the sense of the upper, or giving hand, as opposed to the lower, or receiving hand.

Cf. the rabbinical maxim:

כל מי שה כסף בידו ידו על העליונה

'*Whoever has money (silver) in his hand, his hand is supreme.* See note on أَلْيَدُ ٱلْعُلْيَا in the maqáma of the Yellow', Text p. 230.

2 *I am in a state of affluence:* Metre, *khafif.*

3 *Ceilings of gold:* A boast rather inconsistent with his actual condition. The Constantinople edition has this additional line. 'Sometimes I am a Nabatean at other times an Arab.'

This maqámá is identical in name and theme with *Hariri* v, 49.

4 *The Maqámát of al-Iskanderi.* The first example of the use of the word Maqámát by the author.

5 ٱلْكَهَنَة *Wizards:* pl. of كَاهِن Heb. כֹּהֵן a priest in a degraded sense. In the time of the Prophet it meant a fortune-teller, an interpreter of dreams, etc. See Qur'án, lii, 29 and lxix, 42. This is a word whose origin is not known.

6 *His indifference, etc:* Literally, the sitting down of his resolution with his state.

and fortune. Fortune had made her benefits[1] remote by placing barriers between him and them and continued so to do till I happened to have some business in Ḥimṣ.[2] So I sharpened my greediness of desire to go thither in the company of some individuals, brilliant as the stars of night, and like saddle-cloths cleaving to the backs of the horses. We started on the road eliminating its distance [3] and annihilating its space, and we continued to traverse the humps of the uplands, mounted upon those noble steeds, until they became as lean as walking-sticks and were bent like bows. Now we were fated to pass a valley along the base of a mountain covered with ala and tamarisk thickets which looked like maidens with their flowing tresses and suspended locks.[4] The fierce noonday heat turned us thither to seek a sheltered spot and a midday nap. We had tethered our horses and had addressed ourselves to sleep with the sleepers, when suddenly the neighing of the horses startled us. And I looked towards my steed and behold he had cocked his ears, he was glaring with his eyes, gnawing the strands of the rope with his lips, and scoring the surface of the ground with his hoofs. Then the horses stampeded,[5] staled, broke the ropes and made for the mountains. Every one of us flew to his weapons when lo! there appeared a lion, in the garb [6] of doom, ascending from his lair, with inflated skin, [7] showing his teeth, with an eye full of arrogance, a nose distended with pride, and a breast from which courage[8] never departed and wherein terror never dwelt. We said: 'This is a serious matter and an anxious business.' There advanced to meet him from among the impetuous of the party a youth,

[1] *Her benefits :* Literally, her affairs, or business.

[2] *Ḥimṣ* (Emessa) *:* A well-known city situated half-way between Damascus and Aleppo. The inhabitants of this city were 'Ali's stoutest opponents in Mu'awiya's army in the battle of Siffín (A.D. 657). Yaqût, ii, 334.

[3] *Eliminating its distance :* Literally plundering its distance.

[4] الضَّفائِر و الغَدائِر *Locks and tresses :* غَدائِر are said to pertain to women and ضَفائِر to men.

[5] *Stampeded :* Literally, became agitated.

[6] فَرْوَة *garb :* applied to a garment when it is furred, a well-known kind of garment for preservation from the cold.

[7] *With inflated skin :* Literally, inflated in his skin.

[8] القَلْب *courage :* Literally, the heart.

'Tawny of skin[1] of the family that comprises the nobility of the Arabs,
Who fills his bucket full to the knot of the rope that ties the middle of the cross-bars,'

with a heart urged on by doom, and an all-effective sword, but the fierceness of the lion took possession of him and the ground cheated his feet so that he fell on his hands and face. The lion then crossed over the place of his falling in the direction of those who were with him. Then death summoned the fallen one's fellow in the same manner. He advanced, but terror tied his hands, he fell to the earth and the lion crouched[2] on his chest. But I threw my turban at him and diverted his mouth and thus prevented the shedding of the youth's blood. Then the young man arose and slashed at his stomach until he collapsed with fright and the lion died of the wounds in his stomach. We then went after the horses, found such as had halted, abandoned such as had bolted, and returned to the dead friend to perform the last rites! 'When we had poured the earth upon our *late* fellow-traveller we were grieved, aye and what an hour of grief it was.'[3]

Then we turned again towards the desert and entered it. We journeyed on till the provision bag contracted and supplies were well nigh exhausted. We could neither advance nor retreat, and we dreaded the two slayers, thirst and hunger, when a horseman came in sight. We went towards him and moved

1 *Tawny of skin, etc.:* Metre, *ramal.*

وَأنَا ٱلاخضر ومن يعرفنِى * أَخضَرُ ٱلجِلدَةِ فِى بيت العَرَب

'And I am the tawny: and who knows me?
The tawny of skin (of pure race) of the family that comprises the nobility of the Arabs.'

مَن يَسَا جِلنِى يَسَاجِلُ مَاجِداً * يَملَأ ٱلدَّلو الَى عَقد ٱلكَرَب

'He who contends for superiority (literally vies with me in filling buckets) with me, contends with one possessing glory.
Who fills the bucket up to the tying of the rope attached to the middle of its crossbars.'

These verses are by al-Faḍl Ibn 'Abbás al-Lahabí, *Aghání*, xiv, 171. This poet was a contemporary of Farazdaq (d. 170), *Aghání*, xv, 2-11.

2 *Crouched, etc.:* Literally, made his chest a bed.

3 *Aye and what an hour of grief it was!* Metre, *ṭawil.* Cf. the line of Ka'ah, *Ḥamasah* (Freytag), p. 95, line 3.

in his direction. When we reached him, he alighted from his noble steed,[1] kissed the ground[2] and prostrated himself.[3] He then came towards me, to the exclusion of the company, kissed my stirrup and sought shelter at my side. I beheld and lo! a face that shone like the sheen of the rain-cloud, and a goodly stature,

> 'When the beholder's eye ascends[4] to his head and descends to his feet,
> It is unable to take in all his beauties,'

a cheek upon which the down had appeared and a moustache that had just sprouted; a plump forearm, a supple and slim body.[5] His origin was Turkish[6] and his dress royal.[7] We said: 'Perish thy father!'[8] What has happened to thee?

He replied: 'I am the servant of a king who made a determined attempt to kill me, and so I ran away, I knew not whither, as you see me now.' Now his appearance bore witness to the truth of his statement. Then he said: 'To-day I am thy servant and what is mine is thine!' I said, 'Good tidings for both of us. Thy journey has brought thee to a spacious court and fresh delight.' The company congratulated me, and

1 حُرّ فَرَسِهِ *His noble steed:* The adjective is placed before instead of after the noun.

2 *Kissed the ground:* Literally, he engraved the ground with his lips.

3 *Prostrated himself:* Literally, he met the ground with both his hands.

4 متى مَاتَرَقَّ ٱلعَيْنُ *When the eye ascends:* A quotation from Imral—Qais, p. 25, line 69. Lyall's edition of the *Mu'allaqát*. The text is wrongly vocalized: *for* تَرِقّ *read* تَرَقَّ

5 قضيب ريان *A supple and slim body:* Literally, a well-irrigated branch قضيب a branch cut off and hence a rod.

6 *His origin was Turkish:* Probably an allusion to the line.

لَأَبقَى يَمَاكٌ فِى حَشَاىَ صَبَابَةً * اِلَى كُلِّ تُرِكِىِّ النِّجَار جَلِيبِ

'Verily Yemák hath (by his death) left in my entrails an affection,
For every immigrant of Turkish origin,' Mutanabbí, p. 467.

7 مَلَكِىْ *angelic*, should be vocalized مَلْكِىْ royal.

8 *Perish thy father:* Literally, thou hast no father. A playful term of imprecation expressive of surprise or admiration. Al-Hamádhaní did not think this phrase unworthy of elucidation. He explains, 'the Arabs say thou hast no father concerning anything that is perfect, but it depends upon who says it.' (Letters, p. 249.) For the explanation of the use of the accusative in this and similar expressions, see Wright's Arabic Grammar, ii, 94-5.

he began to look and his glances smote us; he commenced to speak and his words fascinated us. He said: 'O masters! at the base of this mountain there is a spring and ye have entered a waterless desert, [1] so take some water from there.' So we turned rein in the direction he indicated and we arrived there. The noonday heat had melted our bodies and the locusts had mounted the trees.[2] He said: 'Will you not take the noonday nap beneath this spacious shade, and near this fresh water?' We said: 'As thou wilt.' He then dismounted from his horse, undid his belt, removed his tunic [3] so that nothing concealed him from us, except a thin undergarment which did but reveal his body. We doubted not but that he had quarrelled with the ministering angels, [4] evaded the heavenly guards, and fled from the guardian of Paradise. He betook himself to the saddles and removed them, to the horses and fed them, [5] and to the resting-places and sprinkled them with water. Men's perception was bewildered at him, and their eyes were fixed upon him. So I said: 'O young man, how courteous thou art in service and how generally useful! Therefore woe to him whom thou hast forsaken, and blessed is he with whom thou hast become friendly! How is it possible to thank God for His favour through thee?' He said: 'That which you will soon see from me will be even greater. Do my activity in service and my general comeliness please you? What if ye were to see me in company, showing some portion of my skill? It would increase your admiration [6] for me.' We said: 'Go on!' Then he took one of our bows, strung it, braced the bow-string, put it into the notch, and shot it up towards the sky and then

1 *Waterless desert:* Literally, a blind desert, with no عَيْنٌ eye, or spring.

2 *The locusts had mounted the trees:* They were rendered active by the intense heat.

3 قُرْطَقَةٌ *a tunic*, waistcoat or jacket, arabicized from the Persian كرتة

4 أَلْجَنَانَ *ministering angels:* Probably أَلْجِنّ a species of angels who were the guardians of the earth, and of the gardens of Paradise (See Lane, art: جن p. 462).

5 فَحَشَّهَا *Fed them:* Literally, foddered them.

6 شَغَفًا *admiration:* from شَغَافٌ the pericardium and then love which is supposed to tear the pericardium.

followed it up with another and split it in the air. Then he said: 'I will show you another trick.' He then made for my quiver and seized it, went towards my horse and mounted it, and shot one of our number with an arrow which he fixed in his chest, and then a second one which he shot through his back. I cried out 'Sirrah! what art thou doing?' He retorted 'Silence, scoundrel! By heavens, every one of you shall bind his fellow's hands, or I will make his spittle to choke him.' Now with our horses tied up, our saddles off, our arms beyond our reach, he mounted and we on foot, his bow in his hand ready to shoot us in the back, or to pierce our abdomens and chests, we were at a loss what to do. But, when we saw his seriousness, we seized the thong and bound one another. I alone remained with no one to tie my hands. So he said to me: 'Strip!'[1] and I stripped. Then he got down from the horse and began to slap each of us, one after the other, and to take off his clothes, and finally he came to me. Now I had on a pair of new boots and so he said to me: 'Perish thy mother! take them off' I replied: 'I put these boots on when the hide was raw and, therefore, I cannot remove them.' He said: 'I will take them off.' Then he drew near to me to remove them, and I stretched my hand to seize a knife which I had concealed in one boot while he was engaged removing the other. I plunged the knife into his abdomen with such force, that I caused it to appear behind his back, and he uttered but one cry [2] and then bit the dust.[3] Then I arose, went to my companions and untied their hands. And we then divided the spoils [4] obtained from the two dead men. We found our friend had given up the ghost and so we buried him.[5] Then we continued our journey and arrived at Ḥimṣ after five nights' travelling. Now when we reached an open space in the market, we saw a man with a wallet and a small walking-stick in his hand, standing in front of his son and little daughter, and he was saying:—

1 *Strip*: Literally, come out with thy skin from thy clothes.

2 *He uttered but one cry*: Literally, he only opened his mouth.

3 *He bit the dust*: Literally, put the stone in his mouth. Another reading أَلْقَمْتُهُ حَجَرَةً I silenced him. Cf. Freytag, *Arab Proverbs*, i, 120.

4 *We divided the spoils*: A rather unworthy manner of disposing of their dead friend's property.

5 *We buried him*: Literally, he went to his tomb.

'God bless him who fills my wallet [1] with his generous
   gifts,
God bless him who is moved to pity for Sa'id and Fatimah,
Verily he will be your male-servant and she your
   maid-servant.'

Said 'Ísá ibn Hishám : This man is surely al-Iskanderí of
whom I have heard, and regarding whom I have been asking ;
and behold it was he ! [2] So I gently approached him and said :
'Command what is thine.' He replied : 'A dirhem.' I said :—

'Thou canst have a dirhem [3] multiplied by its like
As long as I live.
So make up thy account and ask
In order that I may give what is demanded.'

And I said to him : 'A dinar into two, into three, into four, into
five, until I reached twenty.' Then I said : 'How much dost
thou make it ?' He answered : 'twenty loaves' [4] So I commanded that amount to be given him and said : 'Nought avails
without God's help [5] and there is no device against ill-fatedness.'

VII.   THE MAQAMA OF GHAILAN [6]

'Ísá ibn Hishám related to me and said : 'While we were at
Jurján in a meeting-place of ours discussing, there was with us

---

[1] *God bless him who fills my wallets, etc.* Metre, *khafif*.

[2] فَاذَا هُوَ هُوَ *'And behold it was he !'* There was a controversy between the
schools of Basra and Kúfa as to whether this phrase or فَاذَا هُوَ إِيَّاةُ *And behold it
was him*—was right. The Basrians held that the former, the one used by al-
Hamadhání, was correct. This phrase would call to mind the dispute originated
by Sibawayh, the greatest of grammarians, in the time of the Khalifa Hárún al-
Rashíd (Yaqút, *Dictionary of Learned Men*, vi, 83). Cf. English, It is me, and
the French, *c'est moi*.

[3] *Thou canst have a dirhem.* Metre, *kámil*.

[4] *Twenty loaves :* very defective arithmetic which evokes a well-merited rebuke from 'Ísá ibn Hishám in the concluding sentences of the Maqáma.

[5] الخِذْلَانُ *Without God's help :* See Qur'án, iii, 154.

[6] Abú'l-Haríth Ghailan Ibn 'Uqba Ibn Buhaish, generally known by the surname of Dhú'l-Rumma (the old-rope man) is regarded as the last of the Bedawin
poets. He died in A.H. 117 (A.D. 735-6) and was therefore a contemporary of
Jarir and Farazdaq, see Ibn Khallikan, ii, 447, and Ibn Qutaiba, *Kitáb al-Sh'ir
wa'l-Shu'ará* (De Geoje), p. 333. (The University Press of Cambridge is
publishing for the first time an edition of this poet's work. The editor is Mr. C.
H. H. Macartney of Clare College, Cambridge.)

that chief scholar and narrator of the Arabs, 'Ismat ibn Badr, the Fazárite'.[1] The conversation finally led us to discuss those who pardon their enemies out of gentleness and those who forgive them out of contempt, till we mentioned As-Ṣalatan, al-'Abdi, [2] and al-Ba'ith, [3] and the contempt of Jarir and al-Farazdaq for them.

Said 'Ismat: 'I will relate to you what mine eyes have seen and not what I have got from another. When I was journeying in the country of Tamim, mounted on a noble camel and leading a spare mount, there appeared before me a rider on a dusky camel, frothing thickly at the mouth. He continued to advance towards me till our bodies collided, [4] when he shouted: "Peace be unto you!" I said, "And upon thee peace and the mercy and blessing of God! Who is the loud-voiced rider who salutes with the salutation of Islám?" He answered: "I am Ghailan, ibn 'Uqba." So I said: "Welcome to him of fair renown and famous lineage whose diction is well-known." He replied: "Broad be thy valley and powerful thy associates! but who art thou? I answered, "I am 'Ismat ibn Badr, the Fazárite." He said, "May God prolong thy life! What an excellent friend, associate and companion!" Then we travelled together. When we had journeyed on till noon, [5] he said: "Ísmat, shall we not take a nap, for the sun has melted our brain? I said: "As thou wilt." Se we moved in the direction of

[1] *'Ismat ibn Badr the Fazárite:* I think this character may be identified with Abú 'Abdu'lláh Marwán ibn Mu'awiyah ibn Badr al-Fazári (d. 193 or A.H. 194). Among those who learned traditions from him was Ibn Hanbal (A.H. 164–241) *Ansab of al-Sam'áni*, p. 427, Gibb Memorial Series.

[2] *As-Ṣalatan, al-'Abdi* was a contemporary of al-Farazdaq and Jarír as the following incident shows: 'When as-Ṣalatan, al-'Abdí pronounced al-Farazdaq superior to Jarir in point of lineage, and Jarir superior to al-Farazdaq as poet, Jarír reported with this proverb:

مَتَى كَانَ حَكَمَ اللهِ فِى كَرَبِ ٱلنَّخلِ

'When was God's wisdom in husbandmen and possessors of palm trees?' (Freytag, *Arab Proverb*, ii, 628; Lane, p. 2602 art كرب). The point of this lies in the fact that the region of as-Ṣalatan's tribe abounded in palm trees.

[3] *Al-Ba'ith:* a contemporary of Jarir. He was one of those who had the temerity to satire the great poet's tribe, the Kulayb. *Aghání*, vii, 41.

[4] *Bodies collided:* Literally, form with form.

[5] هَجَّرنَا *We journeyed on till morn:* From هَاجِرَةٌ noon when the heat is fiercest.

some *āla* trees as though they were maidens [1] with their hair down, displaying their charms, and to a collection of tamarisk trees opposite to them. Then we unsaddled and partook of some food. Now Dhú'l-Rumma was a small eater. After that we prayed. Then each of us betook himself to the shade of a tamarisk tree, intending to take the noonday nap. Dhú'l-Rumma lay down and I desired to do as he did. So I lay on my back, but no sleep took possession of my eyes. I looked and saw a short distance of a large-humped camel, jaded by the sun, with her saddle thrown off, and behold a man like a hireling, or slave was standing guarding her. But I turned away from them, for what had I to do with enquiring about that which did not concern me? Dhú'l-Rumma slept for a little [2] while and then awoke. Now this was in the days of his satirizing the tribe of Murri, so he raised his voice, [3] and recited saying:—

"Are the traces of Maiya [4] to be found on the obliterated surface of the sand dune
Which the gale has persistently covered up?
Nought remains but a battered tent-peg,
And a fireplace without a fire-taker,
A cistern with both sides broken,

[1] *As though they were maidens:* Cf. Text, p. 26.

[2] غِرارًا *A little*: Literally, paucity of milk of a camel and then applied to paucity of sleep in which latter sense it is used by al-Farazdaq, نَوْمُهُنَّ غِرَارٌ Their sleep is little (Lane, p. 2239, art غِرار) Cf. *Arab Proverbs*, i, 613: سَبَقَ دِرَّةٌ غِرَارَهُ His abundant milk flow preceded his paucity thereof.

[3] رفع عقيرته *He raised his voice*: Perhaps originally connected with Heb. קרר. For similar examples of transposition Cf. Arabic قَرِعَ = Heb. רקע; Arabic رَقَعَ = Heb. קרע

[4] *In the days of his satirizing the tribe of Murri:* The occasion of this bitter satire was the inhospitable treatment of Dhú'l-Rumma by Hishám al-Murr'í at the village at Mar'at. See *Aghání*, vii, 57.

Are the traces of Maiya to be found. Metre, *mutaqárib*. *Maiya*—The beloved of Dhú'l-Rumma whose beauty he often extolled in his poems, see Ibn Qutaibas Sh'ir wa Shu'ará, p. 334. Mr. Macartney, the editor of Dhú'l-Rumma's Diwán, to whose courtesy I am indebted for much useful information regarding this poet, says, 'although these verses put into the mouth of Dhú'l-Rumma do not exist in the MSS. of the Diwán, still they have a genuine ring and the ideas have their correspondences in the Diwán.'

And an assembly whose traces have been removed and
  effaced.
But I remember it with its inhabitants,
Maiya and the sociable friend
My relations with Maiya were like those of one who scares,
Gazelles when they appear to him at the dawn;[1]
When I would come to her, there turned me away a sulky-
  faced watcher, her guardian and keeper.
There will soon reach Imr al-Qais[2] a widely circulated
  poem
Which traveller and stay-at-home will sing.
Dost thou not see that to Imr al-Qais
Clings his chronic complaint?
They are a people insensible to satire,
But can the dry stone feel pain?[3]
In eminence no knight have they, in war no horseman.
Besmeared and saturated are they in the cisterns of
  reproach,
As the hide is saturated by the tanner.
When men look to them for the performance of generous
  deeds,
Downcast and heavy are their eyes.
The noble abhor marrying their women,
And therefore all their spinsters[4] remain old maids."

[1] عَاطِس *dawn*: Literally, the sneezer; also a gazelle coming before one.

[2] *Soon there will reach Imr al-Qais*: This refers to the tribe of Imr al-Qais, a branch of the Tamim descended from Imr al-Qais ibn Sa'ad ibn Manát ibn Tamím, and not to the poet of the tribe of Kindeh.

This Qaṣída begins with the conventional erotic prologue over the deserted encampment of the beloved, a prelude which was condemned in the poet's own day. It is related that, as Dhú al-Rumma was reciting his verses in the camel market, he said to al-Farazdaq who stopped to hear him: 'Well, Abú Firás! what dost thou think of that which thou hast heard?' Al-Farazdaq replied: 'What thou hast uttered is really admirable.' 'Why then', said the other, 'is my name not mentioned with those of the first-rate poets?' 'Thou hast been prevented from attaining their eminence' answered al-Farazdaq 'by thy lamentations over dunghills, and thy descriptions of the excrements of cattle and their pinfolds.' Ibn Khallikan, ii, 447.

[3] *Can the dry stone feel pain*: A rather poor pun on حَجَر a stone and حُجْر the name of the tribal ancestor.

[4] أَيَامَ *Spinsters*: pl. of أَيِّم a spinster or a widow. Another reading نِسَاؤُهم their women.

When he got as far as this verse, the sleeper awoke, began to rub his eyes and to say: "Does little Dhú al-Rumma [1] deprive me of sleep with an incorrect [2] and unpopular poem?" I said: "O Ghailan, who is this?" He replied: "al-Farazdaq?" Then Dhú al-Rumma waxed hot and said:—

"As for the base men of Majásh‘a [3]
Never has the thunder-cloud watered their pastures.
Soon they will be fettered and restrained from noble enterprises,
And the restrainer shall restrain them!"

Then I said: "Now he will choke and fret and thoroughly lampoon him and his tribe."

But by Heavens! al-Farazdaq only said: "Fie on thee little Dhú al-Rumma dost thou oppose one like me with stolen verses?" [4] Then he went to sleep again, as though he had not heard anything. Dhú al-Rumma went away and I went with him, and verily I perceived in him humiliation until we parted.'

VIII. THE MAQAMA OF ADHARBAYJÁN

SAID ‘ÍSÁ IBN HISHÂM: When wealth girded me with its flowing robe, I was suspected of being possessed of property that I had stolen, or of a treasure [5] that I had found, so the darkness of the night urged me to flee, and the horse carried me away. In my flight I traversed paths that had never been trodden before, and where a bird could not find its way, until I passed through the land of terror, crossed its frontiers, entered the protected domain of safety, and there found tranquility. I arrived at Adharbayján [6] and verily the camel's feet were abraded and the

1 *Little Dhú al-Rumma:* The diminutive is used to express contempt.

2 غير مثقّف *incorrect:* Literally crooked, from مثقّف lit, a spear straightened or made even.

3 *And the base men of Majásh‘a:* Metre *mutaqárib; Majásh‘a:* The name of one of al-Farazdaq's ancestors.

4 *Stolen verses.* This was no libel: Dhú al-Rumma was notorious for appropriating the verses of others, See Ibn Qutaiba, *Sh'ir wa'l Shu'ará*, p. 338.

This was not the only rebuke administered to Dhúal-Rumma by al-Farazdaq. See note on the condemnation of the conventional prelude, p. 49, *supra*.

5 كَنْز *a treasure*—property buried in the earth.

6 *Adharbayján:* The Atropatene of the ancients the north-western and most important province of Persia. It was conquered by the Arabs under al-Mughíra in A.H. 20.

stages travelled had consumed their flesh. And when I reached it,

'We alighted intending the stay to be three days,[1]
But it was so pleasant to us that we stopped there a month.'

Now one day while I was in one of its streets, there suddenly appeared a man with a small drinking-vessel which he had placed under his arm, with a walking-stick with which he supported himself, with a tall round cap[2] which he had donned,[3] and a waist-wrapper[4] which he had put on.[5] He raised his voice and said: 'O God who createth things and causeth them to return again, the quickener of bones and the destroyer of them, the Creator of the sun and who causeth it to revolve; the Maker of the dawn to appear[6] and its Illuminator, who sendeth us bounteous benefits[7] and upholdeth the heavens[8] that they fall not upon us; the Creator of souls, male and female;[9] who hath made the sun[10] for a light,[11] the firmament for a roof[12] and the

1 *We alighted intending the stay to be three days:* This is an allusion to the Tradition: إِنَّ ٱلضِّيَافَةَ ثَلَاثٌ Hospitality is for three days, see De Sacy, *Ḥariri*, i, 177. Metre *táwil.*

2 دَنِّيَّةٌ *Tall round cap:* The kind of head-dress called *Qalansuwah* of a Qáḍi said to be like a دَنّ a wine-jar, because high and round.

3 تَقَلْسَهَا *donned*, the قَلَنْسُوَةٌ a kind of head-dress which, according to Dozy, was worn by the 'Abbásid Khalifas, their ministers, and the Qáḍis, and is still used in Syria.

4 فُوطَةٌ *a waist-wrapper*, a kind of striped Indian cloth unsewn. The commentator says it is arabicized from a Sindhi word.

Cf. the mediaeval Latin *Calantica*, tegumentum capitis ad usum mulierum. A covering for the head of women, a kind of veil.

5 تَطَلَّسَ *He had put on:* Literally, he attired himself with a *Tailisan*, a cloak or mantle. Cf. Hebrew טַלִּית a cover or cloak similar to the Roman pallium, especially the *Talith* the cloak of honour, the scholar or officer's distinction, adorned with fringes. Also the cloak of the leader in prayer (jastrow, *Dictionary of the Targum*, p. 537). It is still worn by many of the professional and learned men in Muslim countries.

6 *The Maker of the dawn to appear:* Qur'án, vi, 96.

7 *Bounteous benefits:* An allusion to Qur'án, xxxi, 19.

8 *Who upholdeth the heavens:* Qur'án, xxii, 64.

9 *Male and female:* Literally, in pairs.

10 *The sun:* ٱلْمِصْبَاحُ Literally, a lamp or its lighted wick. The latter is the proper, though not the more usual meaning, and is the one intended in Qur'án, xxiv, 35.

11 *Who hath made the sun for a light:* An allusion to Qur'án, lxxi, 15.

سِرَاجٌ Light, a lamp, apparently arabicized from the Syriac *Shirágá*, Persian chirágh.

12 *The firmament for a roof:* An allusion to Qur'án, xxi, 33.

earth as a carpet;[1] who hath ordained the night for rest[2] and the day for labour;[3] who formeth the pregnant clouds,[4] and sendeth in vengeance the thunderbolts;[5] who knoweth what is above the stars and what is beneath the uttermost parts of the earth, I beseech Thee to send Thy blessings upon Muhammad, the chief of the prophets, and upon his holy family, and that Thou wilt aid me against exile, that I may rein her round[6] homeward; and against hardship that I may be delivered from its depressing shade, and that Thou wilt make it easy for me to obtain at the hands of one of pious nature and pure origin,[7] blessed with true religion, who is not blind to manifest truth, a camel to traverse this road, provision to suffice me and a travelling companion.' Said 'Ísá ibn Hishám, I whispered to myself, 'This man is more eloquent than our al-Iskanderí, Abú'l-Fath!' Then I turned a glance upon him and lo, by Heavens! it was Abú'l-Fatḥ! So I said: 'O Abú'l-Fath! has thy mischief reached this land and thy hunting for game extended to this tribe?' Then he indited saying:—

'I am a mighty wanderer over the countries,[8]
And a great traverser of the horizons.
I am the toy of time,[9]
And am continually on the road.[10]

1 *The earth as a carpet:* an Illusion to Qur'án, ii, 20.

2 *The night for rest:* an allusion to Qur'án, vi, 96.

3 *The day for labour:* an allusion to Qur'án, lxxviii. 11.

4 *Who formeth the pregnant clouds:* an allusion to Qur'án, xiii, 13.

5 *And sendeth in vengeance the thunderbolts:* an allusion to Qur'án, xiii, 14. This prayer is composed in the style of Qur'án, lxxi, 13-19.

6 *I may rein her round:* Literally, I may turn her rope.

7 أطْلَعَتْهُ ٱلطُّهْرَةُ *Of pure origin:* Literally, purity hath raised him.

8 *I am a mighty wanderer:* Metre, *Khafif.*

9 خُذُرُوفٌ *Toy:* A kind of whirling plaything which a boy turns round by means of a thread causing it to make a sound such as is termed دَوِيّ a small piece of wood in the middle of which is cut a notch and which is then tied with a string which, being pulled, turns round and is heard to make a sound such as is termed حفيف Imr al-Qais likens it to a swift horse. See Lyall's edition of the *Mu'allaqát*, p. 23, verse 59.

10 عَمَّارَةُ ٱلطَّرِيق *Continually on the road.* Cf. عَمَّارُ البيوت The Jinn that inhabit houses.

This maqáma has been translated by De Sacy. See his *Chrestomathie Arabe*, iii, 253.

Blame me not—mayest thou receive right guidance !—
For my mendicity, but taste it.'

IX. THE MAQAMA OF JURJAN

'ÍSÁ IBN HISHÁM related to us and said: While we were at Jurján discussing in an assembly of ours, and there was none among us who was not of us, there stood before us a thick-bearded man, neither tall and lankey, [1] nor short and stunted, [2] and little children in worn-out clothes followed him. He began his speech with a greeting and the salutation of Islám. He approached us graciously and we treated him generously. He said: 'O people, I am a man, a citizen of Alexandria [3] of the Umayyad frontiers; the Sulaim [4] gave me birth and the tribe of 'Abs [5] welcomed me. I have traversed horizons and travelled through the remotest parts of 'Iráq. I have been among the dwellers of the desert and the people of the towns and in the two Houses of Rab'iah and Muḍar.[6] Wherever I have been I have not been slighted. Let not what you see of tattered garments, and threadbare clothes make me appear despicable, for by Heavens! we once were of those that help and reform,[7] giving a camel [8] in the morning and a sheep [9] in the evening.

'And among us there are maqámát [10] whose faces are fair,
And councils where words are followed by deeds.

[1] *Lankey:* Literally, stretched. [2] *Stunted:* Literally, prevented.

[3] *Alexandria* of the Umayyad frontiers. A reference to the importance attached to Egypt by Mu'áwíyah.

[4] *Sulaim:* the name of a tribe.

[5] *'Abs*, the name of a large tribe, the descendants of Sulaim.

[6] *Rab'iah and Muḍar:* the names of tribes.

[7] أَهَلَ ثُمٍّ وَرُمٍّ *Those that help and reform:* A popular saying, i.e. we were the persons to put it into proper order, literally, the repairers and menders.

[8] نُرْغِى وَ نُثْغِى *Giving a camel and a sheep:* Another popular expression, نُرْغِى from رَغَاءٌ a kind of gurgling growl made by the camel when it is being laden; then applied to the camel itself. See *Arab Proverbs*, ii, 327.

[9] نُثْغِى *giving a sheep:* from ثُغَاءٌ the bleating or cry of the sheep goat or the like, and then applied to the sheep, absolutely. Cf. the expression مَالَهُ ثَاغٍ وَلَا رَاغٍ He has neither a sheep nor a camel.

[10] *And there are maqámát:* Metre *táwil.* These lines are taken from the Qaṣída of Zuheir, Shu'ará an-Naṣrániah, pp. 573-4. In the original the first line begins with وَفِيهِمْ and not وَفِينَا. It is correctly quoted on p. 32 of the Letters. The sense of the word *maqámát* here is not known, but the context indicates that it signifies champions and the like

Those of them who have much undertake the support of
them who seek their aid,
And those who have little are generous and liberal.'

Then, O people, fate singled me out from among them and turned the back of the shield [1] towards me. Therefore, I exchanged sleep for wakefulness and rest for journeying. The hurlings [2] have thrown me hither and thither, desert has passed me on to desert and the haps of time have stripped me as gum is stripped from the tree, so that at morn and eve I am barer than the palm of the hand and cleaner than the face of a new-born babe. My courtyard is void and my vessels are empty. There is nought for me but the hardship of travel and the constant gripping of the camel's nose-string. I suffer poverty and I conciliate the deserts. The hard ground is my bed, my pillow a stone.

Now at Ámid [3] and then at Ras-u-'Ainin [4]
And sometimes at Mayyafáriqín.[5]
One night in Syria and then at Ahwaz
Is my camel, and another night in 'Iráq.'

Separation ceased not to hurl me to every hurling-place, till I traversed the stony hill-tract and then it set me down at Hamadhán. Its people received me and its friends craned their necks to look at me. But I inclined to one of them whose dish was most capacious and who was most stinting of roughness.

' His fire is lit upon the hill tops, [6]
At a time of scarcity, when fires are covered up.'

He prepared me a couch and made ready a bed for me. If I felt any languor a son, like a keen Yemen blade, [7] or as the new moon appearing in a clear atmosphere, hastened to attend to me.

1 *Turned the back of the shield:* said of a friend who has become inimical. See *Arab Proverbs*, ii, 258.

2 مرامي *Hurlings:* from مرمى the place of the butt where arrows are shot.

3 *Sometimes at Ámid:* Metre, *Wáfir*.

Ámid: the name of a fortress in Diyar Bakr.

4 *Ras al-'Ain:* a large town in Diyar Bakr between Nasibín and Harran, fifteen parasangs from the former place. It is noted for its numerous springs. The scene of a famous battle between the Tamím and Bakr ibn Wá'il.

5 *Mayyafariqín:* Is a town of Diyar Bakr thirty parasangs from Nasibín.

6 *His fire is lit upon the hill tops:* An allusion to the practice of lighting a fire in a prominent position at night (نار القرى) to indicate to the belated traveller where he might find food and shelter. Metre, *Wáfir*.

7 *Like a keen Yemen blade:* In sharpness and effectiveness.

He bestowed favours upon me which made me straitened as to desert and expansive as to joy. The first of them was house furniture and the last a thousand dinars. But the only thing that made me flee from Hamadhán was the stream of gifts [1] which was continuous, and the rain of generosity which was constant. So I fled from Hamadhán as flees the fugitive, and bolted as bolts the wild animal, [2] traversing the roads, pursuing dangers and suffering hardships in the countries. But I have left behind the mother of my abode [3] and my little one as though he were a precious armlet of silver, broken and thrown down on the playground [4] of the maidens of the tribe. And the wind of need and the breeze of penury have blown me to you. Therefore observe, may God have mercy upon you! one rendered lean and emaciated by travel, directed by need and tormented by want.

> 'A traveller, a mighty traverser of the earth, [5] cast hither and thither,
> By deserts; his hair is matted and he is dust-stained.'

May God grant you a guide to goodness and may He make no way for evil to reach you.

Said 'Ísá ibn Hishám: By Heavens! then did hearts feel compassion for him and eyes streamed with tears at the beauty of his speech. And we gave him what was then ready to hand, and he turned away from us praising us. I followed him and lo! by Heavens, it was our Sheikh Abú'l Fatḥ al-Iskanderí.

X. THE MAQAMA OF ISFAHAN

'ÍSÁ IBN HISHÁM related to us and said: I was at Isfahán [6]

1 *The stream of gifts which was constant:* A very strange reason to assign for leaving Hamadhán. Cf. *The Odes of al-Buḥturí*, ii, 220. (Constantinople edition A.H. 1300) where the same idea is expressed.

2 آبِد *A wild animal:* From أَبَدَ shy or unsociable. Cf. Qaṣida of Imr al-Qais, line 35 (Lyall's edition) where the fleet horse is said to prevent the wild animals from escaping. Also the Tradition اَلنِّعَمُ أَوَابِدُ نَقِّيدُوهَا بِالشُّكْرِ 'Benefits are fugitives, or wild animals, therefore detain them by gratitude.'

3 *The mother of my abode:* The mistress of the house, or a man's wife. See Ibn al-Athír, *Kunya Lexicon*, p. 199.

4 *Broken and thrown on the playground:* And therefore in a condition to excite pity.

5 *A traveller, a mighty traverser of the earth.* Metre, *tawil*.

6 *Isfahán:* A well-known city and a former capital of Persia. Captured during the Khalifate of 'Umar in A.H. 23 or 24.

intending to go to Rayy [1] and so I alighted in the city as alights the fleeting shade. I was expecting to see the caravan [2] at every glance and looking out for the mount to appear at every sunrise. Now, when that which I expected, was about to happen, I heard the call to prayer and to respond to it was obligatory. So I slipped away from my companions, taking advantage of the opportunity [3] of joining in public prayers, and dreading, at the same time, the loss of the caravan I was leaving. But I sought aid against the difficulty of the desert through the blessing of prayer, and, therefore, I went to the front row and stood up. The Imám went up to the niche and recited the opening chapter of the Qur'án according to the intonation of Hamza, [4] in regard to using 'madda' and 'hamza,' while I experienced disquieting grief [5] at the thought of missing the caravan, and of separation from the mount. Then he followed up the Súratal-Fátiḥa with Súrat al-Wáqi'a [6] while I suffered the fire of patience and tasked myself severely. I was roasting and grilling on the live coal

[1] *Rayy:* A town in Persia, 160 parasangs from Qazwín, and the seat of the government of the province known under the Khalifate as the Daylam. Conquered in the Khalífate of 'Umar. During the Arab ascendancy, and under the Seljúks, it was a place of considerable importance. Ibn Fáris, the poet and grammarian and instructor of al-Hamadhání, was born here. The derivative adjective from Rayy is Rází.

[2] أَلْقَافِلَة *The caravan:* The commentator considers it to mean a company of persons returning together from a journey, so called as auguring their safe return but more likely from καπηλος through Talmud ייקפּוּלה a trader.

[3] *Taking advantage of the opportunity:* Because of the greater merit in Islám of public over private prayers. See al-Madhírí, *Kitáb al-Targhib wa Tarhib* (d. A.H. 656) i, 74.

[4] According to the intonation of Hamza in regard to using madda and ḥamza. Al-Madda (أَلْمَدَّة) is the orthographical sign of prolongation = Hamzah (أ) (ا + أ) and written آ as in آمين. For the rules as to its use, in intoning the Qur'án, see Suyúṭí, *Itqán*, pp. 227–31. (Calcutta, edition, 1852). Ḥamza ibn al-Habib (80–156 A H.) buried at Húlwán, was one of the seven recognized readers of the Qur'án. He is charged with exaggerating the use of *madda* and *hamza*. The objection is repudiated, however, by Ḥamza's admirers, see *Manduat al-'Ulúmin Turkish*, i, 483 (Constantinople edition, A H. 1313). Al-Hamadhání evidently believed the charge to be well grounded and hence the appropriateness of the allusion.

[5] *Disquieting grief:* Literally causing to stand up and sit down, hence occasioning restlessness.

[6] *Al-Waqi'a:* The Inevitable. Qur'án lvi. It contains ninety-six verses. According to Sháfi'i, *Umm* 88, the choice of the *Súra* rests entirely with the reader or reciter. See Margoliouth, *Early Development of Muḥammadanism*, p. 21.

of rage. But, from what I knew of the savage fanaticism of the people[1] of that place, if[2] prayers were cut short of the final salutation, there was no alternative but silence and endurance, or speech and the grave. So I remained standing thus on the foot of necessity till the end of the chapter. I had now despaired of the caravan and given up all hope of the supplies and the mount. He next bent his back[3] for the two prostrations with such humility and emotion, the like of which I had never seen before. Then he raised his hands and his head and said: 'May God accept the praise of him who praises Him,' and remained standing till I doubted not but that he had fallen asleep. Then he placed his right hand on the ground, put his forehead on the earth and pressed his face thereto. I raised my head to look for an opportunity to slip away, but I perceived no opening in the rows, so I re-addressed myself to prayer until he repeated the Takbír[4] for the sitting posture. Then he stood up for the second prostration and recited the Súras of al-Fatiḥa[5] and al-Qári'a with an intonation which occupied the duration of the Last Day[6] and well-nigh exhausted the spirits of the congregation. Now, when he had finished his two prostrations and proceeded to wag his jaws[7] to pronounce the testimony to God's unity, and to turn his face to the right and to the left[8] for the final salutation, I said: 'Now God has made escape easy, and deliverance is nigh'; but a man stood up and said: 'Whosoever of you loves the Companions and the Muslim community let him lend me his ears for a moment.' Said 'Ísá ibn Hishám: I clave to my place in order to save my dignity. Then he said: 'It is incumbent upon

[1] *From what I knew of the savage fanaticism of the people.* Cf. Yaqút, i, 296.

[2] أَنْ لَوْ should be vocalized إِنْ لَوْ See Wright, *Grammar*, ii, 348 (*b*).

[3] *His back:* Literally his bow.

[4] *Takbír:* The repetition of the well-known formula—God is great, God is great, there is no god but God.

[5] *Al-Fátiḥa:* The opening chapter of the Qur'án.

Al-Qári'a: The 'striking'. Qur'án ci. It contains eight verses.

[6] *The duration of the Last Day:* Literally 'the hour'. According to Qur'án, lxx, 4, fifty thousand years, and Qur'án, xxxii, 4, a thousand years.

[7] أخدعيه *His jaws:* Literally, the two branches أخدعان of the occipital artery which are distributed upon the occiput branches from the وريد or carotid artery.

[8] *Turn his face to the right and left:* To salute the guardian angels.

me that I should speak nothing but verity and testify to nought but the truth. I have brought you good tidings from your Prophet, but I will not communicate it until God hath purged this musjid of every vile person who denies his prophetic office.' Said 'Ísá ibn Hishám: Now he had bound me with cords and fettered me with bands of iron.[1] Then he said: 'I saw the Prophet in a dream! —May God send His blessings upon him—like the sun beneath the clouds, and the moon at the full. He was walking, the stars following him; he was trailing his skirts and the angels held them up. Then he taught me a prayer and admonished me to teach it to his people. So I wrote it down on these slips of paper[2] with the perfumes of Khalúq,[3] musk, saffron and socc,[4] and whoever asks for a copy as a gift, I will present it to him, but whosoever hands me back the cost of the paper I will accept it.' Said 'Ísá ibn Hishám: Dirhems poured upon him to such an extent that he was bewildered. Then he went out and I followed him wondering at the cleverness of his imposture[5] and his artifice to gain his living. And I determined to question him concerning his condition, but I restrained myself, and to converse with him, but I remained silent, and I pondered over his eloquence with his shamelessness, his pleasantness with his mendicity, his catching men by his artifice and his drawing gold from men by his ingenuity. Then I looked and lo! it was Abú'l-Fatḥ al-Iskanderí. So I asked: 'What set thee on this stratagem?' He smiled and recited, saying:—

'Men are asses,[6] so lead them one after the other,
Compete with, and excel them,
Till thou hast obtained from them
What thou desirest, then quit.'

[1] *Bands of iron:* Literally, with black ropes.

[2] القرطاس *Paper:* Arabicized from the Greek χαρτης.

[3] *Khalúq:* A certain species of perfume also termed Khiláq. It is composed of saffron and other things, and redness and yellowness are the predominant colours.

[4] *Socc:* A sort of perfume prepared from ramik which is a kind of black substance like pitch that is mixed with musk.

[5] زرق *Fraud or imposture:* Seems to be a foreign word, probably borrowed from Persian.

[6] *Men are asses:* فقروز *Then quit:* Literally, then die. Metre, *mujtath*.

This maqáma has been translated by De Sacy, see *Chrestomathie Arabe*, iii 255.

XI. THE MAQAMA OF AHWAZ

'ÍSÁ IBN HISHÁM related to us and said: I was at Ahwaz[1] with some friends—'When the beholder's eye ascends[2] to their heads and then descends to their feet, it is unable at once to take in all their beauties'—among us were none but beardless boys with virgin aspirations,[3] or downy-lipped ones with refined manners, the hope of the days and the nights. We discussed fellowship and the rules we should lay down for it, fraternity and how we should strengthen its bonds, happiness and when we should seek it, drinking and when we should vie with one another therein, sociability and how we should mutually contribute towards it, lost chances and how to recover them, liquor and where we should procure it, and the assembly and how we should arrange it. Then said one of our company: 'I will be responsible for the house and entertainment.'[4] Another said: 'I will undertake to supply the wine and the dessert.'[5] Now, when we had determined to proceed, there met us a man wearing two worn-out garments. In his right hand was a staff and on his shoulder a bier. When we saw the bier we augured ill from it, turned our faces away and avoided it.[6] So he shouted at us with a shout at which the earth was almost cloven[7] in sunder and the stars were about to fall,[8] and he said: 'In abasement ye shall surely see it, and perforce and against your will ye shall mount it. What aileth ye that ye augur ill[9] from a mount which your

[1] *Ahwaz:* The plural of هوز originally خوز the chief town of Khuzistan, famous for its fair and formerly noted for its sugar. Captured by Abú Músá al-Ash'arí in A.H. 17.

[2] *When the eye ascends:* Adapted from line 69 of the *Kaṣida* of Imr al-Qais. Already quoted on p. 29 of the text.

[3] *Virgin aspirations:* Another reading بكرُ الأعمال Virgin actions.

[4] أَلنُّزلَ *entertainment:* Literally food prepared for a guest.

[5] أَلنَّقْلَ *Dessert:* Dried and other fruits, such as nuts, almonds, raisins, dried figs, dried dates, etc., taken as an accompaniment with wine. نُقْل is more common than نَقْل

[6] طَوَينَا دُونَهَا كَشْحًا *We avoided it:* Literally, folded up our flank from it. كَشْح is the flank or the part between the false ribs and the hip. Figure for to turn away from, to avoid contact with, or to withdraw the countenance.

[7] *The earth was almost cloven:* An allusion to Qur'án, lxxxii. 1.

[8] *The stars were about to fall:* An allusion to Qur'án, lxxxi. 2.

[9] *Augur ill:* Cf. Qur'án, xxvii. 48.

ancestors have ridden and your posterity will soon ride ? Wherefore do ye shun as unclean a couch, that your fathers have used[1] and your progeny will use ? Yet, by Heavens ! upon these timbers ye shall surely be carried to those worms, and ye shall be transported by these fleet coursers to those pits. A plague upon ye ! Ye augur ill as if ye were free agents, and ye evince loathing as if ye were sanctified. Vile wretches what profiteth this prognostication ? '

Said ‘Ísá ibn Hishám : Now he had dissolved what we had compacted, and rendered futile what we had determined, so we inclined to him and said : ' How much are we in need of thy admonition and how greatly are we in love with thy words. Now if thou wished thou wouldst say something more ? ' He continued : ' Verily there are behind you watering-places which ye have been travelling towards for twenty years.'—

' And verily a man, [2] who has been journeying to a watering
place for twenty years,
Is near his drinking time.'

' And there is one above you who knows your secrets and could, if He would, expose you. In this world He treats you with kindness, and in the next, He will judge you according to knowledge. Therefore call death to mind lest evil come upon you, for if ye make this thought cleave unto you[3] as an innermost garment, ye will not be refractory ;[4] and if ye remember it, ye will not be frivolous. But if ye do forget it, it will make you remember, and if he be slothful about it, it will wake you up,[5]

1 وَطِئَتْهُ *Used it :* Literally, trodden it.

2 *And verily a man :* Metre, *basit.* The commentator attributes these lines to Ibn Aḥmad the Taymite. The original has fifty and not twenty years. This is an example of تَحرِيفٌ or perversion, to make the sense accord with the youth of the company he is addressing.

3 إذَا أَسْتَشْعَرْتُمُوهُ *If ye make it cleave to you :* Literally, if ye make it your شِعَارٌ inner garment, opposed to دِثَارٌ outer garment. اِسْتَشْعَرَ also means to lay to heart. See H*ariri,* i, 135. Cf. The tradition relating to the Anṣár أَنْتُم شِعَارٌ وَالنَّاسُ دِثَارٌ Ye are the special and close friends and the people in general are less near in friendship.

4 لَمْ تَجمَحُوا *Ye will not be refractory :* From جَمَحَ he (a horse) overcame his rider, bolted.

5 هُوَ ثَائِرُكُم *It will wake you up :* As one who seeks blood revenge (ثَارٌ) or retaliation of the slayer of his kinsman.

and though ye dislike it, it will visit you.' We said: 'But what is thy need?' He replied: 'Too far-reaching to set bounds to, and too manifold to be reckoned up.' We said: 'But for the present time?' He said: 'The bringing back of the past and protection against the accidents of the future.' We said: 'That is not in our power, but thou mayest have what thou desirest of the goods of this world and its vanities.'[1] He said: 'I have no need of them, but my need henceforth is rather that ye should bolt[2] than ye should remember[3] what I say.'

XII. THE MAQAMA OF BAGHDAD

'ÍSÁ IBN HISHÁM related to us and said: When I was in Baghdad,[4] I longed for some of the Azaz date, but I had no cash knotted up. So I went out to the shops seeking an opportunity until my desire put me down at Karkh,[5] when lo!

[1] زُخْرُفُهَا *Its vanities:* From زُخْرُف gold زَخْرَفَة signifies the adorning or embellishing of a thing primarily with gold.

[2] أَنْ تَخِدُوا *That ye should bolt:* From وَخَدَ he went quickly like a camel throwing his legs out like an ostrich. This is an extraordinary use of the verb وَخَدَ and the text is probably corrupt, in fact the sentence is omitted from the Constantinople edition which concludes with the words 'I have no need of them'. Besides the remark is neither witty nor clever.

[3] تَعُوا *To ponder:* Another reading تَعِدُوا to promise, which yields a better sense. Another edition has these additional words: 'Then I approached him and lo! it was our Shaikh al-Iskanderí.'

[4] *Baghdad:* Was the capital of the Khalifate from 762–1258. It was originally a little Persian village on the west bank of the Tigris. Yaqút calls it 'the mother of the world and the queen of cities'. It was founded by the Khalifa Manṣúr who laid the first brick with his own hands and recited on the occasion the following passage from the Qur'án: 'The earth is God's. He giveth it for an inheritance unto such of his servants as he pleaseth, and the prosperous end shall be unto those who fear Him' (Qur'án, vii, 125) adding, 'Build under the blessing of God'. The cost of building the city is said to have been 18,000,000 dinars. Yaqút, i, 677 See also Le Strange, *Baghdad*.

[5] *Al-Karkh:* The business quarter of Baghdad on a site outside the city to which Manṣúr transferred the trades people. Two reasons are assigned for this: (1) A patrician came to Baghdad as an ambassador from the Byzantine court. After he had been taken over the city, Manṣúr asked him what he thought of it. He replied, 'It is a beautiful and well-fortified town, but for the fact that your enemies are within its walls.' Manṣúr asked who they were. The ambassador answered: 'The merchants who come from all parts as spies, find out all they want to know and go away again and you are none the wiser?' After the departure of the Ambassador, Manṣúr had all the trades-people removed outside the city to Karkh. (2) The Khalifa found that the smoke from the shops was spoiling the walls of the gates, and to get rid of this smoke nuisance he had them transferred to Karkh. Yaqút, i, 677.

I chanced upon a rustic[1] urging his ass along his waist-wrapper, tapering on one side with the weight of the money tied up in it. Then I said: ‘By Heavens, we have secured a quarry!’ and I addressed him with, ‘Greeting on thee, Abú Zaid! whence art thou come, and where art thou staying, and when didst thou arrive? Come, let us go to the house.’ The rustic said: ‘I am not Abú Zaid, but Abú ‘Ubaid.’ I exclaimed, ‘Of course; God curse the devil[2] and put away forgetfulness; length of time and distance made me forget thee; and how is thy father? Is he as young as he was when I knew him, or has he aged since I left?’ He answered: ‘The spring pasture[3] has grown over and obliterated the traces[4] of his grave and I hope God may receive him to His paradise.’ I exclaimed: ‘Verily we are God's and to him do we return! There is neither strength,[5] nor power except in God, the High, the Great’; and my hand flew[6] to my undershirt[7] as if I wished to rend it. But the rustic clasped my waist with his hands and said: ‘I adjure thee by God not to rend it.’ Then I said: ‘Let us go to the house and get some food, or to the market and buy some roast meat, for the market is nearer and the food there nicer.’ Thus did I excite in him a fierce craving for meat, and incline him with

1 سَوَادِىٌّ *a rustic:* From the سَوَادُ ٱلْعِرَاقِ the district of towns or villages and cultivated lands of al-‘Iráq, or the district between Baṣra and Kúfa so-called because of خُضْرَةٌ, which means both greenness and a colour, approaching to blackness, of its trees and seed produce. The Arabs call that which is أَخْضَرُ green, أَسْوَدُ black because it appears to be thus at a distance. The meaning here is evidently ‘a greenhorn’

2 *God curse the devil and put away forgetfulness:* An allusion to Qur'án, xviii. 62.

3 ٱلرَّبِيعُ *The spring pasture:* Literally, the spring. Another reading ٱلْمَرْعَى the pasture.

4 دِمْنَةٌ *traces:* Cf. Hebrew דמן

5 لَا حَوْلَ *There is no strength:* A formula used to express consternation or surprise.

6 مددت يد ٱلْبِدَارِ *My hand flew:* Literally, I stretched the hasty hand.

7 صِدَارٌ *undershirt:* Literally, a certain garment with which the head and breast are covered, worn by a woman mourning for her husband, or a small shirt worn next to the body. A proverb says, كُلُّ ذَاتِ صِدَارٍ خَالَةٌ Every female having a ṣidár is a maternal aunt, whom one is under an obligation to respect, and protect. *Arab Proverbs*, ii, 310.

the inclination of gobbling and greed, and he became greedy. But he did not know he had fallen into the trap.

Then we came to a fried-meat seller's whose roasted meats[1] were dripping with fat, and whose cakes were streaming with gravy. I said: 'Put aside for Abú Zaid a portion from this fried meat and then weigh him some of that sweetmeat. Take some of those plates and place upon them some of these wafer-cakes and sprinkle upon them some juice of the Summak[2] berry, in order that Abú Zaid may eat and relish it.' So the fried-meat seller, with his long knife, bent over the choicest productions of his oven, chopped them as small as collyrium grains and pounded them as fine as flour. The rustic sat down and I did likewise. He spoke not neither did I speak[3] till we had eaten all. Then I said to the *halwa-seller*: Weigh for Abú Zaid two pounds of confection of almonds,[4] for it is the easiest to swallow and the quickest to penetrate through the veins.' It should have been made overnight,[5] spread out in the day, crisp, well stuffed, of pearl-like lustre and starry hue, and should dissolve in the mouth like gum, before it is chewed, in order that Abú Zaid may eat and enjoy it. He said: 'And

1 جُوذَابَاتُهُ *Whose roasted meats:* pl. of جُوذَبَة and ذُوبَاج the latter formed by transposition, from the Persian گوداب a dish of meat, rice, vetches and walnuts in which a condiment of syrup vinegar is poured food dressed under roast meat. It is also called أُمّ ٱلفَرَج The mother of Joyfulness, because it removes one's anxiety for seasoning or condiment. See De Sacy, *Ḥariri*, i, 227, and Mas'údí, viii, 405.

2 ٱلسُّمَّاك *Summak: The rhus coriaria of Linnaeus* or its berry, a well-known fruit; a certain acid with which one cooks.

3 لا يَئِسَ وَلا يَئِستُ *He despaired not, neither did I despair.* Another reading to which I have given preference لا نَبَسَ وَلا نَبَستُ He spoke not, neither did I speak.

4 ٱللَّوزِينَج or لَوزِينَجَة *Confection of almonds:* Lozenge and لَوزِينَة from the Arabic لَوز an almond. I think the presumption in favour of the English *lozenge* being derived from this word is strong. Originally لَوزِينَة, Spanish *losanja* in which form it went back to the east. This would explain the termination نج See Mas'údí, viii, 240 for a poem by Ibn al-Rúmi (b. A.H. 221–84) in praise of this sweetmeat. The word lauz occurs in Spanish as *alloza* and in Portuguese as *arzolla*. See Dozy, *Loan words from Arabic*, and Letters, p. 307.

5 لَيلِيّ ٱلعُمُر *Overnight:* Literally, a night old.

he weighed it.'　So we got to work[1] and ate till we finished it.
Then I said : ' Abú Zaid, how badly we need some iced water
to quench this thirst and to allay the heat generated by this
meal.　Sit down, Abú Zaid, till we fetch thee a water-carrier to
bring thee a drink of water.'　Then I went out and sat where
I could see him but he could not observe me, in order to see
what he would do.　When the rustic perceived that I delayed,
he arose and went towards his ass, but the fried-meat seller
clung to his waist-wrapper and said : ' Where is the cost of
what thou hast eaten ? '　Said Abú Zaid : ' I ate it as a guest.'
Then the fried-meat seller struck him a blow with his fist and
followed it up with a cuff, saying : ' Take that, base-born fellow !
When did we invite thee ?　Pay[2] down twenty dirhems.'　The
rustic began to weep and to untie the knots with his teeth
saying, 'How often did I tell that contemptible ape,[3] " I am
Abú 'Ubaid " ', and he would say :—

　　' Nay but thou art Abú Zaid '
Then I indited :—

　　　' To obtain thy livelihood[4] make use of every means ;
　　　Do not be satisfied with any condition,
　　　But be equal to any enormity ;
　　　For man becomes incapable,[5] there is no doubt about it.'

XIII.　THE MAQAMA OF BASRA

'ÍSÁ IBN HISHÁM : related to us and said : I entered Basra[6]
when, as regards age, I was in the prime of youth ; as to attire,
I was clad in the variegated striped stuffs of Yemen, and, in the

---

[1] قَعَدَ وَ قَعَدْتُ وَ جَرَّدَ وَ جَرَّدْتُ We got to work : Literally, he sat down and I sat
down ; he bared his arm and so did I.

[2] زِن Pay : Literally, weigh.

[3] قُرَيْد Contemptible ape.　Diminutive of قِرْد.　Another reading is العُرَيْد diminutive of عَرْد an ass.　See Cambridge MS.

[4] To obtain thy livelihood : Metre, kámil.

[5] Man is incapable there is no doubt about it.　Meidání, Arab Proverbs, ii,
221 (Bulak edition. A.H. 1287).
　Basra was founded by the Arabs in A.H. 17 or 18 in the Khalifate or 'Umar.
It was remarkable during the Khalifate for its population, for the great number of
its mosques and for its famous school of grammar which rivalled that of Kúfa.
Arab scholars were divided into two schools of the Basrians and the Kúfians.

matter of wealth, I had cattle and sheep. And I came to Mirbad[1] with some friends upon whom eyes fastened.[2] We proceeded a short distance to the recreation grounds among the green plains wherein a certain spot arrested us and so we alighted there. We made for the gaming arrows of pleasure and whirled them, throwing off bashfulness, as there was not one among us[3] who was not of us. But in less than the twinkling of an eye, there came in our view the figure[4] of a man which the hollows lowered from, and the ridges exposed to sight. We perceived[5] he was coming towards us and so we craned our necks to see him, till his journeying brought him to us. He greeted us with the salutation of Islám and we returned him the due greeting.[6]

Then he ran his eye over us and said: 'O people, there is not one of you but looks askance at me with excessive caution. Now none can acquaint you concerning me more truthfully than I can myself. I am a man from among the citizens of Alexandria[7] on the Umayyad frontiers.[8] Excellence was generous to me,[9] pleasure hailed me, and a distinguished house bred me.

Then did fortune deny me both her meaner and better gifts, and caused little ones with inflamed crops to follow me,

> As if they were serpents[10] in an arid land,
> Whose venom would be fatal were they to bite.
> When we tarry they send me out to earn,
> And when we travel they ride on me.'

[1] *Mirbad:* Once a famous camel mart and flourishing suburb three miles from Baṣra in the direction of the desert. Here poets and orators contested for superiority as they were wont to do at the fair of 'Ukaz, a practice which gave rise to so much literary emulation that the city became famous for its learning.

[2] *Upon whom eyes fastened:* Because of their attractiveness.

[3] *There was not one among us who was not of us:* Cf. Text, p. 43, supra.

[4] سَوَادٌ *The figure:* Literally, a blackness.

[5] For عمّنا line 3 read عَلمنَا

[6] *The due greeting:* While it is not incumbent upon a Muslim to greet another, to return the salutation is obligatory. See Qur'án, iv. 88.

[7] *I am a man from among the citizens of Alexandria:* Cf. Text, p. 44, supra.

[8] *The Umayyad frontiers:* Alexandria was the western limit of the eastern Khalifate and the eastern boundary of the western Khalifate.

[9] *Excellence was generous to me:* Literally, excellence made its region smooth for me.

[10] *As if they were serpents:* Metre, *rejez*.

The white [1] hath deserted [2] us, the yellow [3] hath become refractory to us; the black [4] hath consumed us, the red [5] hath crushed us. Abú Málik [6] hath come to us. Abú Jábir only visits us when we are barren of strength, [7] and the waters of this Basra promote digestion while her poor are oppressed. Man is occupied in getting something for his teeth and is in anxiety concerning himself. What then is the case of him,

'Who roams and roams [8] and then returns,
To stay with chicks whose sight is made keen, [9]
Whose covering is old, whose hair is matted and dusty so
  that they are ever
Ravenous [10] and lank-bellied.'

Verily to-day they arose in the morning and looked upon a living person who is like one dead, and at a home which was like no home. They wrung their hands longingly, put their ribs out of joint, [11] shed tears and addressed one another by the name of *Hunger*:

'And poverty in the day of the mean, [12]
Is every generous man's badge.
The generous incline towards the mean,
And this is one of the signs of the last day.'

1 *The white:* Silver.

2 نشرت البيض *The white has resisted:* Cf. نشرت المَرأةُ the woman exalted herself against her husband, or deserted him.

3 *The yellow:* Gold.

4 *The black:* Nights.

5 *The red:* Years of severe drought.

Cf. De Sacy, *Ḥarírí*, i, 147, where the names of colours are introduced in a like artificial manner.

For fanciful names of this type see Ibn al-Athír, *Kunya Lexicon* (edition by Seybold).

6 Abú Málik (أبو مَالك) Hunger } Cf. *Harírí*, i, 223–4.
Abú Jábir (أبو جَابِر) Bread }

7 عن عُقْر *Barren of strength:* i.e. when there is no strength left to eat it.

8 *Who roams and roams:* Metre, *wáfir*.

9 مُحَدَّدَة *Made keen:* By expectancy.

10 جياعَ النّاب *Ravenous:* Literally, a hungry canine tooth.

11 *They put their ribs out of joint:* By sobbing violently.

12 *And poverty in the day of the mean:* Metre, *kámil*.

My lords, ye have been chosen by me and I have sworn, verily in them is advantage.[1]

'Now is there a youth who will give them a supper, or cover them? And is there a generous man who will grant them a morning meal, or clothe them?'

Said 'Ísá ibn Hishám: By Heavens! there had never sought the seclusion of my ear a speech more winning, estimable, loftier or more original than that which I heard from him. Perforce we had recourse to our belts,[2] rejecting our sleeves, and eschewing our pockets.[3] And I gave him my ornamented robe[4] and the company followed my example,[5] and we said to him: 'Go and join thy children.' So he turned away from us after thanksgiving, to which he rendered the full meed, and eulogy with which he filled his mouth.

XIV. THE MAQAMA OF AL-FAZARA

'Ísá ibn Hishám related to us and said: I was in one of the regions of the Fazára[6] tribe riding one noble mount and leading another which in turn coursed along with me. And I was making for my native land so that the night with its terrors did not divert me, nor did distance with its deserts turn me from my purpose.

I struck off the leaves of day[7] with the staff of travel, and with the horse's hoofs I penetrated into the maw of night. Meanwhile, in a night so dark that the Qaṭáṭ would lose its way,[8] and the bat could not see[9] in it, I was going swiftly and

1 دَسَم *advantage:* Literally, grease of gravy. Cf. Heb. דשן

2 الأوساط *the belts:* in which travellers place the major portion of their money.

3 الأكمام والجيوب *sleeves and pockets:* in which smaller sums are placed.

4 مُطْرَف *ornamented robe:* a garment of the kind of cloth called خَز woven of silk and wool, or entirely of wool, having ornamental borders.

5 اخذى *my example:* From اخذ a way or manner of life.

6 *Fazára:* The name of an Arab tribe.

7 *The leaves of day:* Figure for the hours of the day.

8 *The Qaṭáṭ would lose its way:* Cf. De Sacy, *Ḥariri*, i, 260, القطاط The bird called (قطا) Qaṭá, is a species of sandgrouse. It is related of this bird that it will leave its young at dawn and go to drink at a place a night's journey off and will return in the morning bringing water to its chicks, that again in the early afternoon it will fly to the place once more returning to bring water a second time without losing its way.

9 *In which the bat could not see:* See *Arab Proverbs*, i, 194.

smoothly along, [1] nothing passing from the right but a lion and nought from the left save a hyena, when suddenly there appeared to my view a rider fully armed; he was making for some tamarisk trees and traversing towards me the intervening stretches of desert. So there seized me because of him what seizes the unarmed in the presence of one bristling with weapons. But I put on a bold front and said: ‘Perish thy father, stand! Before thou canst attain thy object thou wilt have to endure wounds of steel, [2] strip the tragacanth [3] of its leaves, and face a stout foeman with the pride of an Azdite. I am for peace, if thou wilt, or for war, if thou desirest. Tell me, who art thou?’ He replied: ‘Peace hast thou found.’ I said: ‘Thou hast answered well, but who art thou?’ He answered: ‘A counsellor, if thou seekest counsel, an orator if thou desirest converse, but before my name is a veil which the mentioning of no proper name can remove.’ I then said: ‘What is thy trade?’ He replied: ‘I roam about the interiors of the countries, in order that I may light upon the dish of a generous man. I have a mind served by a tongue, and rhetoric which my own fingers record. My utmost desire is a generous person who will lower me one of his saddle-bags and give me his wallet, like the free-born youth that met me yesterday as the rising sun and vanished from my sight with the going down of the same. But although he has disappeared, the memory of him remaineth, and, though he has taken leave of me, the marks of his favour accompany me still.’ Pointing to what he had on, he continued: ‘None can acquaint you of them [4] better than they themselves.’ I exclaimed to myself, ‘by the Lord of the Ka‘ba an importunate, grasping beggar, experienced in the craft, nay but a past master [5] of the art: Thou wilt have

1 *I was going swiftly and smoothly along:* Literally, I flowed with the flowing of water.

2 *The wounds of steel:* The scarifying of sharp edges or points. Cf. the expression sharp tongues. أَلْسِنَةٌ حِدَادٌ

3 *Strip the tragacanth:* Meidání, *Arab Proverbs*, i, 233. (Bulak edition A.H. 1284). Before one can attain it one has to strip the tragacanth, a species of tree with short curved thorns, by grasping each branch and drawing one's hand down it i.e. one has to perform what will be extremely difficult, if not impossible. Literally, less difficult than that would be the stripping of the tragacanth.

4 *Of them:* i.e. the marks of favour.

5 أُسْتَاذٌ *Master:* Arabicised from the Persian استاد a master, or teacher.

to give him something and pay liberally,'[1] so I said: 'Young man, thou hast manifested thy diction; how does thy poetry compare with thy prose?' He replied: 'There is no comparison between my prose and my verse.' Then he summoned aid from his natural ability, raised his voice to such a pitch that it filled the valley, and recited saying:—

'A pure-minded one presented to me by the night, and by the desert,
And by the five so swift that they barely touched the ground.[2]
I applied to his timber[3] the test of the fire of generous deeds.
And he proved to be, both on the paternal and the maternal sides, of high degree.
I sought to cajole him into parting with his property and I succeeded in cajoling him.
I endeavoured to facilitate his giving, and it was made easy to him.
And when we had revealed ourselves to each other, and he found my prose praiseworthy,
He tested me in my versification with what he was disposed to test me.
But, when he shook me, he shook none other than a keen blade,
And he found me not but the first in the race,
While I discovered him to be ever bright and beaming,[4]
And there was beneath him none other than a showy steed, blazed on forehead and feet.'

[1] تَسِحَّ عَلَيْهِ *Pay him liberally:* Literally, pour upon him.

[2] *The five* (*toes*) *that barely touched the ground:* Literally, while one says 'No, No.'

[3] *His timber:* figurative for disposition.

[4] أَغَرَّ مُحَجَّلا *Bright and beaming:* غُرّ is primarily applied to a horse with a white forehead and مُحَجَّل to a horse with white feet, both figuratively mean, bright and cheerful or distinct and clearly marked.

Cf. The lines by Samau'al, *Hamasa* (Freytag), p. 53. * وأَيَّامُنَا مَشْهُورَةٌ فى عَدُوِّنا لِهَا غُرَرٌ مَعْلُومَةٌ وَحُجُولُ 'And our days of victory over our enemies are as conspicuous and remarkable as the blaze on the forehead and feet of a horse.'

حِجْلٌ is from خَلْخَالٌ an anklet as the white on the foot is where the anklet is worn. Another reading أَغَرَّ مُحَجَّبا most honourable and dignified. Metre, *tawīl.*

Then I said to him: 'Gently, O youth, and thou canst command what I have with me.'

He said: 'The provision bag with its contents.' I replied: 'Aye and its bearer too.' Then I clasped him with my hands and said: 'By Him who hath endowed them with the sense of touch, and from one split them into five, thou shalt not leave me, unless I learn thy state.' Then he lowered his veil from his face and lo! by heavens! it was our Sheikh, al-Iskanderí! Without further waiting I said:—

'Abú'l-Fatḥ,[1] in pride hast thou girt on this blade,
But what doest thou with the sword when thou art no warrior?
So melt down into an anklet the gold with which thou hast bedecked this sword of thine.'

XV. THE MAQAMA OF JAHIZ[2]

'ÍSÁ IBN HISHÁM related to us and said: I and a few friends were excited at receiving an invitation to a banquet.[3] I accepted it in accordance with the well-known Tradition of the

[1] *Abú'l-Fatḥ: in pride hast thou girt on this blade:* Metre, *hezej*. The MS. in the Bibliotheque Nationale has the first two lines only. The thought introduced here is taken from the following lines of another poet (See footnote on Text, p. 69).

'Thou hast heard what he said but thou carest not for his speech.
Leave the sword for him who oppresses therewith, the valiant in war.
And melt down into an anklet the sword with which thou hast bedecked thyself,
For what doest thou with a sword when thou art not a fighter?'

Cf. Scott, *Bridal of Triermain*, xxvii.

[2] Abú 'Uthman ibn Baḥr ibn Maḥbáb al-Kináni al-Laithí, generally known by the surname of al-Jáḥiz, a native of Baṣra, was celebrated for his learning. He was the author of numerous works, the three principal ones being *Kitáb al-Haiwán* (the book of animals) *Kitáb al-Baian wa'l-Tabyín* (description and exposition) and *Kitáb al-Bukhalá* (the book of misers), and he also composed a discourse on the fundamentals of religion. An offset of the Mu'tazilite sect was called al-Jáḥizíyya. It is said of the works of Jáḥiz 'that they teach us to reason first, and instruct us in literature next.' He was deformed in person, and the prominence of his eyes, which seemed to be starting out of his head, produced the surnames of al-Jáḥiz (the starer) and al-Ḥadaqí (the goggle-eyed). He died at Baṣra A.H. 255 (A.D. 868–9), at the extreme age of ninety years. Ibn Khallikan, ii, 405. Also Yaqút, *Dictionary of Learned Men* (ed. by Professor Margoliouth), vi, p. 56.

[3] *Were excited at receiving an invitation to a banquet:* Literally, a banquet excited me and a few friends. وليمة a banquet, generally a marriage feast. For the names of the various feasts. See *Khizanat al-Adáb*, iii, 212–13.

Apostle[1] of God, upon whom be the blessings of God and peace —'If I were asked to share the shin-bone of a sheep, I would not refuse, and were I presented with a leg of beef I would accept it.' So we proceeded and reached a house,

> 'Completed and left[2] alone with beauty from which it selected and chose what it would.
> And it had chosen from it its choicest charms, and requested more to give away.'

whose carpets were spread and whose coverings were unfolded and whose table was laid, and we found ourselves among a company who were passing their time amid bunches of myrtle twigs, and bouquets of roses, broached wine vats and the sound of the flute and the lute. We approached them and they advanced to receive us. Then we clave[3] to a table[4] whose vessels[5] were filled, whose gardens were in flower, and whose dishes were arranged in rows with viands of various hues, opposite a dish of something intensely black was something exceedingly white, and against something very red was arranged something very yellow.

Now with us at the feast was a man whose hand wandered over the table playing the rôle of an ambassador between the viands of various hues, seizing the choicest of the cakes and plucking out the centres of the dishes, pasturing on his neighbour's territory,[6] traversing the bowls, as the castle traverses the chessboard, stuffing his mouth with morsel after morsel and chasing mouthful with mouthful. And withal he was silent and spoke not a word. We were conversing the while, until we got as far as the subject of Jáhiz and his oratory and a description of

[1] *According to the Tradition of the Prophet:* This Tradition is cited by Jáḥiz himself. See *Kitáb al-Bayán wa'l-Tabyín*, i, 163.

[2] *Completed and left:* Metre, *kámil.*

[3] عَكَفْنَا عَلَى ٱلْخِوَانِ *We clave to a table:* For the meaning of this verb, see Qur'án, vii, 134.

[4] خِوَانٌ *A table:* Arabicized from the Persian خوان pronounced خَان. Khán; a thing upon which one eats, said not to be so called except when food is upon it, but see Arabic Text, p. 143.

[5] *Vessels:* Literally, cisterns, because of their size.

[6] *Pasturing on his neighbour's territory:* Contrary to كُلْ مِمَّا يَلِيكَ—A Tradition of the Prophet: 'Eat from what is near thee.'

Ibn al-Maqaffa' [1] and his eloquence. Now the commencement of this discussion coincided with the termination of the meal. We then adjourned from that room and the man said to us: 'Where are ye in the discussion which ye were engaged in?' So we began to praise what we knew of Jáḥiz and his language, of the elegance of his style and quality of his rhetoric. Then he said: 'O people, every work hath its men, every situation its saying, [2] every house its occupants and every age its Jáḥiz. If ye were to examine critically, your belief would be falsified.' At this every one curled his lip [3] in disapproval and turned up his nose in contempt. But I smiled encouragingly upon him in order that I might draw him out, and said: 'Inform us and tell us more.' He said: 'Verily Jáḥiz limps in one department of rhetoric and halts in the other. Now the eloquent man is he whose poetry does not detract from his prose and whose prose is not ashamed of his verse. Tell me, do you know of a single fine poem of Jáḥiz?' We said: 'No!' He said: 'Come, let us consider his prose. It consists of far-fetched allusions, a paucity of metaphors and simple expressions. He is tied down to the simple language he uses, and avoids and shirks difficult words. Have you ever heard of a rhetorical expression of his or of any recondite [4] words?' We answered: 'No!' He then said to me: 'Wouldst thou like a sample of speech which would lighten

1 *Ibn al-Maqaffa'*: A Persian convert to Islám renowned for the elegance of his style and penmanship. He made several translations from the Pahlawi into Arabic. The best specimen of his elegant and chaste Arabic is the Book of Kalila and Dimna ultimately derived from the Sanskrit Fables of Bidpai, brought over to Persia in the reign of al-Nushirwan. By command of the Khalifa al-Manṣúr, he was put to a horrible death on a charge of heresy in A H. 142 (A.D. 759-60) by Sufyán the governor of Baṣra. Ibn Kallikan, i, 431.

2 *Every situation hath its saying: Arab* Proverbs, ii, 456.

3 كَشَرَ لَهُ نَابَ ٱلْاِنْكَارِ *curled his lip in disapproval:* Literally, showed him the tooth of denial.

4 غَيْرَ مَسْمُوعَةٍ *Recondite:* Literally, unheard of; rare; another reading كَلِمَةٌ مَسْجُوعَةٌ rhymed speech. Jáḥiz's merits were a subject of controversy. Abú Hayyan Tanḥídí wrote an encomium on him whereas the orthodox attacked him as a Mu'tazilite [See *al-Farq bain al-Firaq*, (A.H. 429), pp. 160 sqq]. Hamadháni evidently shared the orthodox opinion regarding this writer. In this Maqáma we have an indication of Hamadhání's idea as to what constituted a good style. It is evident he preferred rhetorical conceits and the recondite to simple and straightforward language. Of this the Maqámát affords many illustrations,

thy shoulders [1] and disclose what thou hast in thy hands?' I answered: 'By Heavens! Yes.' He said: 'Then open thy little finger [2] for me by means of that which will help in procuring thee thanks.' So I gave him my mantle and he indited:—

'By the life of him [3] who hath thrown over me his garment
By him was that garment filled with glory.
A worthy youth cheated out of his mantle by generosity,
And it threw not a gaming arrow nor cast a gambling dice.
O thou who hast given me thy raiment, look again,
And let not the days bring ruin upon me.
And tell them who, if they appear, appear as the morning sun,
And, if they rise in the darkness, rise as the auspicious star,
Observe the ties of your relationship to nobility and moisten her palate,
For the best of generosity is that whose downpour is prompt.' Cf. أَلْبَادِى أَكْرَمُ —the first is most generous.

Said 'Ísá ibn Hishám: Then the company became expansive towards him and gifts poured upon him. When we became mutually friendly, I enquired, 'Where is the orient of this full moon?' He answered:—

'Alexandria is my home,[4]
If but there my resting-place were fixed,
But my night I pass in Nejd,[5]
In Hijaz my day.'

XVI. THE MAQAMA OF THE BLIND

'ÍSÁ IBN HISHÁM related to us and said: I was passing through one of the towns of Ahwaz when my supreme object was to capture a stray word,[6] or add to my store an eloquent expression. My journeying led me to a vast open space of the town where lo!

[1] *Lighten thy shoulders:* i.e. relieve thee of the responsibility thou hast assumed in thy defence of Jáḥiz.

[2] *Open thy little finger:* i.e. open thy hand and give something. The closing of the little finger indicates avarice, e.g. in counting up to ten, the little finger is the first to be closed and the last to be opened.

[3] *By the life of him:* Metre, *tawíl.*

[4] *Alexandria is my home:* Metre, *mujtath.*

[5] *Nejd:* is ten days journey from, or about two hundred miles east of Yemáma.

[6] *To capture a stray word:* The collecting of (نَوَادِر) rare words was a favourite pursuit.

10

there was a company of people gathered around and listening to a man who was tapping the ground with beats which varied not. I knew there must be a tune with those beats. So I withdrew not, in order that I might enjoy the song or hear a chaste expression, but remained among the spectators, shouldering this one and pushing that one, until I reached the man. I passed my eye over him[1] and I found him to be a person short and portly like a beetle,[2] blind, and wrapped up in a woollen blanket, whirling round like a top, wearing a burnous[3] too long for him, and supporting himself with a staff to which were attached a number of tiny bells. With this he was beating the ground with a rythmical sound, while with plaintive air and pathetic voice proceeding from a straightened breast, he sang :—

'O people my debt weighs down my back,[4]
And my wife demands her dowry,
After abundance and plenty, I have become
A dweller in a barren land and an ally of penury.
O people, is there a generous man among ye,
Who will aid me against the vicissitudes of time ?
O people, because of my poverty my patience is exhausted,
While now no flowing robes my state conceal.
Time with its destroying hand hath scattered
What I had of silver and gold ;
In the evening I repair to a house the size of a span,
My lot is obscure and my pot is small.
If God but seal my affair with good,
He will send me ease after difficulty.
Is there among ye a worthy youth of noble origin,
Who will acquire through me a great reward ?
Even though he value not thankfulness ?'

Said 'Ísá ibn Hishám : By Heavens! my heart became tender towards him and my eyes were filled with tears for him.

1 I *passed my eye over him :* Literally, from him to.

2 كالقرنبى *Like a beetle :* The Qarambá is an insect resembling the beetle called خنفسا *Khanfasá*. It is said 'the *Qarambá* in the eye of its mother is beautiful.' *Arab Proverbs*, ii, 253.

3 *Burnous :* Worn by devotees in the first age of Islám ; any garment of which the head forms a part. Some say it is from ألبرس meaning cotton and the ن is augmentive. It appears to be a foreign word.

4 *O people my debt weighs down :* Metre, *rejez*.

So I gave him a dinar I had with me. And he delayed not but said :—

> ' What beauty is hers [1] and how intensely yellow.
> Light, stamped and round,
> Water almost drops from her lustre,
> A noble mind hath produced her,
> Yea, a soul of a youth possessed by generosity,
> Which makes him do what it will.
> O thou for whom this praise is meant,
> Exaggeration cannot describe the extent of thy worth.
> I therefore refer thee to God [2] with whom is thy reward.
> May God have mercy upon him who will bind her to her pair
> And associate her with her sister.'

The people then gave him what they were disposed to give. Then he left them. But I followed him, for I knew by the quickness with which he recognized the dinar that he was feigning blindness. As soon as we were alone [3] I stretched forth my right hand, seized his left arm and said : ' By Heavens ! thou shalt disclose to me thy secret, or else I will assuredly expose thee.' Then he opened his pair of almonds.[4] I drew his veil from his face and behold—by Heavens ! it was our Sheikh Abú'l-Fath, al-Iskanderí. Said I : ' Art thou Abú'l-Fath ? ' He answered : ' Nay ;

> I am Abú Qalamún,[5] In every hue do I appear,
> Choose a base calling, For base is thy age,
> Repel time [6] with folly, For verily time is a kicking camel.
> Never be deceived by reason, Madness is the only reason.' [7]

---

[1] *What beauty is hers* ! Cf. De Sacy, *Ḥariri*, i, 34. Metre, *rejez*.

[2] *I refer thee to God* : Literally, go to God.

[3] نَظَمَتْنَا خَلْوَةٌ *We were alone* : Literally, seclusion strung us together.

[4] *Pair of almonds* : Figurative for both eyes.

[5] *I am Abú Qalamún* : Metre, *mujtath*.

Abú Qalamún : a kind of variegated Greek fabric. The expression is used to describe a very fickle person. (Ibn al-Athir, *Kunya Lexicon* (*Kitab al-Muraṣṣ'a*, Edited by Seybold, p. 175.)

This maqáma has been translated by De Sacy, *Chrestomathie Arabe*, iii. 251.

[6] زَجِّ الزَّمَانَ *Repel time* : Cf. De Sacy, Ḥariri, i, 304.

[7] Cf. This maqáma with De Sacy, *Ḥariri*, i, 75, where the impostor also feigns blindness.

XVII. THE MAQAMA OF BUKHARA [1]

SAID 'ÍSÁ IBN HISHÁM: One day, joined to a small company of friends bound together in friendship, like the Pleiades,[2] I alighted[3] in the cathedral mosque of Bukhára. Now, when the mosque was filled with its congregation, there appeared before us one clad in a pair of worn-out garments.[4] He had slung his empty wallet over his shoulder, and was bringing behind him a naked boy whose endurance was straitened by calamity, while the cold anon gripped him and let him go.[5] He possessed no covering but his own skin and had nought that sufficed to protect him from a single shivering. The man stood and said: 'None will regard this child except him to whom God has been gracious, and none will be moved to pity by this misfortune but him who is not secure from the like. O possessors of famous fortunes, embroidered robes, lofty houses, and strongly built castles, ye will not be secure from accident, nor will heirs fail you. Hasten then to do good, while ye can and be bounteous unto the world as long as it is bounteous unto you. For, by Heavens! we have eaten "sikbáj",[6] ridden the fleet-footed camel, donned brocaded silk[7] and slept on stuffed couches in the evenings.

1 *Bukhára:* The old Sámanid capital and now the chief city of the State of Bukhára. For ages it has been a great centre of learning and religious life. For a description of the literary splendour of this city at the time of the author, see *Yatima al-Dahr*, iv, 33, and Browne, *Literary History of Persia*, i, 365. It is still the principal book market of Central Asia. Yaqút, i, 517.

2 *Like the Pleiades:* Literally, on the string of the Pleiades, a frequently used simile for being inseparably bound together. Cf. Job, xxxviii, 31.

3 أَحَلَّنِي يَوْمٌ I *alighted:* Literally a day caused me to alight.

4 ذُو طِمْرَيْنِ *In a pair of worn-out garments:* Literally, the possessor of two worn-out garments.

5 *Gripped him and let him go:* As a cat plays with a mouse.

6 سِكْبَاج *Sikbáj:* Arabicized from the Persian سك vinegar and باها arabicized into بَاجٌ food. Fleshmeat cooked with vinegar. It is said that Khusru Perwíz, who is one of the exemplars of magnificence and luxury among the Arabs, was the first for whom *Sikbáj* was cooked and that none fed on it without his permission. De Sacy, *Hariri*, i, 224, and Chenery, *Translation of Hariri*, p. 451.

7 دِيْبَاجٌ *Brocaded silk:* Probably from the Persian ديباى or ديباه The change of the final ه into ج in arabicized words from the Persian is common. A certain kind of cloth or garment made of أبريسم (i.e. silk or raw silk) particularly a name for that which is variegated or embellished. (Lane, *Lexicon*, article ديباج p. 843).

Then, before we knew it, came fortune's treacherous blast and the turning of the back of the shield. Then the fleet camel was changed for the slow short-paced steed, the brocade for wool, and so on until I am reduced to the state and garb in which ye see me. Behold we seek sustenance from barren fortune's breast and ride poverty's sombre steed. We gaze not but with the orphan's eye and stretch forth only the debtor's hands. Now is there any generous one who will dispel the blackness[1] of this want and blunt the edge of this misfortune?' Then he sat down leaning upon his elbows, and he said to the boy: 'Attend to thy business.' The boy said: 'What can I say when this thy speech, did it but come in contact with hair, would clip it, or with a rock would cleave it. Verily a heart not rendered tender by what thou hast said is tough indeed. Ye have heard, O people, what ye have never heard before to-day. Let each one of you engage his hand with charity. Let him think of his own future and shield, through me, his own child. Remember me,[2] and I will remember you and give unto me and I will thank you.' Said 'Isá ibn Hishám, 'In my loneliness I had nought that solaced me but a ring which I placed upon his little finger.[3] As soon as he got it he recited praising, the ring upon the finger, saying:—

O the encircled with itself,[4]
With a necklace like unto the Gemini in beauty!
Like a lover meeting his friend,
And then lovingly and pathetically embraces him.
Selecting one not of his own tribe,
As an ally against fate.
A precious thing whose worth is exalted,
Yet, verily, more exalted is he who gave it.
I swear, if in glory men were words,
Thou wouldst be their meaning.'[5]

Said 'Ísá ibn Hishám: So we gave him what was easy of attainment at once, and then he turned away from us praising us.

1 غَيَاهَب *Blackness:* Plural of غَيهَب darkness, or night: it also means a horse entirely black.

2 *Remember me:* Qur'án, ii, 147.

3 *His little finger:* i.e. the boy's little finger.

4 *O the encircled with itself:* Metre, *kámil.*

5 *Thou wouldst be their meaning:* Cf. *Mutanabbi,* (Dierterici), p. 460.

I followed him, until privacy revealed his face and lo! it was our Shaikh Abú'l-Fatḥ al-Iskanderí, and behold the fawn was his child. I said; 'Abú'l-Fatḥ, thou hast grown old[1] and the boy grown up; 'What of the word of greeting and of converse?'

He answered:—

'A stranger am I[2] when the road doth contain us,
A friend when the tents do enclose us.'

By this I knew he was averse to conversing with me, so I left him and went away.

XVIII. THE MAQAMA OF QAZWIN

'Ísá ibn Hishám related to us and said: In the year A.H. 75[3] I took part in a raid, on the frontier of Qazwín,[4] with those that raided it. We crossed not a rugged upland, but we also descended into a valley, until our march brought us to one of the villages. The scorching noon-day heat impelled us to seek the shade of some tamarisk trees in the centre[5] of which was a spring, like unto the flame of a torch,[6] more limped than a tear, gliding over the stony ground as glides the restless serpent. We took what food we were inclined to take, then we sought the shade and addressed ourselves to the noon-day nap. But sleep had not yet overcome us when we heard a voice more disagreeable than the braying of an ass[7] and a footfall lighter than that of a camel's colt; accompanying these two was the sound of a drum which seemed to proceed from the jaws of a lion and which drove away

1 *Abú'l-Fatḥ thou hast grown old:* Metre, *mutaqárib.*

2 *A stranger am I:* Metre, *mutaqárib.* A pleasing effect is produced here by the Improvisor replying in the same metre and rhyme.

3 *The year A. H. 75:* If we accept this date the author goes back to the raid made by al-Bara ibn 'Azib appointed governor of Rai in A.H. 24. If we take it to be A H. 375 which is the more probable date, that would place the episode five years before Hamadhání is said to have left his native city. De Sacy has adopted the latter view (*Chrestomathie Arabe*, iii, 243.) The year 375 was an eventful one, but there is no allusion to a raid on the frontier of Qazwín. See Ibn al-Athir, ix, 29-33.

4 *Qazwin:* A well-known city and the capital of the province of the same name situated ninety-two miles by road from Ṭeherán.

5 *The centre:* Literally, the enclosure.

6 *The flame of a torch:* Literally, the tongue of a torch, in its purity and sheen.

7 *More disagreeable than the braying of an ass:* An allusion to Qur'án, xxxi, 18.

the scout of sleep from the people. I opened both my eyes[1] and looked towards him, but the trees intervened between us. So I listened and lo! he was reciting to the beat of the drum :—

> ' I invite to God,[2] is there an answerer ?
> To a spacious shelter and luxuriant pasture.
> To a lofty garden[3] the fruits whereof[4] cease not to be near to gather and never vanish from sight.
> O people, verily I am a man returning[5]
> From the land of infidelity, and wondrous is my story.
> If now I have believed, how many nights
> Have I denied my Lord and committed the questionable thing ?[6]
> Ah ! many the swine the ends of whose soft bones I have chewed,
> And the intoxicant of which I have obtained a share !
> Then did God guide me and zealous and effectual endeavour raised me from the baseness of unbelief,
> But I continued to conceal my religion from my people,
> And to worship God with a penitent heart.
> I adored the goddess al-Lát,[7] for fear of the enemy,
> And in dread of the Watcher, I looked not towards the Ka'ba.
> I besought God when night enveloped me and dreadful day wasted me,
> Lord, as Thou hast saved me,
> Now deliver me, for I am a stranger among them.
> Then did I take the night as my steed,
> And I had before me[8] no spare mount, except resolution.

[1] *Eyes :* Literally, twins.

[2] *I invite to God :* Metre, *sari'*.

[3] *To a lofty garden :* An allusion to Qur'án lxix, 22.

[4] *The fruits whereof :* An allusion to Qur'án lxix, 23.

[5] تَائِبٌ *Returning :* In the sense of repenting. Another reading نَابِتٌ bred which is more agreeable to the context.

[6] *And committed the questionable thing :* Another reading, I have adored the Cross.

[7] *Al-Lát :* One of the three goddesses worshipped by the ancient Arabians. The other two were al-'Uzzá and Manáh.

[8] أَمَامِي *Before me* does not yield a good sense : جَانِبِي by my side, would be better.

Suffice thee to know of my journey, that it was in a night,
In which the head of a child would almost turn grey,
Until I passed from the enemy's territory
Into the guarded domain of the Faith, and then I shook
  off fear.
When the signs of the Faith came in sight, I said:
Assistance from God and a speedy victory.'[1]

Now, when he reached this verse, he said: 'O people! I have
entered[2] your dwelling with a resolution which love hath not
excited, nor poverty impelled. I have left behind my back
gardens planted with trees, and vineyards, damsels[3] of equal age
with swelling breasts, and excellent horses,[4] heaped up wealth,[5]
equipments, a numerous tribe, mounts and slaves: But I came
forth as the serpent issues from its hole,[6] and the bird goes forth
from its nest, preferring my religion to my worldly possessions,
bringing my right to my left,[7] and joining my day march to my
night journey.   Now I pray ye will ye combat the fire with its
own sparks,[8] and stone the Byzantine empire with its own
missiles, and with assistance and aid, with support and succour,
and help me in invading them, but not exceeding bounds, every one
according to his several ability and in proportion to his wealth?
I will not regard a bag of ten thousand dirhems too much; I will
accept a mite[9] and not decline a date.   For each one from me

---

[1] *Assistance from God and a speedy victory*: Qur'án lxi, 13.   This text was
the battle cry of the early Muslims.   Cf. De Sacy, *Hariri*, p. 231, line 4.

[2] *I have entered*: Literally, I have trodden.

[3] *Damsels*: Qur'án lxxviii, 32-3.

[4] *Excellent horses*: Qur'án iii, 12.

[5] قَنَا طِيرٍ مُقَنْطَرَةٍ *Heaped up wealth*: Qur'án iii, 12.

قِنْطَارٌ a large quantity or aggregate of property, or much property heaped up.
Its weight in the present day is one hundred pounds. مُقَنْطَرَةٌ aggregated,
the latter word is corroborative. قِنْطَارٌ (centenarius) in the author's time was
equal to 120 ratls (*Mafatih al'Ulūm* p. 179, edited by Vloten).

[6] *As the serpent issues from its hole*: i.e. with nothing.

[7] *Bringing my right to my left*: Either (1) bringing the feet together as a
preliminary to a determination to step forward, opposite of, I advanced one foot and
drew back the other, as a sign of indecision, or (2) bringing the hands together as
a sign of resolution, or (3) clenching the hands as a sign of determination.

[8] *Combat the fire with its own sparks*: This appears to be a proverbial expression.

[9] ألذَّرَّة *A mite*: the weight of an ant.   See Qur'án xxxiv, 3,

there will be two arrows,[1] one of which I will sharpen for future recompense, and the other I will notch with prayer[2] and with it from the bow of darkness[3] shoot at the gates of Heaven.' Said 'Ísá ibn Hishám ' His admirable diction excited me, so I cast off the robe of sleep and ran to the company and lo! it was our Shaikh, Abú'l-Fath al-Iskanderí, with a sword which he had drawn, and in a garb which he had adopted as a disguise. Now when he saw me he winked his eye at me and said: 'May God be merciful to him who from his abundance[4] will help us and apportion to us a share of his favours.' Then he took what he got, then I led him aside and said: 'Art thou of the sons of the Nabateans?[5] He answered:—

'As is my state with fate,[6] such is my state with pedigree.
'My genealogy is in the hands of Time, if it is hard upon it,
it will change.
In the evening a Nabatean am I, in the morning an Arab.'

XIX. THE MAQAMA OF SASAN

SAID 'ÍSÁ IBN HISHÁM: One of my journeys set me down at Damascus. Now one day when I was at the door of my house there suddenly appeared before me a troop of the sons of Sásán.[7]

[1] سَهْمَان *Two arrows:* The primitive meaning of سَهْم is missile with which one draws lots in the game called al-maisar, then applied to the thing won by him whose arrow is successful in the game above mentioned.

[2] بِالدُّعا *With prayer:* for present need.

[3] عَن قوسِ الظّلماء *From the bow of darkness:* A reference to the belief that prayer at night is more effectual; another reading is الظّماء thirst.

[4] *His abundance:* Literally, his superfluous skirts.

[5] أانتَ من أولادِ النّبيط *Art thou of the sons of the Nabateans?* Another, and more appropriate reading in the Constantinople edition, and in the Cambridge MS is 'Art thou of the children of the daughters of the Greeks'?

[6] *As is my state with fate:* Cf. p. 13 of the Text. Metre, *Khafif.*
This makáma is a strange medley of references to paganism, Christianity and Islám based upon the imaginary conversion of a Greek to Muḥammadanism.

[7] *Sásán:* Sásán al-Akbar, son of Bahman, son of Isfandiyar, son of Gushtasp a prince of Western Persia, is the reputed chief and patron of all beggars and mountebanks. The legend mentioned by Ibn al-Múkaffá is that Báhman being near his death sent for his daughter Ḥomaya, who was pregnant, and settled the succession on her and her child, if the child proved a boy, to the exclusion of his own son Sásán. Sásán indignant at this left the court and lived the life of a shepherd among the Kurds so that his name became a proverb for one who leads a vagabond

They had muffled up their faces, and besmeared their clothes with red ochre while each of them had tucked under his armpit a stone with which he beat his breast. Among them was their chief, who was reciting, they alternating with him; he intoning and they answering him. And, when he saw me, he said:—

'I desire from thee[1] a white cake upon a clean table.
I desire course salt, I want plucked greens.
I desire fresh meat, I want some sour vinegar.
I desire a sucking kid, I want a young ram.
I desire water with ice, filled in a rare vessel.
I desire a vat of wine from which I may get up drunk,
And a cheerful cup-bearer, congenial to the minds.
I desire from thee a shirt, a coat and a turban.[2]
I desire thick sandals, with which I may visit the privy.
I desire a comb and a razor, I want a vessel[3] and a bath glove,
O what an excellent guest am I! and what a charming host art thou!
I will be content with this from thee, and I do not wish to impose.'

Said 'Ísá ibn Hishám, I gave him a dirhem and said to him, 'I announce to thee the invitation, and we will soon prepare and

life. Hence 'the people of Sásán, the *Kurd*', is a phrase signifying beggars, prestigiators, people that feign blindness, go about with dogs, monkeys and the like. These people had a cant of their own which was not thought unworthy of study by the learned.

Sheríshí gives another account of the origin of this term. He says that after the Persians had been subdued in the time of the *Khalifa* 'Umar, they submitted peaceably to the conquerors adopting their manners and their religion, and that, being a clever and artful people, they betook themselves to various ways of making a living, one of which was mendicancy. Their way of exciting commiseration was to give out that they belonged to the royal house of Sásán, or, as we call them, the Sásánians, and to describe the cruel change of fortune and their deplorable condition. So that at last people came to call a beggar a Sásání. This may be the true derivation, but it is evident from the forty-ninth maqáma that Ḥarírí adopted the legend which makes Sásán a real person. (Chenery, translation of *Ḥariri*, p. 287-8, and *Ḥariri* i. 23.)

[1] I *desire from thee:* Metre, *mujtath*. Cf. De Sacy *Ḥariri* i. 159.

[2] نَصِيفٌ *A turban:* also a woman's veil or muffler. syn. خِمَارٌ See Aghání ix. 158. Heb. צניף See lexicon. Isaiah iii. 23 and lxii. 3. Probably from انتصف it became halved, alluding probably to the length of the veil.

[3] سَطْلٌ *A vessel:* Probably situla, a bucket for drawing water, indirectly borrowed from the Latin. See Dozy *Supplement aux Dictionaires*, i. 653.

make ready to receive thee. We will do our best endeavour and thou hast our promise for the future. And this dirhem will be a reminder for thee, so take the ready money and expect the promised.' He seized it and went to another man, and I thought he would address him [1] with the same with which he had addressed me, but he recited :—

'O excellent one! [2] who hath appeared,
As if in stature he were a branch.
My tooth desires meat,
Therefore coat it with bread.[3]
And bestow something upon me and give it now down,
Drop thy hand [4] from thy waist and undo the purse's knot,
And put both thy hands [5] under both thy arms for me designedly.'

Said 'Ísá ibn Hishám: When this speech of his had penetrated my ear I [6] knew there was excellence behind it, so I followed him until he reached the mother of his house, and I stood away from him so that he could not see me, but I could see him. The princes lowered their veils and behold their chief was Abú'l-Fath, al-Iskanderí! So I looked at him and said: 'Sirrah, what meaneth this fraud?' Then he indited, saying,

'This age is ill-starred, [7]
And, as thou seest, oppressive;
In it stupidity is estimable
And intelligence a defect and a reproach,
And wealth is a nocturnal visitant [8] but
It hovers only over the ignoble.'

[1] يلقاه *Would address him*: Literally, meet him.

[2] *O excellent one!* Metre, *mujtath*.

[3] *Coat it with bread*: According to the context this seems to be the meaning rather than the explanation given by the commentator, viz., that meat was something forbidden and therefore to desire it was to render him worthy of stripes.

[4] *Drop thy hand*: Lower it to the pocket to undo the knotted money.

[5] *Put both thy hands*: An allusion to Qur'án xx. 23. He uses both hands here designedly so as to be sure of getting out some money, not knowing which side 'Ísá ibn Hishám carried his cash.

[6] *Penetrated my ear*: Literally, split my ear.

[7] *This age is ill-starred*: Metre, *mujtath*.

[8] طيف *Nocturnal visitant*: The Ṭaif al-Khayál or Khayál Ṭaif frequently occurs in Arabic poetry. It is supposed to be the image of the person beloved which appears to the lover in his dream. For an excellent account of the Ṭaif al-Khayál, illustrated by several quotations from the poets, see *Journal Asiatique*, pp. 376-85, April 1838 (M.G. Slane).

XX. THE MAQAMA OF THE APE

'ÍSÁ IBN HISHÁM related to us and said: While I was in the city of Peace,[1] returning from the Sacred Territory,[2] I was swaggering along, with the swaggering of pedestrians, on the bank of the Tigris, observing those rare sights and closely examining those embellishments until, suddenly, I reached a ring of men crowding together, excitement agitating their heads[3] and laughter exploding[4] their cheeks. Curiosity impelled me to do what it had driven them to do, till I stood within earshot of the voice of a man without being able to see his face, because of the intensity of the thronging and the excessiveness of the crowding, and behold! it was a monkey-trainer causing his monkey to dance and making those near him to laugh. So I bounded as bounds the well-trained hound,[5] and went forward, after the manner of one lame, over the necks of the people. This one's shoulder throwing me in that one's stomach,[6] until I made the beards of two men my carpet and sat down after much fatigue.[7] And verily shame choked me with its spittle and the straitness of the place distressed me. When the monkey-trainer had finished his performance and the place of assembly divested itself of its people, I arose, and verily terror had clothed me in its garb, and I stood up that I might see his face, and lo! by Heavens! it was Abú'l-Fath, al-Iskanderí. So I said: 'Sirrah, what meaneth this baseness?' Then he indited saying:—

1 *The city of Peace*: i.e., the city of God. Al-Manṣûr is said to have called Baghdad the city of Peace—Madina al-Salám—because the Tigris had been previously called the valley and river of Peace. It is said 'Abd al-'Azíz ibn 'Alí Ruwwád called it the city of Peace, because in Persian *bagh* is an idol and *dad* a gift which made an impious or ill-omened name. Yaqût, i, 678. See also Le Strange, *Baghdad during the 'Abbásid Khalifate*, p. 10.

2 *The sacred territory*: Mecca.

3 أعناقهم *Their heads*: Literally, their necks.

4 *Exploded* (*literally, split*) *their cheeks*: Cf. English, split their sides.

5 المُحرَّج *Well-trained hound*: Literally, having a collar of white shells such as are worn on the neck to avert the evil eye. It seems that only trained hounds were given this collar.

6 السُّرَّة *Stomach*: Literally, the navel.

7 الأين *great fatigue*: Another reading is بَينَ اثنَينِ between two.

'The sin is the days'[1] not mine,
So censure the vicissitudes of the nights.
By means of folly I obtained my desire
And proudly trailed my embellished skirts.'

XXI. THE MAQAMA OF MOSUL

'ÍSÁ IBN HISHÁM related to us and said: When we were returning from Moṣul[2] intending to go home, the caravan was captured and our baggage and mount were stolen from us The little life I had left carried me to one of its villages[3] and with me was Abú'l-Fath al-Iskanderí. I asked him: 'What shall we devise?' He answered: 'God will suffice.'[4] Now we were impelled to go to a house whose master had just died and the female mourners[5] had already stood up. It was filled with men, whose hearts grief had cauterized, and whose shirts terror had rent, and with women who had unloosed their hair, and were beating their breasts, cutting their necklaces and slapping their cheeks.

Said al-Iskanderí: 'In this mass[6] there is a palm tree for us and in this flock a lamb.' So he entered the house to look at the dead man whose chin was tied up ready to be carried out. The water had been heated to wash him, the bier had been got ready to bear him away, his garments had been sewn that he might be enshrouded and his grave had been dug that he might be buried. Now when al-Iskanderí had observed him, he seized his throat,

[1] *The sin is the days:* Metre, *kámil.*
This maqáma has been translated by De Sacy. See his *Chrestomathie Arabe,* iii. p. 246.

[2] *Moṣul:* A town in Mesopotamia on the right bank of the Tigris. This city reached its greatest prosperity towards the beginning of the decline of the Khalifate when it was for a time an independent capital. The dynasty of the Hamdánids reigned in Moṣul from A.D., 934 but the town was conquered by the Syrian Okailids in 990. Yaqút says the three great cities of the world are 'Nishapur, because it is the gate of the East, Damascus, because it is the gate of the West, Moṣul, because it is on the road between the two.' It appears the city had a notorious reputation for vice in its most degraded form. Yaqút, iv, 682 and *Encyclopaedia Britannica,* xviii, 904.

[3] *One of its villages:* Mosul had a large number of dependent villages.

[4] *God will suffice:* Cf. English, The Lord will provide.

[5] *The female mourners had already stood up:* To bewail and eulogize the deceased. نادبة A wailing woman.

[6] *Mass:* Literally, blackness.

felt his carotid artery, and said: 'O people, Fear God! Do not bury him for he is alive, he is unconcious and a fit has come upon him. I will hand him over with both eyes open in two days.' They said 'Whence knowest thou know that?' He replied: 'Verily, when a man dies his armpit becomes cold. Now I felt this man and I know he is alive.' Then they put their hands into his armpit and said, 'The fact is as he asserts, so do what he commands.' Then al-Iskanderí arose and went to the dead man, stripped him of his clothes, tied on his turban, hung amulets upon him, introduced[1] some olive oil into his mouth, cleared the house for him, and said: 'Leave him alone, and do not interfere with him. If you hear a moan from him, do not answer him.' Then he went out from the presence of the dead. Meanwhile the news had spread and circulated that the dead was raised. Pious gifts came to us from every house, and presents poured upon us from every neighbour, till our purse was swollen with silver and gold and our saddle bags were filled with cheese[2] and dates. We tried hard to seize an opportunity to bolt, but found none, till the appointed time arrived and they demanded the fulfilment of the lying promise. Al-Iskanderí enquired: 'Have ye heard a whisper[3] from the patient or observed from him a sign?' They answered: 'No.' Then he said: 'If he has made no sound since I left him, his hour is not yet come. Let him alone till to-morrow and, verily, if ye hear his voice, ye may be assured he is not dead. Then inform me that I may prescribe for his recovery and rectify what is wrong with his constitution.' They said: 'Do not put it off longer than to-morrow.' He replied: 'No.' Now when the morning beamed[4] and the wing of light spread over the horizon of the atmosphere, the men came in troops[5] and the women in pairs,

1 ألعَقَهُ *Introduced:* Literally, made him lick, from لَعِقَ he licked his fingers, or he gave him as a (لَعُوقٌ) linctus.

2 الأَقِطُ الاقِطُ and الأَقْطُ *cheese:* A preparation of dry curd. See De Sacy, *Ḥariri*, ii. 587.

3 رِكْزاً *A whisper:* An allusion to Qur'án, xix. 98.

4 ابْتَسَمَ ثَغْرُ الصُّبْحِ *The morning beamed:* Literally, the morning smiled so as to show its front teeth.

5 *In troops:* An allusion to Qur'án, cx. 2.

and they said: 'We desire that thou cure the sick man and cease prating.' Said al-Iskanderí: 'Let us arise and go to him.' Then he took the amulets from his hands, removed the turban from his body and said: 'Lay him on his face,' and he was laid upon his face. Then he said: 'Stand him on his feet.' So he was made to stand. He then said 'Let go his hands,' but he fell a lifeless heap.[1] 'Phew!' ejaculated al-Iskanderí: 'He is dead, how can I bring him to life?' Then shoes[2] clave unto him, and palms took possession of him, and it was so, when one hand was raised, another banged down upon him. Then the people busied themselves with the funeral obsequies of the dead man and we slipped away fleeing till we came to a village situated on the edge of a valley whose torrent was eroding it,[3] and whose waters were destroying it. Its people were distressed and had not slept a wink in the night for fear of the flood. Said al-Iskanderí: 'I will deliver[4] you from this flood and its mischief, and will turn away its devastation from this village. So obey me and attempt nothing without me.' They said: 'What is thy command?' He answered: 'Sacrifice in the course of this water a red[5] heifer, fetch me a young virgin, and pray behind me two genuflexions, so that God may divert the direction of this flood to this desert, and, if the waters are not turned away, my blood will be lawful to you.'[6] They said: 'We will do that.' So they immolated the heifer, and married the damsel to him. Then he stood up to pray the two genuflexions and said: 'O people, be careful with yourselves that, when standing, there happen no stumbling, in kneeling no fall, in prostration no slip, in sitting no irregularity, for the moment we blunder our hopes will be disappointed and our action will go for nothing. Be patient over these two genuflexions for their

[1] رَاسِيًا *A lifeless heap:* Literally, stationary, fixed. Another, but less satisfactory reading, رَأْسًا on his head.

[2] خُفّ *a boot*, or جُفّ a concourse of people. I prefer the former reading. Cf. text p. 115. فَأَخِذَتْ مِنَ النِّعَالِ I was attacked with sandals.

[3] *The torrent was eroding it:* In A.H. 376 the town was visited by an earthquake which caused great loss of life and property. Ibn al-Athír, ix. 35.

[4] *I will deliver you:* Literally, I will suffice you.

[5] *Red heifer:* Literally, an intensely yellow; an allusion to Qur'án, ii, 64.

[6] *My blood will be lawful to you:* i.e., you may kill me.

way is long.' Then he arose for the first genuflexion and he stood as rigid as the trunk of a palm tree till they complained of sideache. Then he prostrated himself so long that they thought he had gone to sleep, but they dared not to raise their heads until he repeated the takbír for sitting. Then he returned to the second genuflexion, signed to me, and we made for the valley and left the people worshipping and we know not what fate did with them. Then Abú'l-Fath indited, saying:—

'May God not put far from Him the likes of me,[1]
But where is the likes of me, aye where?
How marvellous was the stupidity of the people,
Which I took advantage of with ease!
I received from them the full measure of good,
While I weighed out to them nought but fraud and falsehood.'

XXII. THE MAQAMA OF THE MADIRAH

'ÍSÁ IBN HISHÁM related to us and said: I was in Baṣra and with me was Abú'l-Fath al-Iskanderí, the man of eloquence who summons it and it responds to him, the man of rhetoric who commands it and it obeys him. We were present with him at a merchant's entertainment and there was placed before us maḍirah[2] which did credit to the townsfolk,[3] oscillated in a large dish, announced health[4] and testified to the Khalifate of

[1] *May God not put far from Him:* Metre, *mujtath.*
It is interesting to observe that the author is said to have been buried in the very state in which he falsely asserted the dead man was in order to defraud the too credulous people of Mosul. See Ibn Khallikan, i. 114.
This maqáma has been translated by De Sacy. *Chrestomathie Arabe*, iii. 247.

[2] *Maḍirah:* From مَضَرَ it (milk) became sour or acid biting the tongue, or, as made by the Arabs, fleshmeat cooked with pure milk that bites the tongue, until the fleshmeat is thoroughly done, and the milk has become thick, and sometimes they mix fresh milk with milk that has been collected in a skin, and in this case it is the best that can be. (Lane, *Lexicon* art. مَضَرَ p. 2720). It is said to have been the favourite dish of Abú Hurayrah, the Traditionalist, and contemporary of the Prophet. For a eulogy on Maḍirah see Mas'údí, viii. 403. For a list of the chief dishes of the Arabs, see the Maqámát of Náṣif al-Yázají, p. 98. (مَجْمَعُ ٱلْبَحْرَيْن)

[3] *Did credit to the town people:* Whose taste was more refined than that of the Bedawín.

[4] *Announced health:* Being easily digested.

Mu'awiya,[1] (may God have mercy upon him!) in a dish which dazzled the eye[2] and wherein beauty was bestirring itself.[3] When it took its place upon the table and its home in the hearts, Abú'l-Fath al-Iskanderí arose[4] cursing it and its owner, manifesting repugnance to it and its eater and reviling it and its cook. We thought he was joking, but behold! the reverse was the fact, and jest was the essence of earnestness. He withdrew from the table and abandoned co-operation with his brethren. So we ordered it to be removed and it was taken away, and with it the hearts; eyes travelled behind it, mouths watered for it, lips were licked for it, livers were inflamed[5] after it and hearts followed in its trail. But we associated ourselves with him in separation from it and we enquired of him the fact concerning it. He answered: 'My story regarding it is more extensive than my misfortune in it and, if I were to relate it to you, I should not be secure from hate and from wasting time.' We said: 'Produce it.' He said: 'While I was in Baghdad a merchant invited me to partake of maḍirah and he clung to me with the clinging of a pressing creditor, and of the dog to the companions of al-Raqím,[6] till I accepted his invitation to it, so we started. Now the whole way he was praising his wife

[1] Mu'awiya ibn Abi Sufyán, the first Khalifa of the House of Umayya. (A.H. 41-60) (A.D. 661-680). An allusion to the reputed gluttony of Mu'awiya (al-Fakhri's History, edition of Ahlwardt, p. 131) and the voluptuousness which is said to have characterized his court. See also *Arab Proverbs*, i, 135.

[2] يَزِلُّ ٱلطَّرْفُ *which dazzled the eyes*: Literally, the eye slipped from it.

[3] يَمُوجُ فِيهَا ٱلطَّرْفُ *Wherein beauty was bestirring itself*: Another reading is تَمْرَحُ فِيهَا ٱلطَّرْفُ The hand moved briskly to it.

[4] *Abú'l-Fatḥ arose*: Cf. De Sacy, *Ḥarírí*, xviii, 199, which is a very close imitation and, in parts, almost a literal copy of this maqáma.

[5] *Livers were inflamed*: Arabic writers suppose the liver to be the seat of affection and the heart to be that of reason. Cf. Merx's article on the Foie in the volume dedicated to de Vogue.

[6] *The dog to the companions of al-Raqím*: See Qur'án, xviii, 8–18. What is meant by this word the commentators cannot agree. Some will have it to be the name of the mountain, or the valley, wherein the cave was; some say it was the name of their dog and others, who seem to come nearest the true signification, that it was a brass plate, or stone tablet placed near the mouth of the cave in which the young men, the companions of the cave, were. Baiḍáwí's *Commentary* (edited by Fleischer), p. 555. Sale, *Translation of the Qur'án*, xviii, 217. Hamadhání certainly did not think that al-Raqím was the name of their dog.

and ready to sacrifice his heart's blood[1] for her, eulogising her cleverness in her art, and her excellent taste in cooking, saying, 'Sir, if thou wert to see her with the apron[2] tied round her waist, going about the rooms, from the oven[3] to the cooking-pots, and from the cooking pots to the oven, blowing the fire with her mouth, pounding the spices with her hands; and if thou wert to see the smoke discolouring that beautiful face and affecting that smooth cheek, thou wouldst behold a spectacle at which eyes would be dazed. I love her because she loves me, and it is a mark of a man's good fortune that he should be given a lawful helpmeet and that he should be aided by his spouse, and especially when she is of his own clay. In near relationship she is my paternal uncle's daughter, her clay is my clay, her town is my town, her paternal uncles are my paternal uncles and her origin is my origin. But in disposition she is more generous than I am, and in form more beautiful. He bored[4] me with his wife's virtues till we reached his quarter, whereupon he said: 'Sir, seest thou this quarter? It is the best quarter in Baghdad. Worthy men vie with one another for settling in it, and the great ones jealously compete with one another for finding quarters in it; but none but merchants live in it. Verily a man is known by his neighbour.[5] My house is in the middle of its belt[6] of buildings and is the point in the centre of its circle. How much dost thou think, Sir, was spent upon each house in it? Say approximately, if thou dost not know for certain.' I replied: 'Much.' Said he: 'Good gracious, what a terrible mistake!' thou sayest 'much' only! and he heaved a deep sigh and ejaculated: 'Praise Him who knoweth all things!' And we reached the door of his house and he said 'This is my house, how much dost thou reckon I spent on this window? By heavens! I spent upon it beyond my means

1 مُهْجَةٌ *Heart's blood*: Also the soul or spirit, e.g. خَرَجَتْ مُهْجَتُهُ His spirit went forth. Cf. مَهَجَ He sucked the breast of his mother.

2 الجُرْزَقَةُ *Apron*: Literally, a piece of cloth torn off.

3 تَنُّورٌ *An oven*: Old Persian tanura. Assyrian tenura. Hebrew תנור (Genesis, xv. 17). In Arabic a loan word from Aramaic.

4 صَدَعَنى *He bored me*: Literally, he split me. Cf. صُداعٌ a splitting headache.

5 *A man is known by his neighbour*: Cf. *Arab Proverbs*, i, 303.

6 *Its belt*: Literally, its necklace.

and what exceeded the limits of poverty. How dost thou find its workmanship and shape? I adjure thee by God, hast thou ever seen its like? Observe the fine finish of it. Ponder its curves which seem to have been drawn with a compass.[1] Regard the skill of the carpenter in the make of this door. Of how many planks[2] did he make it? Say, How do I know? It is made of teakwood[3] from one piece which was neither worm-eaten nor rotten. When it is moved it creaks, and, when it is struck with the finger, it rings. Who made it, Sir? Abú Isḥáq ibn Muhammad the Baṣarian made it, and he is, by Heavens! a man of clean reputation,[4] well acquainted with the art of making doors, deft of hand in the work. What a splendid man[5] that is! By my life I shall employ none but him for such work as this. Now this knocker; dost thou observe it? I bought it in the fancy bazaar from 'Imrán, the curiosity dealer, for three Mu'izzí dinars.[6] How much brass[7] does it contain, Sir? There are in it six pounds. It revolves on a pin in the door. I adjure thee by God, turn it, then sound it and observe it. By the preciousness of my life to thee, do not buy knockers except from him, for he sells only the best.'[8] Then he knocked at the door, we entered the vestibule[9] and he said: 'May God prosper thee, O house! and not destroy thee, O wall! How strong are thy walls, substantial thy superstructure, and how firm thy foundations! By heavens! observe its staircase, the entrance and the exit, and ask me 'How didst thou get it?

[1] اَلبِرْكَارُ *A compass:* Arabicized from the Persian پرکار or پرگار

[2] مِن كَمْ *Of how many planks?:* Literally, of how many?

[3] سَاجٌ *Teakwood:* Arabicized from the Sanskrit *saka*. Hindustani ساکوان

[4] *Clean reputation:* Literally, of clean clothes.

[5] لِلّٰهِ دَرُّ ذٰلِكَ آلرَّجُلِ *What a splendid man that is!:* A well-known expression of admiration. See Wright's Grammar, ii, 150.

[6] *Mu'izzí dinars:* The coin of Mu'izz al-Daula (A.H. 303–56). The Buwayhid prince who ruled at Baghdad from A.H. 334–56. The life of this sovereign is given by Ibn Khallikan, i, 555.

[7] اَلشَّبَةُ *Brass:* read اَلشَّبَهُ

[8] اَلأَعْلَاقُ *the best:* plural of عِلْقٌ a precious thing.

[9] اَلدِّهْلِيزُ *vestibule:* Arabicized from the Persian داليج and داليز an entrance or passage of a house, between the outer door or gate.

How many devices didst devise before thou didst appropriate it?' I had a neighbour surnamed Abú Suleyman, who lived in this quarter. He had of live stock[1] more than enclosure could contain, and of dead stock more than could be weighed. He died—may God have mercy upon him!—and left a son who squandered[2] it on wine and music[3] and scattered it between backgammon[4] and dice. I was afraid lest excessive need should compel him to dispose of the house and he should sell it while in a state of vexation, or expose it to ruin, in which case I should see the chance of buying it lost, and wear myself out with vain regrets to my dying day. So I took some stuff not in demand, carried it to him and offered it to him, and I bargained with him to buy it on credit; and the unfortunate one counts credit a gift, and the promise breaker considers it a present. And I asked him for a bond for the goods, so he granted it, and signed[5] it in my favour. Then I pretended to be indifferent in demanding payment till the extremities of the garment of his state became frayed, and then I came to him and asked him to pay the debt. He begged for time and I respited him.[6] He next asked for some stuff besides that; so I brought it and asked him to mortgage his house to me as a security in my hands, and he did so. Then I gradually involved him in bargains till it came to selling the house and it was acquired by me through rising fortune, and helping fate, and the strength of my arm. '*There is many a toiler for an idle sitter.*[7] And, praise God, I am exceedingly lucky, and in such matters worthy of commendation,

1 أَلمَالُ *Live stock:* Wealth, gold or silver, primarily camels or cattle, or sheep or goats, because most of the wealth of the Arabs of the desert consisted of these. It is here used in the primitive sense as appears from the context أَلصَّامِتُ the dumb, as opposed to أَلنَّاطِق having the faculty of producing sound.

2 مَزَّقَهُ *Squandered it:* He scattered it, or tore it to pieces. Cf. Qur'án, xxxiv, 18.

3 *Music:* Literally, playing upon the reed or pipe.

4 أَلنَّرْدُ *Backgammon:* or trick track: A Persian word also called نرد شير, because invented, as some say, by Ardeshir, son of Bábak, a Persian King.

5 عَقَدَهَا *He signed it:* That is, he drew up and signed the bond in my favour. For this meaning of this verb, see Qur'án, iv, 37.

6 *I respited him:* An allusion to Qur'án, vii, 13 and 14.

7 *There is many a toiler for an idle sitter:* Freytag, *Arab Proverbs*, i, 544, used for a person whose wealth passes to some one who has done nothing for it. 'Unearned increment'. See Constantinople edition, p. 5.

and this will suffice thee, Sir. For many nights I had been sleeping in my house with those therein when lo! there was a knock at the door, I said, 'who is the wandering nocturnal visitor?' And behold it was a woman with a pearl necklace with a surface as clear as water, and in fineness like unto the mirage, which she offered for sale! So I snatched it from her with a plundering snatch and bought it for a low price and soon there will be derived from it a manifest gain and plentiful profit, by the help of God, the most High, and thy good fortune. I have only related this story to thee that thou mightest know the propitiousness of my fortune in commerce. 'Luck brings forth water from stones.'[1] Great God! None can inform thee more truly than thyself and naught is nearer to thee than thy yesterday. I bought this mat in an auction. It was taken from the house of the Furát family[2] at the time of sequestration and plundering. For a long time I had been seeking one like it, but had found none. But time is pregnant and it is not known what it will bring forth.[3] Then it so happened I was at the Táq gate and

[1] *Luck brings water from stones:* Apparently a proverbial expression. It occurs again in a slightly modified form on p. 205 of the Text.

[2] آل الفرات *The Furát family:* A highly distinguished family in the service of Khalifate during the fourth century, remarkable for their official and administrative ability for several generations. There were four brothers who rose to eminence during the reign of Muqtadir b'illáh (A.H. 295-320) namely, Aḥmad Abú'l-'Abbás, 'Abdulláh Ja'far, Abú 'Ísá Íbráhim, Abú'l-Ḥasan 'Alí. Their father was Muḥammad Ibn Músá, an agent to the Khalifa Muntaṣir (A.H. 247).

Abú'l-Ḥasan 'Alí, the most celebrated of the four, was three times wazir to al-Muqtadir. He was a man of great natural gifts, an excellent administrator, and liberal to extravagance. In A.H. 299 the Khalifa dismissed him and seized all his vast wealth. This is the incident Hamadhání refers to. From the time of his dismissal to his reinstatement in 304 the income from his estates to the public treasury amounted to no less than seven million dinars. On his reappointment in 304 the Khalifa showed him the highest favours, sending him seven cloaks of honour and 300,000 dirhems. Two years later he was again arrested and thrown into prison. In 311 he was restored to his post for the third time and marked his resumption of office by acts which have left a stain on his memory. He exacted large sums from many people and allowed his son, Abú'l-Muḥássin, to put to death Ḥamid ibn al-'Abbás, the late wazir. The following year he fell for the third time, when it was found that he possessed upwards of a million dinars, and that his landed property produced an annual income of a million dinars. A few days later he and his son Muḥássin were put to death by Nazuk the chief of the police. (See Ahmedroz, *Wazirs of Hilál.* Chenery's translation of *Ḥarîri*, p. 469 and al-Fakhri (edition, Ahlwardt), p. 311.

[3] *It is not known what it (Time) will bring forth:* Cf. English, we know not what a *day* may bring forth.

this was being offered for sale in the streets. So I weighed out for it such and such a sum of dinars I adjure thee by God observe its fineness, softness, workmanship, and colour, for it is of great worth. Its like is found but rarely. If thou hast heard of Abú ‘Imrán, the mat-weaver, it is his handiwork. And he has a son who will succeed him and who is now in his shop. Fine mats can only be had of him. By my life! do not buy mats except at his shop. Now the righteous man is his brethren's counsellor, especially of him whose person is rendered inviolable by eating at his table. Let us return to the story of the Maḍirah for noontide has approached. ‘Boy! the basin and the water!’ I said ‘Great God! perhaps deliverance is nigh, and escape has become easy.’ The slave came forward. He asked: ‘Dost thou see this slave, he is of Greek origin, brought up in ‘Iráq. Step forward boy, uncover thy head, bare thy calf, tuck up thy sleeves, expose thy teeth, advance, retire!’ The slave did so. Said the merchant: who bought him? ‘By Heavens! Abú'l-‘Abbás bought him from the slave dealer. Put down the basin[1] and bring the ewer.’[2] The slave put it down and the merchant picked it up, turned it round, looked it over, sounded it and said: ‘Look at this brass,[3] it seems like a burning brand, or a piece of gold. Its brass is Syrian and it is of ‘Iráq workmanship. It is not a worn-out curio. It has known and made the round of the palaces of kings; consider its beauty and ask me ‘When didst thou buy it?’ ‘I bought it, by Heavens! in the famine year and I have preserved it for this hour. Boy, the ewer!’ And he brought it. And the merchant took it up, turned it over and said: ‘The spout is of one piece with it. This ewer is fit only for this basin, and this basin is only suitable for this company[4] and this company suits only this house and this house is not adorned except by this guest. Boy! pour the water, for food time is

1 الطست *The basin*: Arabicized from the Persian طشت or تشت, Zend *tasta*, a basin, a ewer-stand.

2 ابريق *The ewer*: Arabicized from the Persian آبريز a water-pot with a spout The word occurs in the plural أباريق in Qur'án, lvi, 18.

3 شَبَةٌ *Copper*: read شَبَهٌ

4 الدست *Company*: Arabicized from the Persian دست the upper end of a chamber, hence a place or seat of honour, and then the company itself. It also means a game. Cf. the remark of Imr al Qais, ‘I did not wish to spoil thy game.’ (*Aghání*, viii, 65.) For other uses of this word see *Ḥaríri*, i, 276.

nigh. I adjure thee by God, dost thou see this water? How pure it is! Blue as the eye of the cat, clear as a crystal wand, drawn from the Euphrates, and it is used after standing for the night when it has become like the flame of a torch and translucent as a tear. And the importance is not in the water carrier, but in the vessel. Nothing proves to thee the purity of the vessel more correctly than the purity of the liquid. Now this napkin, ask of me its story. It is a fabric of Jurján and a production of Arraján. It fell to my lot and I bought it. My wife took a portion of it for drawers [1] and I made some of it into a napkin.[2] Her drawers took twenty cubits [3] and I forcibly wrested this much from her hand, gave it to the embroiderer [4] to make and embroider it as thou seest it. Then I brought it back from the market and stored it away in a box and preserved it for refined guests. The common Arabs have not defiled it with their hands, nor women with the corners of their eyes, for every precious thing has its day [5] and every instrument its people. Boy! the table! for the delay is great, and the bowls! for the discussion has been long, and the food! for words have been multiplied.' The slave brought the table. The merchant then turned it over

[1] سراويل pl. of سروال *Drawers or trowsers:* Arabicized from the Persian شلوار probably from the stem شل a thigh and the suffix وار an inner breeches or drawers reaching to the feet. Cf. Greek *σαραβαρα*. Suidas regards it as a Persian garment. Cf. Hebrew סַרְבָּלֵיהוֹן Daniel, iii, 27. A tradition of the Prophet enjoins the wearing of the سراويل by both sexes. (*Ḥariri*, i, 78.). *Ḥariri*, i, 78, uses the word سربال with سروال in the phrase بسربال و سروال 'With a shirt and trowsers'. Although, conceivably, سربال may be a corruption of سروال the words appear to have connoted different articles of dress. See Text, p. 240; و سربلوها من القار 'and they coated it with pitch'.

[2] منديل *a napkin*, kerchief or towel: Arabicized from the Latin mantele (mantile). Spanish mantilla. Cf. The mindil or kerchief of St. Veronica delivered up in A.H. 331 by the Khalífa Muttaqí (A.H. 322-29) to the Byzantine emperor, Romanos I, at the request of the latter, in exchange for a large number of Muslim prisoners of war. *Annals of Abú'l-Fida*, p. 424.

[3] ذراع *Cubits:* The space from the extremity of the elbow to the extremity of the little finger. It is divided into six قبضات (fists), the measure called a cubit, about eighteen inches.

[4] طراز *Embroidery:* Arabicized from the Persian تراز from ترازيدن to embroider, to embellish.

[5] ***Every precious thing has its day:*** Apparently a proverbial expression.

sounded it with his fingers, and bit' it[1] with his teeth and said: 'May God prosper Baghdad, how excellent are her goods and skilful her artisans! By Heavens! observe this table, look at the breadth of its surface, the lightness of its weight, the soundness of its timber and the beauty of its make.' Said I: 'This is the make but when is the meal?' He answered: 'Immediately. Boy! quick, the food! But the table, its legs are a part of it.' Said Abú'l-Fatḥ, 'My spirit boiled,[2] and I said: 'There remaineth the baking and its implements, the bread and its properties, the wheat and whence the grain was first bought, and how the transport was hired for it, in which mill it was ground and the vessel in which it was kneaded, which oven was heated and which baker was hired; and there remaineth the wood, whence it was gathered, when it was brought in, how it was stacked till it was seasoned and how it was stored until it dried. Then there are left the baker and his description, the apprentice[3] and his qualification, the flour and its praise, the leaven and its tale, the salt and its savour; and then there remain, the dishes[4] and who had them, how he procured them, who used them and who made them. Then the vinegar, how its grapes were picked, or how its ripe dates were bought, how its press was plastered, how the essence was extracted, how its jar was besmeared with pitch and how much its vat is worth. Then there remain the vegetables and the devices whereby they were picked, in which vegetable garden they were arranged, and the skill displayed to produce them free from impurities. Then there remaineth the Maḍirah[5] and how its meat was bought and its extra fat was got, how its cooking pot was set up, how its fire

1 عَجَمَهُ *Bit it:* Tested its soundness.

2 تَجَاشَتْ نفسي *My spirit boiled:* Another possible rendering, my soul (stomach) heaved.

3 تلميذٌ *An apprentice:* Borrowed from Hebrew or Aramaic תַּלְמִיד; Aramaic *talmadá* a pupil or attendant. (*Ḥariri*, i, 20.)

4 السُّكُرُّجَات *The dishes:* Said to be arabicized from the Persian سكرجه and سكر a saucer, a short of small bowl-shaped vessel out of which one eats (Lane, p. 1392). Cf. Armenian, *skavarák*.

5 *There remaineth the Maḍirah:* Hamadhání here gives the recipe for this dish, and, following in the strain of the bore, he cleverly holds up to ridicule the incoherent garrulousness of his tormentor.

was kindled, how its spices were pounded, till, finally, it was well-cooked and its gravy became consistent. But this is a mighty matter and a never-ending affair?' So I arose. He asked: 'Whither dost thou intend to go?' I replied, 'I intend to go to discharge a need.' He enquired: 'Sir, dost thou want a privy that makes the spring quarters of the prince, and the autumn residence of the wazir appear contemptible? Its top has been plastered[1] with gypsum and its bottom with mortar, its roof has been made flat and its floor paved with marble. The ant slips down from its wall and cannot cling, and the fly tries to walk upon its floor but slides. It has a door whose venetians are made alternately of teak and ivory and joined together with an excellent joining so that the guest desires to eat in it.' Said I: 'Eat thou from this bag, the privy was not in the reckoning.' And I went out towards the door, quickened my pace and began to run, while he was following me and shouting: 'Abú'l-Fatḥ! the Maḍirah! 'And the boys thought Maḍirah was a title of mine, and took up his cry. So out of excessive vexation I threw a stone at one of them, but a man received it on his turban and it sank into his skull. Therefore I was attacked with sandals,[2] old and new, and with cuffs good and bad; and then I was placed in prison and remained in that unfortunate plight for two years. So I vowed not to eat Maḍirah as long as I lived. Now ye men of Hamadhán[3] am I unjust in this?' Said 'Ísá ibn Hishám 'So we accepted his excuse, we vowed the same vow and said· "Long since did Maḍirah sin against the noble and prefer the base[4] to the good."'

[1] مَهرج *Plastered:* Arabicized from the Persian ماروج plaster, or quicklime.

[2] فَأُخِذتُ مِنَ ٱلنِّعَالِ *I was attacked with sandals:* Cf. The maqáma of Moṣul, Text, p. 98.

[3] يا آلَ هَمَذانَ *Ye men of Hamadhán:* The scene of the incident is Baṣra and that of the narration Hamadhán. On page 340 of the Letters there is an allusion to one who swore he would not partake of Maḍirah and then ate a dog's tail with monkey's milk!

[4] ألأَراذِلَ *The base:* Another reading ألأَنذَالَ the vile.

This maqáma is all in prose and is remarkable for the large number of foreign words. It contains no less than thirteen,

'ÍSÁ IBN HISHÁM related to us and said: When exile had taken me as far as Báb al-Abwáb[1] I was content with return as a booty,[2] but there intervened between it the bounding main[3] with its lofty waves, and the ships going out of their courses with their passengers. But I sought a good omen from God concerning returning, and I sat in a most dangerous place in the ship. Now when the sea had got the ascendency over us, and the night enveloped us, there overwhelmed us a cloud raining in torrents[4] and marshalling mountains of mist with a wind which sent the waves along in pairs and the rain in hosts.[5] Thus we were left in the hand of death between two seas,[6] while we possessed no equipment but prayer, no device except weeping, and no protection save hope, and we spent a night of Nabigah![7] and in the morning we cried and complained to one another. Now there was among us a man whose eyelid was not wetted

1 *The Gate of Gates*: or Darband, a town in the province of Daghistán on the western shore of the Caspian Sea. To the south lies the seaward extremity of the Caucasian wall (fifty miles long) otherwise known as Alexander's wall, blocking the narrow pass of the Iron Gate, or Caspian Gates. This, when entire, had a height of twenty-nine feet and a thickness of about ten feet and with its iron gates and numerous watch towers formed a valuable defence of the Persian frontier. The walls and the citadel are believed to belong to the time of Anushirwán (A.D. 531–579). Yaqút says the breadth of the wall was 300 cubits or about 150 yards. It was captured in A.H. 19 by the Arabs under Suraqa ibn 'Amr, also called Dhú'l-Nún. In A.D. 728 the Arabs entered into possession and established a principality in the city which they called Bab al-Abwáb, or the Chief Gate. Harún al-Rashid lived here at different times and made it famous as a seat of arts and commerce. It was noted for its linen manufacture. (Yaqút, i, 437. *Encyclopaedia Britannica*, viii, 64.)

2 *I was content with return as a booty*: That is, I was content with return as my only return. *Arab Proverbs*, i, 537.

3 *The bounding main*: The sea referred to was the Caspian and this is no exaggerated description of its stormy character. The winds from the north and the north-west sometimes blow for days together with great violence, rendering navigation extremely dangerous.

4 *Raining in torrents*: Literally extending ropes of rain.

5 *In hosts, or troops*: An allusion to Qur'án, cx, 2.

6 *Between two seas*: i.e., the torrents above and the sea beneath.

7 *A night of* Nabigah: An allusion to the oft-quoted lines of Nabigah.

فَبِتُّ كَأَنِّي سَاوَرَتْنِي ضَئِيلَةٌ * مِنَ ٱلرُّقْشِ فِي أَنْيَابِهَا ٱلسُّمُّ نَاقِعُ

And I passed a night as I should have passed had one of the spotted snakes attacked me, the poison of whose fangs is deadly.

and whose eye was not moistened; he was expanded and dilated of bosom,[1] light-hearted and glad. Now by Heavens! we were perfectly astonished, and so we said to him! 'What hath given thee security from destruction?' And he said: 'An amulet whose possessor will not drown, and, if I wished to give each of you a charm,[2] I could do so.' So all inclined towards him and were persistent in demanding from him. But he said: 'I will not do so till every one of you gives me a dinar now, and promises me another when he is saved.' Said 'Ísá ibn Hishám: 'We paid him down what he demanded and promised him what he stipulated. Then his hand returned to his pocket and he drew forth a piece of silk in which there was an ivory box whose interior[3] enclosed some billets, and he threw each of us one of them.

When the ship got safe to shore and we landed in the city,[4] he demanded of the people what they had promised him, so they paid him. It finally came to my turn, but he said: 'Leave him.' Then I said to him, 'That is thine after thou acquaintest me with the secret of thy condition.' He said, 'I am from the city of Alexandria.' I asked, 'How was it that patience helped thee but forsook us?' He said:—

> 'Woe, to thee![5] were it not for patience I had not
> Filled my purse with gold.
> He will not obtain glory who is impatient
> At what befalls him.
> Again, what was given me has not now resulted in harm to me.
> Rather with it do I strengthen my loins
> And bind up the broken.
> And if I were to-day among the drowned,
> I should not have been troubled for an explanation.'[6]

[1] رَخِيُّ الصَّدر *Expanded of bosom:* That is, easy in mind.

[2] *A charm:* The commentator says (Text, p. 117) that Islám forbids the use of charms, but the statement is unsupported by authority.

[3] صَدرُهَا *Whose interior:* Literally, whose breast.

[4] *We landed in the city:* Literally, the city caused us to alight. A very common construction where the adverb is made the subject of the sentence.

[5] *Woe to thee!:* Metre, *ramal*.

[6] Compare this maqáma with Ḥarírí, pp. 130 and 494.

XXIV. THE MAQAMA OF THE ASYLUM

‘ÍSÁ IBN HISHÁM related to us and said: I entered the asylum[1] of Baṣra and there was with me Abú Dá’úd the scholastic divine.[2] And I beheld a madman[3] who was glancing at me. Said he: ‘If the augury bird is right ye are strangers.’ And we answered: ‘It is so.’ He said: ‘Who are the people? How excellent are their fathers!’ I replied: ‘I am ‘Ibn Hishám and this is Abú Dá’úd the theologian.’ He enquired: ‘Al-’Askari?’ I said: ‘Yes.’ Then he exclaimed: ‘May the faces be disfigured and the possessors thereof! Verily free-will[4] belongs to God and not to his slave, and affairs are in the hands of God and not in his. Ye Magians of this community[5] ye live predestined lives, and die victims of a merciless fate. Ye are forcibly driven doomwards. ‘And, if ye had been in your houses,[6] verily they would have gone forth to fight, whose slaughter was decreed, to the places where they died.’[7] If the fact be as ye describe it, why are ye not just? Ye assert, the

1 اَلْمَارِسْتَان *The asylum:* Arabicized from the Persian بيمارستان a hospital.

2 *Abú Dá'úd the scholastic divine:* The person referred to is evidently Abú Bakr Muḥammad ibn Abdulláh al-'Askarí the chief Qáḍí of the Khalifa Al-Mahdí (A.D. 775-84) at Ruṣafa. He was one of the most famous of the Mu'tazilás (*al-Ansáb* of al-Sam'aní, p. 392).

3 مَجْنُونٌ *a madman:* Literally, possessed by a jinn, demon, or demoniac.

4 اَلْخِيَرَةُ *Free-will:* The doctrine of free-will was no new idea, for we are told that al-'Aasha, a contemporary of the Prophet, was a believer in it and that he had been instructed therein by the 'Ibádites, or Christians, of al-Ḥira from whom he used to buy wine. *Aghání*, viii, 76. The orthodox belief is expressed in *Arab Proverbs*, ii, 405. 'Had I been given free choice, I should have chosen'. لَو خُيِّرتُ لَا خترتُ [Cf. *Life of Muhammad* (Wüstenfeld) Band, iv, 1011]. The Mu'tazilís were the partisans of free-will (قَدْر) as opposed to orthodox fatalism or predestination (جَبْر). For an excellent account of the origin and development of this sect, see Professor Browne, *Literary History of Persia*, i, 281-92; *Hibbert Lectures*, v, 214; Shahrastání, *al-Milal wa'l-Nihal* (Cunton's ed.), pp. 29-30 and Sell, *The Faith of Islám* (3rd ed.), pp. 194-206.

5 *Magians of this community:* An allusion to the spurious tradition اَلْقَدَرِيَّةُ مَجُوسُ هٰذِهِ ٱلْأُمَّةِ 'The partisans of free-will are the Magians of the Church', quoted by Abú'l-Ḥasan al-'Ash'arí (A.H. 270-330), in the *Ibána*, p. 73, as a genuine tradition.

6 *If ye had been in your houses:* Qur'án, iii, 148.

7 *The places where they died:* Literally, sleeping-places.

creator of oppression is an oppressor, then why do ye not say, the creator of death is mortal? Do ye not surely know that, as to religion, ye are viler than the Devil, who said, ' Lord because thou hast seduced me,'[1] for he confessed, but ye have denied; he believed but ye have disbelieved. Ye say man has been given free choice and so he chooses. Never! for the free agent would not rip open his stomach, nor pluck out his eye, nor hurl his son from a crag. Is, therefore, compulsion aught but what ye perceive it? Now compulsion is sometimes enforced by reason and sometimes by the scourge. Let it be to your shame that the Qur'án rouses hatred in you and the Tradition angers you. When ye hear, ' he whom God causeth to err[2] shall have no guide, ye pervert it.'[3] And when ye hear, ' The earth contracted for me[4] and I was shown its east and its west', ye disbelieve it. When ye hear, ' Paradise was so manifested to me[5] that I attempted to pluck its fruits, and Hell fire was so exhibited to me that I shielded myself from the heat thereof with my hand,' ye wag your heads and turn your necks awry. If it be said ' The torture of the tomb,' ye presage evil, or if it be said, ' The bridge,' ye wink at one another. If the ' balances '[6] are mentioned, ye say : ' Its two scales consist of emptiness '. If the ' Book ' be spoken of, ye say : ' The two sides of it are of leather.'[7] Ye enemies of the Book and the Tradition! of what do ye presage evil? Do ye mock God and his signs and his Apostle?[8] A faction seceded[9] and they were the dross of the Tradition. Then ye separated yourselves from it, therefore ye

[1] *Because thou hast seduced me :* Qur'án, xv, 39.
[2] *Whom God causeth to err :* Qur'án, vii, 185.
[3] ألْحَدتَم *Ye pervert it :* Literally ye turn away from the apparent meaning and twist it. This is an allusion to the Bátinites who assert that the Qur'án has an outward sense and an inward meaning differing from the former and known to them, i.e. the literal and the allegorical.
[4] زُوِيَت ٱلَى ٱلأَرضُ *The earth contracted for me :* Íbn al-Athír, *Niháyah,* ii, 82.
[5] عُرِضَت عَلَىَّ ٱلْجَنَّةُ *Paradise was manifested to me :* ibid.
[6] *The balances :* Of Justice and equity in mutual dealings. Qur'án, iv, 6.
[7] من القد *Of leather :* i.e., something created and not uncreate. An allusion to the dogma that the Qur'án is uncreate and the belief of the heterodox that it is something created.
[8] *God and His signs and His Apostle:* Qur'án, ix, 66.
[9] مَرَقَت مَارِقَةٌ *A faction seceded :* An allusion to the withdrawal of Wáṣit ibn 'Aṭá the founder of the Mu'tazila sect.

are the dross of the corrupt. Hermaphrodites of the Khárijites![1]
Ye are of their opinion except as to fighting, and thou, Ibn
Hishám, thou believest in part[2] and rejectest in part. I have
heard thou hast selected for thy bed a fiend from among them.
Hath God not forbidden thee to take an intimate associate[3]
from among them? Woe to thee! makest thou not a good
selection for thy seed? And dost thou pay no regard to thy
posterity?' Then he prayed: 'O God! Give me in exchange
for them better than they and place me with thy heavenly
messengers.' Said 'Ísá ibn Hishám: 'I could not, nor could
Abú Dá'úd return a reply and we went away from him in disgrace and verily I was conscious of humiliation in Abú Dá'úd
until we desired to separate. He said: ''Ísa, by thy father!
This is the fact, but what did he mean by a female fiend?' I
answered, 'By Heavens! I know not, except that I had resolved
to ask one of them in marriage, but I had not mentioned what I
intended to any one. By God! I will never do it.' Then he
said: 'By Heavens! this is none other than a devil in bonds.'
So we returned and stood before him. And we hastened to
speak and we began questioning. He said: 'Perhaps you both
wish to know of my affair that which you denied.' We said ·
'Thou wert previously acquainted with our affairs and now thou
art not mistaken as to what is in our minds.[4] So explain thy
affair to us and reveal thy secret to us. He recited:

'I am the fountain of wonders.[5]
In my devising I am the possessor of high degrees.

---

[1] الخَوارِج The Khárijites: 'The Seceders, or Theocratic Separatists'. The
pious fanatics in 'Ali's army who forced him to submit to arbitration at the battle
of Siffin (A.D. 657) and afterwards blamed him for doing so, and, because he would
not publicly confess, what they denounced as his disloyalty to God for having submitted the question of the succession to the Khalifate, for which he and Mu'áwiya,
the Governor of Syria, were contending, to arbitration, they seceded from him. No
less than twelve thousand of these fanatical malcontents separated themselves from
him and adopted as their war-cry, لا حُكَم إلا لله 'Arbitration belongs to God alone'.
Browne, Literary of History of Persia, i, 220. Al-Fakhrí (Ahlwardt), p. 114.

[2] Thou believest in part: An allusion to Qur'án, ii, 79.

[3] بِطانَة an intimate associate: Literally the lining of a garment; metaphorically an intimate and familar friend. In the text it means a wife. See Qur'án, iii,
114.

[4] Minds: Literally, breasts.

[5] I am the fountain of wonders: Metre, ramal.

In truth, I am the camel's hump.[1]
In vanity, I am its withers.[2]
Alexandria is my home, an aimless
Wanderer am I on God's earth.
In the monastery I am an abbot,
In the masjid an ascetic.'[3]

XXV. THE MAQAMA OF THE FAMINE

'ÍSÁ IBN HISHÁM related to us and said: I was in Baghdad in a famine year,[4] and so I approached a company, united[5] like the Pleiades, in order to ask something of them. Now there was among them a youth with a lisp in his tongue and a space between his front teeth. He asked: 'What is thy affair?'[6] I replied: 'Two conditions in which a man prospers not: that of a beggar harassed by hunger, and that of an exile to whom return is impossible.' The boy then said: 'Which of the two breaches dost thou wish stopped first?' I answered: 'Hunger, for it has become extreme with me.' He said: 'What sayest thou to a white cake on a clean table, picked herbs with very sour vinegar, fine date-wine with pungent mustard, roast meat ranged on a skewer with a little salt, placed now before thee by one who will not put thee off with a promise nor torture thee with delay, and who will afterwards follow it up[7] with golden goblets of the juice of the grape? Is that preferable to thee, or a large company, full cups, variety of dessert, spread carpets, brilliant lights, and a skilful minstrel with the eye and neck of a gazelle?

[1] سَنَامٌ *The camel's hump:* Figure for height or prominence.

[2] *Withers:* Figure for less high, or less prominent.

[3] In this maqáma the author introduces an extremely polemical subject, the doctrines of free-will and predestination. Abú'l-Fatḥ in the character of a madman in bonds champions the orthodox opinion, and Abú Dá'úd and 'Ìsá ibn Hishám, the partisans of free-will, are silenced and discomfited. Hamadhání's own opinion was clearly against the doctrine of free-will. See his Letters, pp. 27-8.

[4] *A famine year:* Probably A.H. 382 when famine prices prevailed in Baghdad and bread was 40 dirhems a pound (Ibn Al-Athir, ix, 66). A.H. 373, 376 and 377 were also years of severe drought in 'Iráq, Ibn Al-Athir, ix.

[5] *United:* Literally, bound together with the string of the Pleiades.

[6] *What is thy affair?* Cf. Qur'án, xx, 96.

[7] يُعَلِّلُ *Follow up with;* Literally, give thee to drink a second time.

'If thou desirest neither this nor that, what is thy verdic regarding fresh meat, river fish, fried brinjal,[1] the wine o Quṭrubbul [2] picked apples,[3] a soft bed on a lofty place, opposit a rapid river, a gushing fountain, and a garden with streams i it?' 'Ísá ibn Hishám related: So I said: 'I am the slav of all three.' The boy said: 'And so am I their servant, if the were only present.' I then said: 'May God not bless thee Thou hast revived desires which despair had destroyed, and nov thou hast gripped their palate.[4] From which ruins dost tho hail?' He said:—

'I am of the citizens of Alexandria,[5]
Of sound and pure stock among them.
The age and the people thereof are stupid,
Therefore I made my stupidity my steed!'

XXVI. THE MAQAMA OF THE EXHORTATION

'ÍSÁ IBN HISHÁM related to us and said: when I was in Baṣr I was going proudly along until my walk led me to an ope space in which many people were assembled before a man wh was standing, admonishing them and saying: 'O people, ye hav not been left without control.'[6] Verily joined to to-day i to-morrow.[7] Ye are descending into a deep place, therefor prepare against it what force ye are able. And verily afte this life is the judgement,[8] therefore get provisions ready for it Behold there is no excuse, for the highway has been mad clear unto you. God's case against you is clear,[9] by revelatio from Heaven and by examples on earth. Lo! Verily He, wh with knowledge created the race, maketh the dry bones live

[1] بَاذَنجَان *Brinjal:* Arabicized from the Persian بادنگان, Sanskrit *Banganah* English Brinjal; the *Solanum melongena*, mad-apple; or egg-plant.

[2] *Qutrubbul:* A village situated between Baghdad and 'Okbara noted for th excellence of its wine. It was much frequented by the people of the former city i their parties of pleasure and debauch.

[3] *Pickled apples:* Cf. Qur'án, xx, 25.

[4] قبضت لها ثها *Thou hast gripped their palate:* Deprived them of realization.

[5] *I am of the citizens of Alexandria:* Metre, *kamil.*

[6] *Left without control:* An allusion to Qur'án, lxxv, 36.

[7] *Verily joined to to-day is to-morrow:* Freytag, *Arab Proverbs*, i, 45.

[8] معادا *Judgement:* Literally, return.

[9] *God's case against you is clear:* Cf. Qur'án, iv, 163.

Is not the world indeed a house of probation and a bridge to cross? He who traverses it is saved, but he who hoards up the world repenteth. Behold it has laid the snare and spread the grain for you. Therefore whoever pastures there will be entrapped, and whoever picks up the grain will be ensnared. Lo! poverty was the garb of your Prophet,[1] therefore wear it; but wealth is the robe of rebellion against God, therefore put it not on. False are the imaginations of the perverters of the truth[2] who have denied the Faith and made the Qur'án discordant.[3] Verily after life is the grave, 'and ye were not created in sport.'[4] Therefore beware of the heat of Hell-fire and hasten to the eternal home. Verily knowledge, whatever its failings, is good, and ignorance is bad under all conditions. Ye are surely the most wretched overshadowed by the heavens if, through you, the learned are in distress, for men are judged by their leaders, and, if the people are led by their influence,[5] they are saved by their responsibility.

Men are divided into two classes, the observant scholar and the striving student, as for the rest, they are abandoned ostriches and beasts pasturing at pleasure. Woe to him of high degree commanded by one beneath him, and woe to the knower of something who is ruled by one ignorant of it! I have heard that 'Alí ibn al-Ḥusain[6] was standing admonishing the people and saying: 'O soul, how long wilt thou rely upon life, and depend upon the world and its building up? Hast thou not taken warning from those of thy ancestors who have passed away, from

[1] *Poverty was the garb of your Prophet:* An allusion to the tradition (الفقر فخري) 'Poverty is my glory'. For poverty of the Prophets, see Tha'álibí, *Thamar al-Kutub*, p. 49.

[2] ظنون الملحدين *The imaginations of the perverters of the truth:* مُلحِد from لحد he disputed or wrangled, is applied to one who swerves from the truth and introduces into it that which does not belong to it. الملحدون is especially applied to the Esoterics (Báṭinites) who assert that the Qur'án has an outward and inward sense, the latter differing from the former and known to them. According to al-Farq bain al-Fir'aq, they denied the resurrection. Hibbert Lectures, p. 218.

[3] *Who have made the Qur'án discordant:* Qur'án, xv, 91.

[4] *Ye were not created in sport:* Qur'án, xxiii, 117.

[5] *Led by their influence:* Literally, by their reins.

[6] *'Alí ibn al-Ḥusain:* (A.H. 38–94), generally known by the appellation Zain al-'Abidín, was the grandson of 'Alí. Ibn Khallikan, ii, 209–11.

those of thy friends whom the earth has covered up, from those of thy brethren who have been smitten, and from those of thy fellows who have been transported to the house of decay ?

In the bowels of the earth [1] are they after having been upon its back.
Their virtues decaying and forgotten therein.
Their houses are emptied of them and their enclosures are void,
And the Fates have driven them deathwards.
They have left the world and what they had collected therein,
And under the earth the pits have embraced them.'

How many ages, one after the other, have Death's hands snatched away, and what changes have they produced by their calamities and how many great men have they concealed beneath the dust !

'And thou art intent upon the world,[2] vying
With its suitors for her, covetous and boasting of thy superior substance.
Thou goest into danger and art unmindful.
Didst thou but understand, wouldst thou not know to what danger thou exposest thyself ?
And verily the man, who endeavours and strives after this world,
And neglects the next, is without doubt a loser.'

Mark the dead nations and defunct kings, how the days overthrew them, and death destroyed them, so that their traces have been obliterated [3] and but a tale of them remaineth.

'They are decayed in the dust [4] and devoid
Of them are the assemblies, and the spacious apartments have become desolate.

[1] *In the bowels of the earth :* Metre, *ṭawil.*

[2] *And thou art intent upon the world :* Metre, *ṭawil.*

[3] فانمحت آثارهم *Their traces have been obliterated :* Contrast this statement with the lines :

تلك آثارنا تدل علينا * فانظر بعدنا الى الآثار

'These are our works (literally remains, or traces) which prove what we have done, look, therefore, at our works when we are gone.'

[4] *They are decayed in the dust ;* Metre, *ṭawil.*

They have left the world and what they had collected therein,
And none of them succeeded but the perseveringly patient.
And they have alighted in an abode where there is no exchange of visits;
For how can there be intercourse between the tenants of the tomb?
Thou seest nought but the level grave, in which they abide,
And over which the whirlwind carries the dust.'

Many a man hast thou seen possessed of might and power, armies and allies who has gained the world and obtained from it his desire. He built fortresses and castles[1] and collected precious things and forces.

'But the treasures diverted not death's hand[2] when it appeared suddenly desiring him.
Nor did the fortresses surrounded by moats and the castles, which he had built, protect him!
No device overcame death for him, nor were his armies eager to defend him.'

O people beware! beware! and hasten, O hasten away from the world and her mischiefs, and from the traps she has laid for you, from her appearing in her adornment before you and in her loveliness raising her eyes towards you.

'But less affliction than thou seest[3] sufficeth to summon thee to abandon it and to exhort thee to piety.

[1] ٱلدَّسَاكِرُ *Castles*: Plural of دَسْكَرَةٌ. Arabicized from Talmud. דיסקרתא name of various villages, probably originally from Διοσκουριας or the like, from Διοσκοῦροι (Stephanus Byzanthinos). A country seat. See Bukhárí (edited by Krehl) i, 9. Also a wine hall or saloon (*Ḥariri*, i, 140). The word also occurs in the lines of Ibn al-Ḥájib on the Aiwán (ايوان) quoted by Yaqút, i, 426.

هَذى ٱلْمَصَانِعُ وَالدَّسَاكِرُ والْبِنَا * وَقُصُورُ كِسرَانَا أَنُوشِرْوان

These pavilions, pleasure houses, buildings and castles of our Kisra Anushirwán. It is probable Hamadháni had the Aiwán in mind when he composed or quoted these lines.

[2] *But the treasures diverted not death's hand*: Metre, *ṭawil*.

[3] *But less affliction than thou seest*: Metre, *ṭawil*.

So strive and be not negligent, for thy life is fleeting, and thou art returning to the abode of death.
And seek not the world, for the pursuit of it, even if thou obtainest thy desire from it, injures thee.'

How can a wise man covet, or a sagacious person be pleased with it, when he is sure of its perishing? Do ye not wonder at him who sleeps, while he fears death, and hopeth not for escape?

'Nay, nay, but we delude our own souls[1] and worldly delights preoccupy them to the exclusion of what they apprehended.
And how can he enjoy pleasure who is certain of the standing-place of justice where all secret thoughts and actions shall be examined into?[2]
It is as though we thought there is no resurrection and that we are left at liberty and that, after dissolution, there is no future state for us.'[3]

How many of those, who have inclined towards it, hath the world deceived, and many a one of those intent upon it has fallen, and it raised him not from his stumbling,[4] nor excused him for his falling. It healed him not of his sickness, nor relieved him of his pain.

'Rather has it brought him down,[5] after his possessing might and rank,
To evil watering-places from which there is no climbing out.[6]
So when he saw there was no escape, and that

[1] *Nay, nay, but we delude our own souls:* Metre, *ṭawil.*

[2] *Secret thoughts and actions shall be examined into:* An allusion to Qur'án, lxxxvi, 9.

[3] مَصَائِرُ *Future state:* Plural of مَصِيرٌ; literally, a place or state to which a person or thing eventually comes.

[4] *It raised him not from his stumbling:* Another and better reading: لَم تَقلهُ من عَثرَتِهِ وَلَم تُنعِشهُ مِن صَرعَتِهِ. It excused him not his stumbling, nor raised him from his falling.

[5] *Rather has it brought him down:* Metre, *ṭawil.*

[6] *From which there is no climbing out:* Cf. *Kitáb al-Bayan wa'l-Tabyín,* i, 119.

It was death, from which the helpers could not save him,
He sought repentance, if length of repentance could avail him,
And his heinous crimes caused him to weep.'

He wept over his past sins, and felt regret for what he was leaving of the world, when weeping profited him not, and excuse delivered him not.

'His sorrows and cares encompassed him,[1]
And, when excuses baffled him, he despaired.[2]
Therefore he hath no saviour from the pains of death,
Nor helper from that which is avoided.
His throat rattled [3] before death,
While the uvula and the larynx re-echoed it.'

How long wilt thou mend thy present condition at the expense of thy future state, and, in so doing, ride upon thy desire? Verily I perceive thee to be weak in assurance, O patcher of thy present condition with thy religion. Has the merciful God commanded thee to do this, or the Qur'án guided thee so?

'Thou destroyest that which remaineth,[4] and buildest that which perisheth,
But neither is this complete nor that abiding.
If then thy end come suddenly upon thee,
When thou hast acquired no good, hast thou an excuser with God?
Art thou content that life should pass and end,
While thy religion is deficient and thy wealth complete?'

Said 'Ísá ibn Hishám: I asked one of those present: 'Who is this?' He replied: 'A stranger who arrived by night? I

[1] *His sorrows encompassed him:* Metre, *ṭawíl.*

[2] أَبْلَسَ *He despaired*: The Muslim name for the Devil is said to be derived from this verb because he despairs of God's mercy. Iblís is probably a corruption of diabolos.

[3] *His throat rattled:* From خَسَأَ; literally, he drove away a dog. The explanation of this sentence seems to be, his soul fled before death while the uvula and the larynx turned it back. Figurative for death throes.

[4] *Thou destroyest that which remaineth:* Metre, *ṭawíl.*

know him not personally, so 'wait for the end of his discourse,[1] perhaps he will tell his name.' So I waited. Then he said: 'Adorn knowledge with practice and show gratitude for power by practising forgiveness. Take the clear and leave the muddy.[2] May God forgive you and me!' Then he started off. So I followed in his track and said to him: 'O Shaikh, who art thou?' He replied: 'Good Gracious! art thou not satisfied with pondering over externals, that thou madest for the truth and then failed to recognize it?[3] I am Abú'l-Fath al-Iskánderi.'

I said: 'May God preserve thee, but what is this hoariness?' He answered:—

'A warner, but a silent one,[4]
And a guest, but a gloating one,
The messenger of death, but
Verily he will stay on[5] till I accompany him.'[6]

XXVII. THE MAQAMA OF AL-ASWAD[7]

'ÍSÁ IBN HISHÁM related to us and said: I was suspected on account of some property I had gotten and so I fled, I knew not whither, until I came to a desert, and my wandering led me to the shade of a tent. I found near the pegs thereof a youth playing in the sand with those of his own age, and reciting a

[1] فَاصْبِرْ عَلَيْهِ إِلَى آخِرِ مَقَامَتِهِ *So wait for the end of his discourse:* Here Hamadhání uses the word maqáma for a religious discourse or sermon.

[2] *Take the clear and leave the muddy:* Take what is free from trouble and leave what is attended therewith.

[3] غَيَّرْتَهَا *Failed to recognize:* Literally, thou didst change it, that is thy mind. Abú'l-Fáth chides 'Ísá ibn Hishám for thinking him to be some one else when he knew who he was.

[4] *A warner, but a silent one:* Metre, *mutaqárib.*

[5] ثَابِتٌ *will stay on:* Unlike any ordinary messenger who delivers his message and departs.

[6] An excellent example of a sermon in rhymed prose and verse on the vanity of human life and the certainty of death and judgement, of which the eleventh maqáma of Hariri is a close imitation. There is little reference to future reward or punishment. Cf. *Ḥariri*, i, 14 and 121.

[7] *Al-Aswad ibn Qinán:* A famous Bedawin Shaikh. He belonged to the family بَنُو قَنَان of whom an account is given by Ibn Duraid in his *Kitáb al-Ishtiqáq*, p. 240.

poem which was in keeping with his condition but did not accord with his powers of improvisation.[1]

And I felt it to be far from him to be able to weave its fabric, so I said: 'Young Arab, dost thou recite or compose this poem?' He said: 'Nay, but I compose it.' Then he recited saying:—

'And verily though I be young[2]
And the eye disdain me,
My demon[3] is the chief of the *Jinn*
And he takes me through all the range of the poetic art,
Until he drives away what occurs of doubt.
Therefore go at thine ease and depart from me.'

I said: 'O young Arab, terror has brought me to thee. Is there, therefore, safety or hospitality with thee?' He replied: 'Thou hast descended in the very house of safety and alighted on the land of hospitality.' He said: 'Then he arose and seized me by the sleeve and I went with him to a tent whose curtains were lowered.' Then he shouted: 'O damsel of the tribe, here is a neighbour whose country has rejected him, and whose ruler has oppressed him. Fame, which he has heard, or a report, which has reached him, has driven him to us, so give him shelter.' The damsel said: 'Stay, O townsman.'

'O townsman, stay and fear no ill,[4]
For thou art in the house of al-Aswad ibn Qináni
The mightiest son of woman from Maa'd and Ya'rub,
And the most promise-keeping of them in every place.
The best striker with the sword among them in defence of his neighbour,
And the greatest smiter with the spear in protecting him.
It is as though death and bounty were in his hand

[1] *Did not accord with his powers of improvisation:* That is, his powers of improvisation were greater than could be expected of a youth of his age.

[2] *And verily though I be young:* Metre, *rejez.* This poem is quoted by Jáḥiz. See Jáḥiz, *Ḥaywán*, i, 146, and Letters of Abú'l 'Alá al-Ma'arrí, p. 66, line 22.

[3] *My demon:* (my muse). The ancient Arabs believed that the poet was in league with spirits (Jinn), or satans and that he derived his inspiration and supernatural powers from them. Cf. Qur'án, xxvi, 224-6 on the poets; also, Letters of Abú'l 'Alá al-Ma'arrí, pp. 66, 73-4.

[4] *O townsman, stay:* Metre, *ṭawíl.*

Two clouds connected and combined.
Fair of countenance of noble forehead. And, when he mentions his pedigree,
It goes back to illustrious Yemeni origin.
So go to the house of refuge in which seven have alighted
And thou wilt make them the even number eight.'[1]

Then the young man took me by the hand to the house which she had indicated. I beheld and lo! there were seven persons in it. But my eye fastened upon none among them except Abú'l-Fáth al-Iskanderí. So I said to him: 'Sirrah in what land art thou?' He recited:—

'I have alighted in the house of al-Aswad.[2]
I choose the choicest of its fruits.
And I said I am a terrified man,
Fear hath pursued me for her blood-wit—
The device of the likes of me against
The likes of him in this and like conditions—
Until he clothed me, repairing my need,
And removing its manifest signs.
So take from Time and get what is pure,[3]
Before thou art transported from its abode.
Beware that thou keep back no desire,
Nor permit any milk to remain in the udders[4] of the camels.'

[1] شَفَعْتَهُم بِثَمانِ *Thou wilt make them the even number eight* —

(1) from شَفَعَ he made it an even number or pair.

(2) وَتَرَ he made it an odd number.

Example: كَانَ ٱلْقَوْمُ وَتْراً فَشَفَعْتُهُمْ وَكَانُوا شَفْعاً فَوَتَرْتُهُمْ

'The people were an odd number and I made them an even number; and they were an even number and I made them an odd number.' Cf. Qur'án, lxxxix, 2. (وَٱلشَّفْعِ وَٱلْوَتْرِ) 'By that which is double and that which is single', and *Aghâni*, iv, 176, line 20.

[2] I *have alighted in the house:* Metre, *sar'i*.

[3] وَنَلْ مَاصَفَا *So take what is pure:* Cf. Text p. 135.

[4] *Nor permit any milk to remain in the udders:* الشَّوْل A small quantity of milk in the udder. اغْبَار plural of غُبْر milk remaining in the udder. كَسَعَ throwing cold water upon a camel's udder to make her return or increase her milk. Therefore the literal meaning is to wet the camel's udder with what should remain

Said 'Ísá ibn Hishám: I exclaimed: 'Good gracious! What way of mendicity[1] hast thou not trodden?'

Then we lived together in that abode for a season until we were safe from danger, and then he fared eastwards and I westwards.

XXVIII. THE MAQAMA OF 'IRAQ[2]

'ÍSÁ IBN HISHÁM related to us and said: I travelled about the world till I reached 'Iráq. I had turned over the pages of the *díwáns* of the poets until I thought to myself I had not left in my quiver a victorious shaft. And I alighted at Baghdad.[3] Now, while I was on the river bank, there suddenly appeared before me a youth in worn-out garments begging from the people who disappointed him. Now his eloquence astonished me, so I arose, went to him and asked him of his origin and home. So he said: 'I am of 'Abs[4] origin, and Alexandria is my home.' I said: 'What is this language and whence this eloquence?' He replied: 'From knowledge whose refractoriness I have subdued and into whose seas I have plunged.' I asked: 'With which of the sciences art thou adorned?' He said: 'I have an arrow in every quiver. Which of them dost thou like best?' I replied: 'Poetry.' He said: 'Have the Arabs uttered a verse which cannot be paraphrased? Have they composed a eulogy whose subject is unknown? Have they a verse unseemly in original intent but is made proper by punctuation? What

therein. A figure for improvidence, or indifference to the needs of the future. There is a tradition of the Prophet: دَعْ دَاعِيَ اللَّبَنِ 'Leave in the udder what will induce the milk flow.'

[1] *Mendicity:* I have read الكُدْيَة mendicity being more consistent with the context and the word other editions give preference to, instead of الكَرَاهَة disagreeable.

[2] *'Iráq:* the name applied since the Arab conquest in the seventh century to designate that portion of the valley of the Tigris and the Euphrates known in older literature as Babylonia. With the advent of the Arabs 'Iráq entered on a new period of prosperity, several important new cities were founded Kúfa, Basra and Baghdad which became under the 'Abbásid *Khalífas* not only the capital of 'Iráq, but, for a time, the metropolis of the world. *Encyclopaedia Britannica*, xiv, 740; Yaqút, iii, 628.

[3] *I alighted at Baghdad:* Literally, Baghdad caused me to alight.

[4] *'Abs:* 'Abs the name of the tribe to which the poet 'Antara belonged. This is the first time the improvisor mentions his tribe.

verse is it whose tears cease not to flow? What verse is it whose fall is heavy? What verse is it the last foot of whose first half verse wounds, and the final foot of whose second half heals? What verse is it whose intimidation is formidable and whose subject is insignificant? What verse is more sandy than the desert? What verse is like the mouth of the person with pearly teeth and a serrated saw? What verse is it whose beginning pleases and whose end displeases thee? What verse is it whose interior slaps thee and whose exterior deceives thee? What verse is it whose hearer is not sure until the whole of it is mentioned? What verse is it that cannot be touched? What verse is it whose transposition is easy? What verse is longer than its fellow, as though it were not of its kind? What verse is rendered contemptible by a letter and established by the omission thereof?' Said 'Ísá ibn Hishám: 'By Heavens! I did not venture to reply to him [1] and I was not guided to a right answer other than 'I know not.'

He said: 'And what thou knowest not is yet more.' So I said: 'How is it that with this excellence thou consentest to this base livelihood?' He recited:—

'A plague on this age for an age,[2]
Marvellous are the courses of its affairs.
It is inimical to every man of culture,
As though culture were guilty of an impropriety with its
mother.'

Then I caused my eye to move over him and I looked again at his face and lo! it was Abú'l-Fath al-Iskanderí. I said: 'God prosper thee! and raise thee up when thou fallest![3] If thou dost think fit to oblige me with a commentary on what thou hast sent down,[4] and with a full explanation of what thou hast epitomized, thou wilt do so.' He said: 'This is the

1 *I did not venture to reply to him:* Literally, I shuffled not a gaming arrow. An allusion to the well-known game of meisar (الميسر) forbidden by Islám. See Qur'án, v. 92.

2 *A plague on this for an age:* Metre, *munsereh.*

3 *When thou fallest:* Literally, thy falling.

4 *What thou hast sent down:* That is what thou hast revealed like, as it were, the Qur'án which is also called *Tanzíl* (تنزيل), the downsending.

explanation: As for the verse that cannot be paraphrased[1] there are many. An example of it is the verse of al-A'shá[2]:—

'All our dirhems are good,[3]
Delay us not therefore by testing them.'

As for the eulogy, whose subject is unknown, there are many. An example of it is the saying of Al-Hudhallí:—

'I knew not who threw his cloak over him[4]
Except that he was verily of illustrious and pure stock.'

But as for the verse which is unseemly in its original intent[5], but is made proper by punctuation, it is the verse of Abú Núwás[6]:—

'And we passed the night,[7] God regarding us as the vilest company,
Trailing the skirts of wickedness, and no boast.'

But as for the verse whose tears cease not to flow, it is the verse of Dhú al-Rumma:—

'What aileth thine eye[8] that water poureth therefrom
As if it were kidneys split and running?'

For it comprehendeth either water, or an eye, or pouring, or urine, or a cloud, or the bottom of a provision bag, or a split, or a torrent.

[1] *The verse that cannot be paraphrased:* The point is that there is no way wherein the first three words can be twisted so as to alter the metre e.g.:

كُلُّ دَرَاهِمِنَا جَيِّدٌ - دَرَاهِمُنَا جَيِّدٌ كُلُّهَا - جَيِّدٌ كُلُّ دَرَاهِمِنَا

See p. 225 of the text.

[2] *Al-A'ashá:* The 'sweet singer of the Arabs' (صَنَّاجَةُ ٱلْعَرَبِ) was a contemporary of Muḥammad (ob. A.H. 6 or 7). A life of this poet will be found in De Sacy, *Chrestomathie Arabe*, ii, 471. See also *Aghání*, viii, pp. 74–84.

[3] *All our dirhems are good:* Metre, *mutaqárib*.

[4] *I know not who threw his cloak over him:* Metre, ṭawíl.
Abú Khirásh al-Hudhallí, the author of the elegy from which this line is quoted, flourished during the Khalifate of 'Umar ibn al-Khaṭṭáb. *Ḥamása*, (edited by Freytag) pp. 365-6.

[5] *The verse which is unseemly in its original intent:* That is, if we take the verse to the end of the sentence, as far as 'wickedness' it is unseemly, but it is rendered seemly by the additional words, 'and no boast'.

[6] *Abú Núwás:* born at Ahwaz A.H. 145 and died at Baghdad A.H. 195, the well-known witty and talented but profligate court poet of Harún al-Rashíd. Ibn Khallikan, i, p. 391.

[7] *And we passed the night:* Metre, *ṭawil*.

[8] *What aileth thine eye:* Metre, *basit*.

But as for the verse whose fall is heavy. It is like the verse of Ibn al-Rúmí[1]:—

'When he gives[2] he makes not his gift an obligation,
And he says to my soul, O soul respite me.'

But as for the verse the last foot of whose first half verse wounds, and the final foot of whose second half heals. It is like the verse of the poet:—

'I advanced[3] with a glittering mashrafí[4] sword,
As one who shakes hands and approaches to greet.'

But as for the verse whose intimidation is formidable, but whose subject is insignificant. An example of it is the verse of 'Amr ibn Kulthúm[5]:—

'As though our swords, ours and theirs,[6]
Were wooden blades in the hands of the players.'

But as for the verse which is more sandy[7] than the desert. It is like the verse of Dhu al-Rumma:—

'Venturing upon[8] the vehement heat of the pebbles, striking them with his foot.

1 *Abú'l Ḥasan 'Ali ibn al-Rúmi* was born at Baghdad A.H. 221. This celebrated poet's verses are admirable for their beauty of expression and originality of thought. He was poisoned in A.H. 283, or 284 at Baghdad at the instance of al-Qasim ibn 'Ubeidalláh The Wazir of al-M'utaḍid (A.H. 279–89). Ibn Khallikan, ii, 297.

2 إذا منّ *When he gives:* The point as to weight is the repetition of the word *mann* (منّ) which means 'he bestowed', and a certain weight which is generally considered as equal to two pounds troy. Metre, *ṭawil.*

3 *I advanced with a glittering mashrafi sword:* Metre, *wáfir.*

4 *Mashrafi:* Belonging to Mushárif the name of a collection of Arab villages near the cultivated part of 'Iráq. It is said that مَشرف was a blacksmith who made swords (Lane). I think the word should be vocalized مُشرَفِي See *Yaqút*, iv, 538.

5 *'Amr ibn Kúlthúm:* The author of one of the Mu'allaqát (No. 6 in Lyall's edition).

6 *As though our swords, ours and theirs:* Metre, *wáfir.*

7 *More sandy than the desert:* The point here is the play on the word رَمَل literally *sand*, and technically 'poetry lacking beauty and containing words which are not pleasing to the ear.' (Freytag's *Arabische Verskunst*, p. 530.) Note the collection of *ḍáḍs* (ض), the most difficult letter to pronounce in the whole alphabet, in the first half verse.

8 مُعرَوْرِيًا *venturing upon:* Metre, *basit.* Literally, riding barebacked. In this verse the poet refers to the insect called *Jundak*, a species of locust.

When the noonday sun revolves[1] as though perplexed in its course.'

But as for the verse which is like the mouth of the person with pearly teeth[2] or a serrated saw. It is like the verse of al-A'ashá:—

'I went betimes to the wine-shop[3] while there followed me,
A man, brisk, active, quickish, agile, rapid.'

But as for the verse whose beginning pleases but whose end displeases thee. It is like the verse of Imr al-Qais:—

'Attacking, fleeing, advancing, retiring, simultaneously,
Like a mass of rock hurled from a height[4] by the torrent.'

As for the verse whose interior slaps thee, and whose exterior deceives thee. It is like the verse of the poet:—

'I reproached her,[5] she cried and said, O youth,
May the Lord of the empyrean deliver thee from my reproach.'

But as for the verse whose hearer is not sure until the whole of it is mentioned. It is like the verse of Tarafa:—

'My companions, stopping their camels near me,
Saying, do not die of grief, but endure patiently.'

For the hearer imagines thou art reciting the verse of Imr al-Qais.

But as for the verse that cannot be touched. It is like the verse of Al-Khubzuruzzí[7]:—

[1] *Revolves:* The sun does not seem to be inclining towards the horizon.

[2] *Like the mouth of the person with pearly teeth:* I have given preference to the meaning derived from أَظْلَمَ. It glistened, e.g. أَظْلَمَ ٱلثَّغْرُ the front teeth glistened, to that adopted by 'the commentator, namely, 'the teeth of the oppressed', which does not yield a satisfactory sense. The point lies in the repetition of the letter six times with its implied primary meaning, a tooth.

[3] I *went betimes to the wine-shop:* Metre, *basit*. Ibn Qutaiba criticises the poet for introducing in this verse four synonyms for the word *active*. Sh'ir wa Shu'ará, p. 12.

[4] كَجُلْمُودِ صَخْرٍ *Like a mass of rock hurled from a height:* The criticism is that the second half of the verse does not suggest a horse under control ready 'to attack, retreat, advance, or retire.'

[5] *I reproached her:* Metre, *kámil*.

[6] *My companions stopping their camels near me:* Metre, *ṭawil*.

[7] *Naṣr al-Khubzuruzzi* (d. A.H. 317) the rice-bread baker was a native of Baṣra. This poet could neither read nor write. He baked rice-bread in a shop

'The cloud of separation[1] has cleared away from the moon of love,
And the light of peace has risen from the darkness of reproach.'

And also like the verse of Abú Núwás ·—

'The saffron-scented breeze[2] in a watery garment,
A stature of light upon etherial parchment.'

But as for the verse whose transposition is easy. It is like the verse of Ḥassán[3] :—

'Of fair countenances,[4] their pedigrees are noble,
Haughty, of the most noble extraction.'

But as for the verse which is longer than its fellow as though it were not of its kind. It is like the folly of Al-Mutanabbí[5] :—

'Enjoy,[6] live on, be exalted, be a chief, be generous, be a leader, command, forbid, be manly, speak, be asked, be angry, shoot, hit, protect, raid, take captive, terrify, stop, give the blood-wit, govern, divert, obtain.'

But as for the verse which is rendered contemptible by a letter and established by the omission thereof. It is like the verse of Abú Núwás :—

situated at the Mirbad of Baṣra and he used to recite there to crowds of enthusiastic admirers, verses of his own, all of them amatory. Ibn Khallikan, iii, 530 ; *Yatima*, ii, 132.

1 *The cloud of separation :* Metre, *ṭawil.*

2 *The saffron scented breeze :* Metre, *ṭawil.*

3 *Ḥassán :* (ibn Thábit) d. A.H. 54 was one of the poets that espoused the cause of Muḥammad. He belonged to a family of poets and is said to have lived to the great age of 120 years. His *Diwán* has been published by the Trustees of the Gibb Memorial. Ibn Khallikan, iv, 259.

4 *Of fair countenances :* Metre, *kámil.*

5 *Like the folly of* Mutanabbi *:* Twenty-three imperatives in two lines ! See diwan of Mutanabbí, ed. by Dieterici, p. 495, and for an example of another collection of fourteen imperatives, p. 493.

Mutanabbi : (A.H. 303-354). The well-known court poet of Saif Al Daula is generally admitted to be the greatest of all Islámic poets. As the poets of the Mu'allaqát illustrated the spirit of the sons of the desert, so does Mutanabbí represent the sentiments of the Muslim Arabs. See *Yatima*, i, 78 ; Browne, *Lit. Hist. of Persia*, i, 369 ; Nicholson, *Lit. Hist. of the Arabs*, p. 304 ; Ibn Khallikan, i, 102.

6 *Enjoy, live on, etc. :* Metre, *ṭawil.*

'My verse is lost upon your door [1]
As pearls are lost on Khaliṣa.' [2]

Or, like the verse of another:

'Verily the sentence which thou perceivest to be praise, [3]
Was a sentence that $\frac{\text{shone upon him}}{\text{was lost upon him}}$
That is to say when "lost" is read it is satire, but when "shone" is recited, it is praise.'

Said 'Ísá ibn Hishám: 'By Heavens! I was astonished at his discourse and I gave him what would assist him against his changed condition. Then we separated.'

XXIX. THE MAQAMA OF HAMDAN [4]

'ÍSÁ IBN HISHÁM related to us and said: We were present one day at the court of Saif al-Daula ibn Hamdán,[5] and they brought before him a horse—'when the eye looks up at him [6] it wants to look down again in order to take in all his beauty.' The company looked at it and Saif al-Daula said: 'Whoever of

[1] *My verse is lost upon your door:* Metre, *mutaqárib.*

[2] *Khaliṣa:* An extremely ill-favoured damsel of whom Harún al-Rashíd was passionately fond. To compensate for her natural defects the Khalifa furnished her with rich apparel and costly jewels. Abú Núwás became aware of this and wrote these lines over her door. The damsel complained to Harún and Abú Núwás was summoned to the presence of the Khalifa to explain his presumptuous conduct. On his way to the audience-chamber he passed the door over which the offending lines were written and erased the lower curve of the *'ain* so that only the upper one (ء), the sign for *hamza*, remained, so that the word read ضاء shone, instead of ضاع was lost. (*Núfḥat al-Yemen.* Story 13.)

[3] *Verily the sentence:* Metre, *basít.* The letter *'ain* is manipulated in a similar manner in this line. See note 2 on Khálíṣá.

[4] *Abdallah ibn Ḥamdán:* The name of Saif al-Daula's father.

[5] *Saif al-Daula the Ḥamdánid:* A.H. 333-56 (A.D. 916-67), made himself master of Aleppo in 944 and founded an independent kingdom in northern Syria.

He was an accomplished scholar and poet himself, a lover of fine poetry and a renowned patron of letters. For notices of his life, see Ibn Khallikan, ii, 334 and Tha'alibí, *Yatíma*, i, 88.

[6] *When the eye looks up:* An allusion to the Qaṣída of Imr al-Qais, p. 25, verse 69, Lyall's edition of the Mu'allaqát. The text is incorrectly vocalized the ق and هـ should be doubled.

I have varied the translation of these lines in accordance with the different meanings suggested by Tabrízí. Hamadhání has already twice quoted this line, but this is the first occasion he has done so appositely.

you describes it best, I will make him a present of it.' So every one tried his best endeavour and expended what ability he possessed. One of his attendants said: 'May God prosper the Amir! Yesterday I saw a man who put eloquence under his feet [1] and upon whom men's eyes rested. He was soliciting the people and getting nothing.[2] Now, if the Amir would summon him, he would excel them in his repartee.' Said Saif al-Daula: 'Bring him to me as he is.' Then the attendants flew in search of him and they forthwith brought him, but they did not tell him with what object he had been summoned. Then he was taken near and was brought close up. He was wearing a pair of worn-out garments upon which time had long eaten and drunken.[3] When he reached the front rank he kissed the carpet and stood still. Saif al-Daula said: 'The report of thy eloquence has reached us so exhibit it on this horse and its description.' He said: 'May God prosper the Amir! How can it be done before riding him and seeing his jumping, and disclosing his defects and his latent qualities?' He said: 'Mount it.' So he mounted it, made it go and then he said, 'God prosper the Amir! He is long in both ears, scanty of two, spacious in the rectum, soft of three, thick in the shank, depressed of four, strong-winded, fine of five, narrow in the gullet, thin of six, sharp of hearing, thick of seven, fine of tongue, broad of eight, long in the ribs, short of nine, wide of jaw, remote of ten. He grips with his forefeet, kicks out with his hind ones, appears with a bright face and laughs exposing his permanent corner nipper. He cracks [4] the face of the earth with hoofs of iron,[5] he rises like the ocean when it is rough, or the torrent when it

1 *Put eloquence under his feet:* Literally, tramples upon it, figuratively for having eloquence in subjection.

2 *Getting nothing:* Literally, he made them to drink despair; this is capable of two explanations :—

(*a*) If we take the verb يَسْأَلُ to mean he was asking the people for something, يَسْقِى ٱلْيَاسَ would signify he made them despair of giving him sufficient.

(*b*) if يَسْأَلُ means he was questioning the people, then يُسْقِى ٱلْيَاسَ signifies he made them despair of answering him. I think the second explanation is more in consonance with the context.

3 *Eaten and drunken: Arab Proverbs,* i. 61. Figure for old and much used.

4 يجز *He cracks:* Another reading يَخُدُّ he scores.

5 *Hoofs of iron:* Literally, an iron pounder.

rages.' Saif al-Daula said: 'Thou art welcome to the horse.' He said: 'Mayest thou cease not to get precious things and to give away horses!' Then he turned away and I followed him and said: 'I will undertake to supply thee with the equipment necessary for this horse, if thou explain what thou hast described.' He answered, 'Ask what thou desirest.' I said: 'What is the meaning of thy saying, Remote of ten?' He replied: 'Remote of sight, of pace, of space between the two eye sockets, and between the two hind quarters, and remote of space between the two extremities of the haunches, between the nostrils, wide in the space between the two hind legs,[1] and between the navel[2] and the operating point.[3] Remote of goal in the race.' I said: 'May thy teeth not be broken! And what is the meaning of thy saying, Short of nine?'[4] He replied: 'Short of hair, short of hair on the pastern, short of tail bone, short in the arms, short in the pasterns, short in the sciatic artery, short in the back, short of shank.' I said: 'How excellent! And what is the meaning of thy saying, Broad of eight?' He answered: 'Broad of brow, broad of haunch, broad of back, broad of scapula, broad of flank, broad of sinew, broad of breast, broad of neck.' I said: 'Well done! And what is the meaning of thy saying, Thick of seven?' He answered: 'Thick in the fore-leg, stout of girth, thick in the tail root, thick of skin in the head, thick in the pastern, thick in the thighs, thick in the back.' I said: 'How wonderful! And what is the meaning of thy saying, Thin of six?' He answered: 'Thin of eyelid, thin in the fore-part of the neck, thin in the lip, thin-skinned, thin in the tips of the ears, thin in the sides of the neck.' I said: 'Well done! And what is the meaning of thy saying, Fine of five?' He replied: 'Fine in the uppermost part of the neck, fine in the frog, fine in the forehead, fine in the knee, fine in the foreleg sinew.' I said: 'May God prolong thy life! And what is the meaning of thy saying, Depressed of four?' He answered

[1] *Wide in the space between the two hind legs:* Such a horse is called مُجَنَّبْ

[2] اَلصِّفَاقُ *Navel:* The point on the navel where the farrier operates to extract a yellow fluid.

[3] مَثْقَبْ *The operating point:* That is, the thin skin next to the navel which the farrier perforates in order that a yellow fluid may issue forth.

[4] *Short of nine:* Only eight are mentioned, one having been omitted on grounds of decency.

‘Depressed in the top of the shoulders, depressed in the knee joints, depressed in the eyebrows, depressed in the arm-bone.’ I said: ‘And what is the meaning of thy saying, Soft of three?’ He said: ‘Soft in the upper parts of the shoulder blades, soft of mane, soft in the mouth.’[1] Then I said: ‘And what is the meaning of thy saying, Scanty of two?’ He answered: ‘Scanty in the flesh of the face, scanty in flesh on both sides of the back.’ I asked: ‘Whence the origin of this excellence?’ He replied: ‘From the frontiers of the Umayyads and the city of Alexandria.’ Then I said: ‘Dost thou with this excel lence expose thy self-respect[2] to this extravagance?’ Then he recited saying:—

> ‘Befool thy time well, for time is a fool,[3]
> Consign honour to oblivion and live in comfort and plenty,
> And tell this thy slave to bring us a cake.’[4]

XXX. THE MAQAMA OF RUSAFA

‘ÍSÁ IBN HISHÁM related to us and said: I sallied forth from Rusáfa[5] to go to the capital when the fervent summer sultriness[6] boiled in the breast of irritation. Now when I had traversed half the road, the heat became intense, patience failed me and so I turned towards a masjid which had appropriated to itself the secret of all beauty.[7] And in it there were people

1 *Soft in the mouth:* Literally, soft of, i.e. obedient to, the rein.

2 *Expose thy self-respect:* Literally, expose thy face, a common figure for risk of self-respect.

3 *Befool thy time:* Metre, *mujtath*. Cf. p. 128 of the Text.

4 Saif al-Daula died about two years before Hamadhání was born. This maqáma is, therefore, based on an imaginary incident or a popular story. See Ibn Khallikan, ii, 139, where there is a description of a horse presented by this prince. Also cf. p. 124 of the same volume. For an example of riddling with numbers, see Ecclesiastes, xi. 2.

5 *Rusáfa:* A famous quarter to the east of Baghdad. In the time of al-Manṣúr (A.D. 754–75) it was the cantonment of the city. It was built by the Khalifa's son al-Mahdi, in A.H. 159, and in time grew to the size of the capital itself. It was also the necropolis of the ‘Abbásid Khalifas. (Yaqút, ii, 783. See also Le Strange, *Baghdad*.)

6 حَمَارَّةُ ٱلْقَيْظِ *Fervent summer sultriness:* Another reading جَمَارَةُ ٱلْقَيْظِ The live coals of the intense summer heat.

7 *Which had appropriated to itself the secret of all beauty:* The cathedral masjid of Ruṣáfa was larger and more magnificent than that of Baghdad itself.

contemplating its ceilings and discussing its pillars. Finally the discussion led them [1] to the mentioning of thieves and their artifices, and cut-purses and their practices.

They mentioned among thieves, forgers of seals, the light-fingered, and palmers, him who gives short weight, him who robs in the ranks, him who throttles by the sudden attack,[2] him who hides in the locker till lifting is possible, him who substitutes by cajoling,[3] him who steals in jest, him who steals by the confidence trick, him who invites to compromise,[4] him who sweeps off the change,[5] him who induces sleep,[6] him who confounds with backgammon,[7] him who deceives with the monkey, him who gets the better by means of the mantle [8] and a needle and thread, him who brings thee a lock,[9] him who

1 *Finally the discussion led them:* Literally عَجُزُ ٱلْحَدِيث 'the *end* of the discussion led them' عجز means the hinder part of anything, particularly the buttock or rump. In poetry it signifies the second half of a verse or couplet, the first half being called ṣadr (صَدْر).

2 *Him who throttles by the sudden attack:* From دَفَّ he went lightly or stealthily, and دَفَّ عَلَيْهِ he despatched him. (Lane's Lexicon, article دَفَّ, p. 887.)

3 *Him who substitutes by cajoling:* For this use of the word مَسَحَ rather than that adopted by the commentator, see Letters of the author, p 329, line 8.

4 *Him who invites to compromise:* In a case where he has no legal claim.

5 *Who sweeps off the change:* The explanation of this trick is as follows: the thief goes to a money changer on the pretext of changing a dinar then snatches what the man has before him and decamps.

6 *Him who induces sleep:* The thief being in company with some one who has money pretends to be drowsy and thus induces his victim to go to sleep, he then robs him of his property. But, literally, 'him who puts to sleep with the eye.' More probably, therefore, hypnotic suggestion.

7 *Him who confounds with backgammon:* The thief takes with him into the house he intends to rob a backgammon or chess-board, usually made of cloth, and spreads it out. In case he is discovered by the master of the house he raises a cry that he has been cheated at the game and his opponent refuses to pay his losses.

8 *By means of the mantle:* The thief observes a man wearing a mantle, goes quickly behind him, raises the skirt of the garment, in order to get at the purse usually carried underneath, and begins sewing it to the collar. If he is discovered, and the man turns round, he says, 'Do not be afraid, I was only mending thy cloak; dost thou not want it done?' In this way he manages to escape with or without the purse.

9 *Him who brings thee a lock:* The thief contrives to sell the shopkeeper a defective lock. If the latter uses it to lock up his shop, the thief takes advantage of the first opportunity to effect an entrance and to help himself to the merchant's goods.

makes a subterranean passage, him who renders men unconscious with hemp,[1] or cheats by juggling,[2] him who changes his shoes,[3] him who ties his two ropes,[4] him who overpowers with the sword, him who ascends from the well,[5] him who accompanies the caravan,[6] the gentry of the cloth,[7] him who enters the assemblies,[8] him who flees from the night patrol,[9] him who seeks refuge from danger, him who flies the bird,[10] him who plays with the strap [11] and says 'Sit down, there is no harm!' him who steals by playing upon people's modesty, him who

[1] *Hemp* (بنج): Arabicized from the Persian بنگ (Sanskrit *bhangā*). Baron Hammer Purgstall is wrong in identifying it with the Coptic *bendj*, plural *nebendj*, which he says is the same plant as the *νηπενθης* which so much perplexed the commentators of Homer (Odessey, 4. 221 sq.), for two reasons:

(*a*) There is no such word as *bendj* or *nebendj* in Coptic.

(*b*) It is a good Sanskrit word and is found in the Athara-Veda Samhita (xi. 6. 15). Also see Monier Williams' Sanskrit and English Dictionary, article *Bhangā*.

[2] بنيرج *By juggling*: Arabicized from the Persian نيرنگ literally anything new; also magic and enchantment.

[3] *Him who changes his shoes*: A very easy thing to do at the masjid or the bath where shoes and sandals have to be left outside.

[4] *Him who ties his two ropes*: the *modus operandi* is this: The thief climbs upon the terrace or roof of a house, ties to the end of a rope what he wishes to steal, descends quickly and pulls his booty down.

[5] *Him who ascends from the well*: Which he has been using as a place of concealment.

[6] *Him who accompanies the caravan*: As if he were one of the travellers.

[7] *The gentry of the cloth*: That is, the wearers of the ascetic garb. This is still a very popular form of disguise in the East.

[8] *Him who enters the assemblies*: By virtue of being well-dressed and of respectable appearance. This is the fourth time the author uses the word **M*aqáma***. Here it means companies of respectable people.

[9] *From the night patrol*: The thief enters a house to rob it. If he is surprised, he declares he has run away from the night patrol and is the victim of an injustice. If he is believed he waits for an opportunity to help himself and then disappears.

[10] *Him who flies the bird*: The thief causes his pigeon to fly into a house and then follows it. If he is discovered he pretends he has come for his bird. This is like the excuse of the poacher who, when found trespassing, asserts he is looking for his sheep!

[11] *Him who plays with the strap*: The explanation of this trick is as follows: The thief starts a game which consists of one hiding something and asking another to say where it is. If he fails he is beaten on his hand or leg with a strap. Such a game is bound to end in a quarrel which the sharper takes advantage of to appropriate whatever he can.

takes advantage of a panic, him who gets a meal[1] in the street by blowing his trumpet, him who brings a pitcher,[2] the master gardeners,[3] those who rob through the windows,[4] him who scales lofty houses, him who climbs[5] upon the roof, him who creeps stealthily with the knife along the mud wall, him who comes to thee suddenly with a sweet-smelling nosegay,[6] the men of the axe[7] like official attendants, him who comes by stealth and moans after the manner of madmen, the possessors of keys,[8] the men of cotton and wind,[9] him who enters the door in the guise of a guest, him who goes into the house like a visitor, him who passes in humbly in the garb of the destitute, him who steals at the cistern when the plunge makes it

---

[1] *Him who gets a meal*: Literally, to blow the trumpet, which means to indulge in vain and empty talk. (See Taj al-'Arús, vi, 301.) In order to obtain this rendering, requiring the reflexive use of the verb, a slight emendation of the text is necessary, *for* أَطْعَم *read* أَطْعِم (p. 161, line 1).

[2] *Him who brings a pitcher*: As though he had come to fetch water. If he can lay his hands on anything, he steals it. بُسْتُوق *Bastúq*: Arabicized from the Persian بستو or پستو a small glazed earthenware vessel.

[3] *The master gardeners*: The thief represents himself to be an expert gardener. If you employ him he soon begins to help himself to the produce of the garden and this he does without arousing suspicion, because he is thought to have your authority to do so بَسَاتِين *Gardens*: Arabicized from the well-known Persian word بوستان *Bústán*.

[4] *Those who rob through the windows*: روازين plural of رَوْزَنَة arabicized from the Persian روزن a hole.

[5] *Him who climbs*: By means of a rope.

[6] *Him who comes with a sweet-smelling nosegay*: As if he were bringing it as a present to the master. Should he get an opportunity he steals something. The practice of presenting flowers in this way is still common in the East.

[7] *The men of the axe*: That is, the policemen. طَبَرزِين and طَبَرزَن arabicized from the Persian تبر an axe and زن imperative form of زدن to strike; literally something struck with an axe, or the striker with an axe or a hatchet and then the tool itself.

[8] *The possessors of keys*: Those who carry about a number of keys with which they endeavour to open doors, boxes, etc.—pickers of locks.

[9] *The men of cotton and wind*: The plan is as follows: the thief scatters some cotton so that the wind may blow it into certain houses and then, on the pretext of collecting his cotton, he goes in and robs them. The word قُطُن is probably of foreign origin.

possible,[1] him who robs with two sticks,[2] him who swears to a debt,[3] him who cheats with the pledge,[4] him who gives a bill of exchange,[5] him who changes the purse,[6] him who palms off in fraud, him who gives to bankrupts,[7] him who clips his sleeve[8] and then says, 'Observe and decide', him who stitches the breast,[9] him who says 'Dost thou not know?'[10] him who

1 *When the plunge or dip makes it possible:* I think أَمْعَنَ 'to go deep' would make better sense than أَمْكَنَ 'to make possible', i.e. when the bathers plunge into the water.

2 *Him who robs with two sticks:* The thief stands upon the roof of his house and lies in wait for the caravan. When it comes opposite the house, he lowers a long stick on the end of which is a hook like a grapnel and pulls up what he can of cloth, etc.

3 *Him who swears to a debt:* This is a species of black-mailing. The swindler swears that a certain person of importance owes him money. The latter rather than run the risk of being haled before the Qáḍi pays the amount.

4 *Him who cheats with the pledge:* The rogue buys goods from a merchant and leaves in pledge with him a sealed casket supposed to contain valuable jewels which, of course, it does not.

5 *Him who gives a bill of exchange:* The fraud is perpetrated as follows: The thief sees a traveller with a large sum of money in cash and offers to relieve him of the trouble of carrying it by giving him a bill of exchange on some one in the town to which he is journeying. The bill is, of course, worthless. (سُفْتَجَةٌ) Arabicized from the Persian سُفته literally, pierced; a consignment made by a person of one country to a person of another.

6 *Him who changes the purse:* The swindler bargains for some goods, produces a purse and counts out in gold or silver a sum which the shopkeeper declines to take, he then puts the purse back into his pocket. The haggling continues, and eventually he persuades the shopkeeper to accept the amount first counted. He then pulls out a purse exactly like the first, but which contains only coppers. If the merchant accepts the purse without counting the contents, the thief makes off with the goods.

7 *Him who gives to bankrupts:* The swindler contrives to secure the confidence of some merchants, takes a quantity of goods and sells them on credit to impecunious traders, at double the prime cost, and leads the public to believe he is doing a flourishing business. Then, when he has sold them articles of the value equal to what he owes his creditors, he announces he has gone bankrupt and that his outstandings represent exactly the amount of his liabilities. In this way he benefits by precisely half the amount of goods he has taken from his creditors.

8 *Him who clips his sleeve:* When the sharper sees a man placing some money before a shopkeeper, or a money changer, he seizes him and accuses him of having robbed him and exhibits his cut sleeve as evidence.

9 *Him who stitches the breast:* This is similar to the mantle trick.

10 *Him who says 'Dost thou not know?'* The swindler goes up to his dupe and says, 'Art thou not aware of what happened to so and so to-day? A thief seized his clothes thus'—suiting the action to the word—pulls him and, in the pulling, contrives to rob him of his money.

bites,[1] and him who ties,[2] him who substitutes when he counts, him who enters with his accomplices and says, 'He is not asleep',[3] him who deceives thee with a thousand,[4] him who passes behind,[5] him who steals in fetters,[6] him who shams pain to defraud, him who beats with the shoe,[7] him who questions the truth,[8] him who steals with a cleft stick, him who enters by the underground passage, him who takes advantage of mining,

[1] *Him who bites:* The sharper picks a quarrel with some one and, when they come to blows and seize each other he contrives, in the struggle, to tear with his teeth his antagonist's clothes where he thinks the money is put away.

[2] *Him who ties:* The thief being seated near some one he wishes to rob, attaches to a piece of string, which he retains hold of, whatever he finds it possible to relieve the individual of. When the man gets up and goes away, the article is left behind.

[3] *'He is not asleep':* The robber and his accomplices find a man asleep and make a noise until they wake him by saying, 'He is asleep' or 'He is not asleep', and in their conversation they lead him to believe that they have buried a treasure there, and so now he pretends to be asleep. Then to prove whether or no he is asleep they begin to feel him and, during the process, rob him. After they have gone he gets up only to find that he has been both robbed and hoaxed and the buried treasure consists of worthless shells.

[4] *Him who deceives thee with a thousand:* The sharper deposits for safe custody with a merchant a bag supposed to contain a thousand dinars. On the top he has put a layer or two of dinars while the remainder consists of coppers. He returns later and takes out a few pieces. This is repeated until the silver is exhausted. Then he buys largely from the merchant who unhesitatingly gives him credit in the belief that he has a large sum in deposit. He then bolts. After some time has elapsed the merchant gets suspicious, opens the bag and discovers that he has been duped.

[5] *Him who passes behind:* The thief goes with an accomplice to a shop and asks for something which he cleverly passes unobserved to his fellow who immediately runs away with it. He then pretends to be very much upset and exclaims: 'What am I to do? The fellow has gone off with it!'

[6] *Him who steals in fetters:* The robber appears as an escaped prisoner in fetters and tells a pitiful tale how he has been unjustly dealt with. You pity him, loose his bonds, and treat him kindly. He repays your kindness by robbing you the first opportunity he gets.

[7] *Him who beats with the shoe:* The sharper takes off his old shoes to beat some one who has a good pair. The latter takes his off to retaliate and in the struggle that ensues the former makes off with the good shoes of the latter!

[8] *Him who questions the truth:* The thief knows you have a certain sum of money with you. He approaches you and says he has goods to sell of greater value than the money you possess, but he is willing to take what you actually have. He then asks if you have the amount with you and you say 'Yes'. He will retort 'Never'. Then you produce it and count it. If he can contrive to get hold of it he will swear it does not belong to you. Then he either bolts with all or makes a compromise with you.

the masters of the grapnels and the rope of coconut fibre; and the conversation turned on to him who got the better of them.[1]

Here follows a story of Abú'l-Fatḥ al-Iskanderí, which, on grounds of decency, has been omitted. The only thing in it that may be mentioned is 'the moonlight night', regarding which he says, 'in other than his own garb'.

'And a phantom[2] paid a nocturnal visit when night was in a garb not his own[3]
And the full moon met him and brightened the parting of his hair.'

XXXI. THE MAQAMA OF THE SPINDLE

‘ÍSÁ IBN HISHÁM related to us and said: I entered Baṣra when I was wide of fame and abundant of reputation, and there came to me two young men. One of them said: 'May God strengthen the Shaikh! this youth entered our house and seized a kitten[4] with vertigo in its head, with the sacred cord[5] and a whirling sphere around its middle. Gentle of voice, if it cries; quick to return, if it flees; long of skirt, if it pulls; slender of

1 *Him who got the better of them:* That is, the thieves. This story has been suppressed on grounds of decency.

2 *And a phantom:* Metre, *ṭawíl.*

3 *In a garb not his own:* The usual garb of night is darkness, so that '*not his own*' would mean brightness, i.e. moonlight. Night personified is here regarded as masculine.

This maqáma may be compared to Hariri, xxx, 372, in which we have examples of the cant of beggars, mountebanks, prestigiators and the like. Here Hamadhání gives illustrations of the methods pursued by the fraternity of burglars, thieves, sharpers, swindlers, pickpockets and the like. Cf. Gaubari, *Endickte Geheimnisse* (von de Goéje Z.D.M.G.), xx, 504.

4 قَبَج سِنَّوْر *A kitten:* The commentator does not consider that قَبَج arabicized from the Persian كبك a partridge, makes good sense and says that the text is corrupt. He suggests that the correct word is فَنَج from the Persian فنك a furred animal and, as the context shows, a kitten. I think his view is correct. If we accept فَنَج as the arabicized form of فنك the slight error in pointing is the kind of one a copyist might easily make.

5 زُنَّار *Zunnar:* Greek ζωναριον a cord or girdle worn by the Eastern Christians, the Jews, Magi, and the Brahmins. Originally the lower girdle worn by a woman just above the hips over which the gown was drawn and fell in folds.

waist, weak of chest,[1] of the size of a plump sheep. Staying in the town, yet not abandoning travel. If it be given a thing, it returns it. If it be tasked with a journey, it goes energetically, and, if it is made to draw the rope, it lengthens it. There it is, bone and wood. It contains property, immoveable and moveable, a past and a future.'[2] Said the young man: 'Yes, may God strengthen the Shaikh! for he forcibly took from me:—

'Pointed is his spearhead,[3] sharp are his teeth,
His progeny are his helpers, dissolving union is his business.
He assails his master, clinging to his moustache;
Inserting his fangs into old and young.
Agreeable, of goodly shape, slim, abstemious.
A shooter, with shafts abundant, around the beard and the moustache.'

So I said to the first: 'Give him back the comb in order that he may return to thee the spindle.'

XXXII. THE MAQAMA OF SHIRAZ[4]

'ÍSÁ IBN HISHÁM related to us and said: When I was returning from Yemen and making for my native land, a fellow-traveller joined me with his baggage and we journeyed together for three days, until the highland attracted me, and the lowland swallowed him. So I ascended and he descended. I fared eastwards and he went westwards, but I regretted separating from him after the mountain and its ruggedness took possession of me, and the vale and its depth seized him.

'By Heavens! separation from him left me desiring him, and he left me suffering from his absence after him. Now when I parted from him, he was a man of wealth and beauty, of goodly appearance and perfection. Well, Time dealt us its

[1] *Weak of chest:* Literally, weak in the place of the shirt. المَمَرّ gives no sense. Probably جَزُور a fat sheep fit to be slaughtered.

[2] قَبْلٌ وَبَعْدٌ *Past and future:* That is, ancestral and passing to posterity.

[3] *Pointed is his spearhead:* Metre, *rejez*. Cf. *Ḥarîri*, i, 87.

[4] *Shiráz:* The capital of the province of Fárs situated 112 miles from Bushire and 220 parasangs from Nishapur.

blows, but I pictured him to myself at all times, and called him to mind every moment, and I did not think Time would help me to him or through him, till I came to Shiraz.

'Now one day, while I was in my chamber,[1] suddenly there appeared before me an old man, whose countenance poverty had marred,[2] whose lustre Time had entirely exhausted, whose erectness[3] disease had bent, and whose nails destitution had clipped; with a face more wretched than his actual state, and a garb more dreadful than his condition, with dry gums and parched lips, muddy feet, with a blistered hand,[4] with canine teeth that misfortune had destroyed, and a bitter existence. And he saluted me. My eye disdained him, but I returned his greeting. So he said: 'O God make us better than we are suspected to be.' Therefore I smoothed out for him the wrinkles of my face,[5] opened my ear to him and said: 'Proceed[6] with thy story!' Then he said: 'I have suckled thee on the breast of covenant, and shared with thee the rein of protection[7] and, in the opinion of the wise, acquaintance is sacred and friendship is kinship.' I then said: 'Art thou a fellow-townsman, or a fellow-tribesman?' He said: 'Nought unites us save the land of exile, and nothing binds us together but the relationship of neighbourhood.' Then I asked: 'Which road bound us both with one cord?' He replied: 'The road to Yemen.' Said 'Ísá ibn Hishám: So I asked: 'Art thou Abú'l-Fath al-Iskanderí?' He replied: 'I am that person.' I said:

[1] حُجْرَتِى *My chamber:* Literally, an enclosure for camels.

[2] غَبَّرَ *had marred:* Literally, had covered with dust.

[3] *Whose erectness:* Literally, whose lance, which is a figure for straightness.

[4] وَيَدٍ مَجِلَةٍ *And a blistered hand:* Cf. طَحَنْتُ حَتّى مَجَلَتْ يَدَاىَ I had ground at the mill till both my hands were blistered (Musnad, p. 106).

[5] I *smoothed out for him the wrinkles of my face:* That is, I ceased to knit my brows and to frown.

[6] إِيهِ *Proceed:* also إِيهًا and إِيهٍ. It is a word denoting a desire for one to speak. With ه quiescent, إِيهْ, it is used for chiding or checking, and means حَسْبُكَ—sufficient for thee is such a thing.

[7] عِنَانَ عِصْمَةٍ *The rein of protection:* An allusion to the co-partnership of two persons in one particular thing exclusive of the rest of the articles or property of either.

'How thin thou art become since parting from me, and thou hast changed beyond my recognition; therefore lay before me thy whole case and the cause of thy disordered condition.' He said: 'I have married a beautiful woman of base stock,[1] and I am afflicted with a daughter by her. So because of her I am in affliction, and she has despoiled me of my living and sapped my youthful vigour.' I said: 'Why dost thou not absolutely divorce her and be at rest?'[2]

XXXIII. THE MAQAMA OF HULWAN

'ÍSÁ IBN HISHÁM related to us and said: When I was coming back from the Pilgrimage with those who were returning, and I alighted at Ḥulwán[3] with those who alighted, I said to my slave: 'I find my hair is long and my body somewhat dirty,[4] so chose for us a bath that we may enter it, and a barber whom we may make use of. Let the bath be of spacious yard, of clean locality, of pure atmosphere and the water of moderate temperature; and let the barber be deft of hand, with a sharp razor and clean dress, and little given to gossip.' So he went out for a long time,[5] returned late, and said: 'I have chosen it as thou described it.' Then we took the direction of the bath and arrived there, but we did not see the keeper. But I went in, and there entered in my track a man who betook himself to a lump of clay, besmeared my forehead with it, and then placed it on my head. Then he went out, and in came another and he began to rub me with a rubbing that grazed my bones, to knead

[1] خَضْرَاءُ دِمْنَةٍ *A beautiful woman of base stock:* Literally, the greenness of a dungheap. Cf. Hebrew דֹּמֶן dung, i.e. of the enclosure where the camels were kept during the stay of the tribe at a certain place. When the tribe moved on, the place became covered with rich but rank green grass, very pleasant to the eye but coarse and unpalatable. A tradition of the Prophet says: إِيَّاكُم وَخَضْرَاءَ الدِّمَن 'Beware of the green dungheaps', which he explained to signify 'a beautiful woman of base stock.' See *Ḥariri*, i, 48; and *Arab Proverbs*, i, 48.

[2] *Why dost thou not absolutely divorce her?* See Qur'án, ii, 229–30. This maqáma does not conclude with the conventional lines of poetry.

[3] *Ḥulwán:* A town in 'Iráq in the mountains east of Baghdad.

[4] *My body somewhat dirty:* Cf. *Ḥariri*, i, 46.

[5] *He went out for a long time:* Cf. Qur'án, xix, 47.

me[1] with a kneading which crushed my joints, and to whistle with a whistling that scattered spittle. He next aimed at my head to wash it, and at the water to pour it. Then without delay the first entered and greeted the branch of the occipital artery of the second with a blow of his clenched fist that made his canine teeth rattle, and he said: 'Wretch! what hast thou to do with this head when it is mine?' Then the second turned on the first with a blow of his fist that destroyed his dignity,[2] and he said: 'Nay, but this head is my right, my property, and is in my hands.' Then they fought each other with fisticuffs till they were both exhausted, and, then, with what life was left, they summoned each other to arbitration and came to the keeper of the bath. And the first said: 'I am the owner of this head for I besmeared its forehead and placed upon it its clay.' The second asserted: 'Nay, but I am its owner, for I rubbed its bearer and kneaded his joints.' Said the keeper of the bath: 'Bring me the possessor of the head and I will ask him, "Is this thy head or his?"' So they both came to me and said: 'We want thy evidence, therefore undertake the duty and impose upon thyself the task.'[3] So I arose and went willy nilly. Said the keeper of the bath: 'Man, speak nothing but the truth and witness nought but the fact, and tell me to which of the two belongs this head?' I replied: 'God bless thee![4] this is my head, it has accompanied me upon the road, and encompassed the Ancient House[5] with me, and I have never doubted but that it was mine.' He said: 'Silence! garrulous fellow;' and then turned to one of the disputants and said: 'Sirrah! how long this contending with the people for this head? Be satisfied, so valueless is it, let it go instead to

[1] *To knead me:* Literally, to pinch or squeeze me.

[2] هَتَكَ حِجَابَهُ *Destroyed his dignity:* Literally, rent his veil.

[3] فَتَجَشَّمْ *Impose upon thyself the task:* From جَشْمٌ a difficult or inconvenient affair. It means to undertake something in spite of the inconvenience.

[4] عَافَاكَ ٱللهُ *God bless thee!* Literally, may God preserve thee from sickness, etc.

[5] ٱلْبَيْتُ ٱلْعَتِيقُ *The Ancient House:* The name given to the *Ka*'ba in Qur'án, xxii, 30, because Muslims believe that this was the first edifice built and appointed for the worship of God. See also Qur'án, iii, 90.

the curse of God and the heat of His hell. Suppose that this head was not, and that we have never seen this he-goat.' Said 'Ísá ibn Hishám: 'I arose from that place mortified, put on my clothes in terror, and quickly slipped away from the bath. And I reviled the slave with evil-speaking and contumely and pounded him after the manner of the pounding of gypsum.'[1] Then I said to another: 'Go and fetch me a barber to remove from me this load;' and he brought me a man of delicate build, agreeable make, like an image,[2] and I took to him quickly. Then he came in and said: 'Peace be to thee! From which town art thou?' I replied: 'Qúm'.[3] He said: 'May God prosper thee! From a land of plenty and comfort, the city of the Sunnis.[4] I was present there in its cathedral mosque in the month of Ramaḍán when the lamps had been lit and the *taráwih*[5] prayers were inaugurated, but, before we knew it, the Nile rose and came and extinguished those lights, but God made me a shoe which I put on when it was green, but there was no embroidery produced on its sleeve. And the boy

[1] ألجصّ *Gypsum:* Said to be arabicized because (ج) and (ص) do not ordinarily occur in an Arabic word. Probably from the Persian گچ.

[2] ألدُّمية *An image, or a likeness:* Metonymically applied to a woman or anything that is deemed beautiful. A loan word from Aramaic דְּמְיוֹן from the root דמה *damá* To be like. Cf. *Ḥariri*, ii, 611 and *Arab Proverbs*, i, 408.

[3] *Qúm:* A town south-west of Hamadhán; next to Meshed it is the most important place of pilgrimage in Persia. Yaqút writing in the thirteenth century says there was no trace of a non-Muslim in it.

[4] *The city of the Sunnis:* Literally, of the practice and the agreement. The point here is that the people of Qúm were exclusively Shí'ah, there was not a Sunní in the city. (See Yaqút, iv, 175.) 'And all its inhabitants are Shí'ah of the Imámí sect?' وأهلها كلّهم شيعة إمامية. Also de Goeji, *Collection of Arabian Geographers*, iii, 259, line 7 where Ibn Ḥauqal, a contemporary of the author, says: 'Shí'ism prevails at Qúm'; also see Letters, p. 423. This is the first of a number of amazing malapropisms.

[5] *Taráwiḥ prayers:* A form of prayer performed at some period during the night in the month of Ramaḍán, after the ordinary prayer of nightfall, consisting of twenty or more *rak'as*, according to the different persuasions, so called because the performer rests after each ترويحة which consists of four *rak'as*, or because they used to rest between every two pairs of salutations. (Lane, *Lexicon*, p. 1183; See also Letters, p. 424.)

returned to his mother, after I had performed the evening
prayer[1] when the shadow is equal.[2] But how was thy pilgrimage? Didst thou perform all its ceremonies as was incumbent? And they cried out: " A marvel! a marvel!" So I looked
at the beacon, and how light a thing is war—to the spectators!
And I found the *Harísah*[3] in the same state, and I knew that
the matter was decreed and pre-ordained by God. And how
long this vexation? And to-day, and to-morrow, and Saturday
and Sunday, but I will not be tedious, but what is this prating?
And I like thee to know that Mubarrad[4] in grammar wields
a keen razor, so do not occupy thyself with the speech of the
common people. Now if ability preceded action,[5] I should have
shaved thy head. Dost thou consider it advisable that we
begin?' Said 'Ísá ibn Hishám: 'I was bewildered at his
fluency with his malaprop loquacity, and I feared he might
prolong his sitting, so I said: "Till to-morrow, if God will."
Then I asked those present concerning him, and they said:
"This is a man from the country of Alexandria, this climate
has disagreed with him and madness has overtaken him, so that

---

1 العَتَمَة‎ *The evening prayer:* Literally, the first part or third of the night,
after the setting of the light of the شَفَق‎ and the time of the prayers of nightfall;
but the calling of that prayer the prayer of the عَتَمَة‎ as the Arabs of the desert
named it, instead of calling it عِشَاء‎ is forbidden by the Shafa'í code (*Minhadj
at-Talibín*, ii, 61). Hence the malapropism.

2 *When the shadow is equal:* Another malapropism.

3 *Al-Harísah:* A kind of thick pottage prepared of cooked bruised wheat,
fleshmeat, butter, almonds, vegetables, etc. (See Mas'údí, viii, 402-3.) It is said
to have been invented by the Sasanians and to have been the favourite dish of
Anushirwán.

4 *Al-Mubarrad* (A.H. 210-286): The well-known eminent philologer and
grammarian, author of the *Kámil* (edited by Wright). Ibn Khallikan, iii, 31.

5 فَلَو كَانَتِ ٱلاستِطَاعَةُ قَبْلَ ٱلفِعْلِ‎ *Now if ability preceded action:* A reference
to the technical language of the Ash'arite school representing the orthodox opinion
that ' the ability (*istitá'a*) to do the action goes along with the action and is the
essence of the power (*Qudra*) by which the action takes places'. (Macdonald,
Muslim Theology, p. 310.) This was how the orthodox disposed of the doctrine
of free will. On the other hand, the partisans of the Freedom of the Will main-
tained that the ability to do is always present. It is possible that Hamadhání may
have been aware of the Aristotelian treatment of the question of ἐνέργεια and
δύναμις. Translations of Aristotle's works were to be found in the library of the
Sáhib to which the author probably had free access during his stay at the Wazír's
court from A.H. 380.

he babbles the whole day, as you observe, but behind him there is much excellence." I said, "I have heard of him, and his madness grieves me." Then I recited and said:

"I make a firm promise[1] to God in a binding vow,
I will not shave my head as long as I live, even though I
suffer inconvenience."'

XXXIV. THE MAQAMA OF FRESH BUTTER

'Ísá ibn Hishám related to us and said: I turned aside with a few[2] of my friends to the front of a tent to ask hospitality from its occupants, and there came out to us a portly little man[3] and asked: 'Who are you?' We replied: 'Guests who have tasted nothing for three nights.' He related: 'He coughed and then said: "O young men! What do you say to fresh butter of the flock, like the head of a bald man, in a broad shallow dish adorned with the dates of Khaibar,[4] taken from the bunch of a branch of a tall, young, and large palm-tree? One of them would fill the mouth of one of a hungry company five days without water;[5] the tooth is lost in it, and its stone is like

[1] *I make a firm promise:* Metre, *ramal.*

[2] نَفَر *A few (Individuals):* A number of persons from three to nine.

حُزُقَّة *A portly little man:* Literally, large-bellied and short, short in step, or a niggard. I think Hamadhání had both meanings in his mind; the man's appearance would justify the former and his behaviour the latter, e.g. he began by coughing and on p. 187 of the text we find that coughing is indicative of a disinclination to give. Cf. also Text, p. 218: 'O coughing of the host when the bread is broken.'

[4] *Khaibar:* A well-known town in the district of Ḥijáz and four days' journey, or about fifty-four miles north-west of the city of Madína. In the time of Muḥammad the name *Khaibar* was borne by a whole province which was inhabited by various Jewish tribes. It comprised seven fortresses, meadows, and numerous groves of palm-trees. It was noted for the abundance and excellence of its dates. Cf. the line of Ḥassán ibn Thábit quoted by Yaqút, ii, 505.

فَإِنَّا وَمَنْ يَهْدِي ٱلْقَصَايِدَ نَحْوَنَا * كَمُسْتَبْضِعٍ تَمْرًا الَى أَرْضِ خيبر

'Verily as for us, he who presents *qasidas* to us,
Is like him who exports dates to the land of Khaibar.'

In A.H., 6 or 7, Muḥammad made himself master of the place and all its castles and strongholds, and took spoils to a great value. Yaqút, ii, 504. *Jewish Encyclopædia*, vii, 480.

[5] عِطْشِ خِمْسٍ *Five days without water:* An allusion to the drinking of camels on the fifth day counting the day of the next preceding as the first; their

the tongue of a bird, and they scoop up the butter with it, taken with deep wooden drinking-bowls of milk drawn from good milking-camels pastured on *haram*[1] and *rabl.*[2] O young men, do ye like it ?"' We answered: 'Yes, by Heavens! we like it.' 'Ha, ha,' laughed the old man, 'Your uncle also likes it.' Then he said: 'O young men! What is your opinion of white flour like unto a piece of molten silver collected on a round piece of hide with the odour of the qaraẓ ?[3] From among you one springs forward, a young, comely and active man, and mixes it without violently disturbing or scattering it. Then he leaves it before it is well kneaded. After a while he mixes it thoroughly with milk, more or less diluted with water. He next proceeds to work it up and then leaves it around the pan[4] till it is leavened without becoming dry; then he betakes himself to the *ghaḍa*[5] wood and kindles it. Then, when the fire subsides, he spreads it over his oven,[6] goes to his dough, flattens it out, after he has well kneaded it, lays it upon the hot ashes and then covers it up.'

'Then, when it has dried and risen,[7] he places on it hot stones sufficient to unite the two heats.[8] He covers them up over the bread, in the form of a round plate, until it cracks and splits and its crust resembles that of a circular cake, and its

drinking one, then pasturing three days, then coming to the water on the fifth day, the first and last days on which they drink being thus reckoned. Lane, p. 810.

1 هرم *Haram:* The name of a plant whose leaves are intensely acid, a species of sorrel.

2 ربل *Rabl:* The name applied to certain sorts of trees that break forth with leaves in the end of the hot season. They are intensely green.

3 القرظ *Qaraẓ:* A species of mimosa the leaves and fruit of which are used for tanning.

4 الصيداء *The pan:* Literally, a stone cooking-pot.

5 *Al-Ghaḍa:* A wood proverbial for making a powerful and lasting fire. This shrub, which is of the genus Euphorbia, is said to be peculiar to the Arabian Peninsula. See *Palgrave in his Travels*, i, 38; cf. De Sacy, *Ḥarírí*, i, 60 and ii, 632.

6 قرموص *Oven:* Literally, a hollow which a man digs wherein to sit to protect himself from the cold.

7 قبب *Risen:* Literally, became domelike.

8 الأوران *The two heats:* That is, the heat above and the heat below.

brownness[1] looks like that of the Ḥijáz date,[2] famous as Umm al-Jirdhán[3] or 'Idq ibn Ṭáb.[4] Wild honey, white as snow, is then poured over it till it penetrates the brown crust[5] and the pith absorbs all it has upon it. It is then brought before you, and you gobble it with the gobbling of Juwain,[6] or Zankal.[7] Young men, do you desire it?' He related: 'Each one of us stretched his neck towards what he had described, his mouth watered and he licked his lips and smacked them,' and we answered: 'Yes, by Heavens! we like it.' 'Ha! ha!' laughed the old man, and said: 'And your uncle, by Heavens! does not hate it.' Then he said: 'What is your opinion, O young men, of a wild she-kid of Nejd and Aliya[6] which has fed upon the artemisia Judaica of Nejd, the artemisia abrotanum and hashim,[9] nibbled at the thick herbage and is filled with tender grass? Her marrow is abundant, her inner membrane is covered with fat[10] and she has been slaughtered without blemish. Next it is suspended head downwards in an oven till it is perfectly baked without being either burnt or underdone, and then it is placed before you with its skin cracked, exposing white fat, on a table with thin cakes disposed thereon, as though they were unfolded Egyptian linen, or fine cloth of Kohistán coloured with red clay. It is surrounded with vessels containing mustard

[1] احمرارها *Its brownness :* Literally, its redness.

بُسر *Date :* The term applied to dates that have become coloured but have not become ripe. Cf. Heb. בֹּסֶר, unripe dates.

[3] *Umm al-Jirdhán :* Literally, mother of the field mice. A large kind of date and the last to ripen. It is cultivated in Ḥijáz. It is said that, before the fruit is cut from the tree, the field mice collect beneath.

[4] *'Idq ibn Ṭáb :* The name of a species of palm-tree in Madína.

[5] الدِّهَان *Brown crust :* Literally, red leather. For the use of this word to describe red colour, see Qur'án, lv, 37.

[6] *Juwain :* Diminutive of Juwán, is the name of a man who was notorious for making free with other people's property. *Fara'id Al-La'ál,* i, 134.

[7] *Zankal :* Ibn 'Alí ibn Abú Fazara is mentioned on page 362 of the Taj al-'Arús, but there is nothing to connect him with greedy feeding.

[8] *Aliya :* Belonging to the region above Nejd.

[9] *Hashim :* A plant that is dry and brittle.

For الحَمِيم in the text *read* الجَمِيم from جَمَّ it became much or abundant.

[10] *Her inner membrane is covered with fat :* That is, from tail to throat.

and raisin sauce[1] and divers kinds of fluid seasonings.[2] Then it is served to you exuding fat and dripping with gravy. O young men, do you like it?' We replied: 'Yes, by Heavens! we like it.' He said: 'And your uncle, by Heavens! will dance for it.' Then one of us sprang towards him with a sword and said: 'Does not our hunger suffice thee that thou mockest us?' Then his daughter brought us a tray upon which were a piece of dry bread, scraps and leavings, and she entertained us well. So we departed, praising her and blaming him.

XXXV. THE MAQAMA OF IBLIS

'Ísá ibn Hishám related to us and said: I lost some camels of mine and I went forth in search of them. I alighted in a verdant valley and behold there were running brooks,[3] tall trees, ripe fruits, blossoming flowers and broad plains, and lo! an old man was seated there. Now that which terrifies a solitary person from his like made me afraid of him, but he said: 'Have no fear.' Then I saluted him and he ordered me to sit down, and I obeyed. Then he asked me concerning my condition and I informed him. Then he said to me: 'Thou hast got thy guide and found thy stray. Dost thou recite anything of the poems of the Arabs?' I answered: 'Yes,' and I recited from Imr-al-Qais, 'Obeid, Labid, and Tarafa. But he was not pleased with anything of that and he asked: 'Shall I repeat some of my poetry?' I said to him: 'Produce it.' Then he recited ·

> 'The co-partners have separated,[4] but had I obeyed,
>   they would not have parted.
> And they have severed our cords from the bonds of union,'

---

1 منَاب *Raisin sauce :* Made of mustard and raisins.

أَصْبَاغ *Fluid seasonings :* See Qur'án, xxiii, 20.

Cf. Maqáma twenty-five of the Text, p. 125 ; the themes are identical.

This maqáma is remarkable for its collection of recondite words and technical terms ; the disquisition on Bedawín baking being extremely difficult to render into English. The conventional concluding lines of poetry are wanting.

3 أنهَارٌ مُصَرَّدَةٌ *Brooks :* Literally, little streams, from صَرَّدَ he made it little.

4 *The co-partners have separated :* Metre, *basit.* See Ibn Qutaiba's Sh'ir wá Shu'ará, p. 9.

أَقْرَانَا *Co-partners :* plural of قَرَن and قَرْن literally, a cord of twisted bark with which camels are tied.

until he went over the whole qaṣída. I said: 'O Shaikh! this is Jarír's poem, the boys have conned it, the women know it, it has entered the tents and reached the assemblies.' He said: 'Stop this but if thou dost know a poem of Abú Núwás repeat it to me.' So I recited to him:—

'I will not lament over the deserted abode,[1]
Nor will I yearn after the drivers of the white camels.
The dwelling most worthy of abandonment is that one;
In which union with the beloved is not long enjoyed.[2]
What a splendid night was that which is past. How delightful it was!
When the cups took effect upon our haughty brethren;
And a young gazelle[3] whose eye spoke enchantment,
Girded with a girdle,[4] an ally of the rosary and sanctification.
I strove with him for a kiss, and the wine was pure and ruddy,
In the garb of a Qáḍi and with the piety of Shaikh Iblis.[5]
When we became intoxicated, and all the people were drunk,
And I feared his overthrowing me with the cups,
I snored, feigning slumber, that I might put him to sleep,

[1] I *will not lament over the deserted abode*: Metre, *basit*. Abú Nuwás was one of the first to condemn the time-honoured prelude in the form of the erotic prologue to the qasida. Allusion has already been made in the note on Dhú al-Rumma, p. 49, to al-Farazdaq's condemnation of it.

[2] غَيرُ مَلْبُوسٍ *Is not long enjoyed*: Literally, is not enduring, from لَبِسَ he lived with.

[3] هادِن *A young gazelle:* That has become strong and has no need of its mother from هَدَنَ he became strong.

[4] مُزَنَّرٍ حلفِ تَسْبِيحٍ وَتَقْدِيسٍ *Girded with a girdle, an ally of the rosary and sanctification.* In this line the poet seems to refer to Christianity (the girdle), Islám (the rosary), Judaism (تقديس) which refers to that part of the Jewish Liturgy where God's name is sanctified. Cf. Waráqah's exclamation to Khadíja قُدُّوسٌ قُدُّوسٌ 'Holy! Holy!' *Life of Muḥammad* (Wüstenfeld), p. 153.

[5] *The piety of Shaikh Iblis*: An allusion to the piety of Iblís *per contrarium*. For the use of 'Shaikh' as a title for Iblís, see *Ḥariri*, p. 144.

And both his eyeballs clad themselves with sleep from my bag.
Then he stretched himself on a couch which was finer to me,
In spite of its disordered condition, than the throne of Balqís[1],
And I visited his sleeping-place before the dawn,
And when the sound of the church bells[2] indicated the morning.
So he asked, "Who is that?" I answered:
"The priest has come.[3]
And thy convent[4] must be ministered[5] by the priest."[6]
He said: "By my life thou art a vile sort of a man."
But I said: 'Never! I am not one to be blamed."'

He related: 'Then he rejoiced, cried out and shouted.' So I said: 'God disfigure thee for an old man! I know not whether thou be more stupid in arrogating to thyself Jarír's poetry, or in thy delight at the poem of Abú Núwás who is a libertine[7] and a vagabond.' He said: 'Stop this! Go thy way

1 عَرش بَلقيس *The throne of Balqís:* (Queen of Sheba) See Qur'án, xxvii, 23. Baiḍáwí says this throne was made of gold and silver and crowned with precious stones. Its surface was eighty cubits square and its height eighty cubits. Baiḍáwí', *Commentary* (edited by Fleischer), ii, 66.

2 ألنّواقيسُ *The bells:* Plural of نَاقُوس arabicized from the Syriac *naqusha*, an oblong piece of thick wood with several holes bored through it struck with a mallet called رَبيل *rabil*, used by Christians in Muslim countries instead of church bells to summon people to prayer. Hence, in the present day, applied to a bell, and particularly to the bell of a church or convent.

3 ألقَسّ *The priest:* Arabicized from the Syriac qashá a presbyter.

4 دَيرٌ Probably دَور plural أديار a convent, monastery or cloister. From the Syriac *dairá*, Chaldaic. דיר

5 تَشْميش *Ministered:* The context shows that the poet has evidently used the Hebrew תַשְׁמִישׁ from שָׁמַשׁ to minister, the *double entendre* of which suits the line.

6 قسيس *A priest:* From the Syriac qashíshá, from qash, to be old.

These verses are a sample of the thinly veiled obscene allusions in which Abú Nuwás revelled. They are not found in the published Díwán of this poet.

7 فُوَيسِق *A libertine:* The diminutive is used for aggrandizement.

and when thou dost meet on the road a man with a leathern bottle, who goes about in the houses, around the cooking-pots, boasts of his form and glories in his beard, say to him: "Direct me to a bound fish in a sea, slender in the waist, that stings like a wasp, and turbans with light." His father is a stone, his mother a male. Gold is his head and flame is his name, and the rest of him is tail. He acts upon clothes with the action of the moth. In the house he is the bane of the oil, a greedy drinker never satisfied, and a glutton never sated. A bountiful giver whom none forbids; he climbs the acclivity, and his property does not decrease through generosity. What pleases him grieves thee, and what benefits thee injures him. I was going to conceal from thee my story and live with thee in comfort, but thou didst refuse, now hear the truth.[1] There is not a poet[2] but has a helper from among us. And I dictated this qaṣida to Jarir. I am the Shaikh Abú Múrrah.'[3] Said 'Ísá ibn Hishám: 'Then he vanished and I saw him not. And I went on headlong and met a man with a fly-whisk[4] in his hand. I said to myself,[5] "By Heavens! this is my man." So I told him what I had heard of him. Then he handed me a lamp, pointed to a dark cave in the mountain and said: "There is the cave and thou hast with thee the lamp."' He related: 'I entered it and behold I found my camels and they had taken the other direction, but I turned their heads and drove them back. Now, while I was in that situation in the wood, creeping stealthily through the thicket, lo! Abú'l-Fatḥ al-Iskanderí met me with a greeting.' I said to him: 'Sirrah! what has driven thee to this place?' He answered: 'The injustice of the days in decisions, and the non-existence of generous men.' I said: 'O Abú'l-Fatḥ, give then thy command.' He said: 'Bear me

[1] *Now hear the truth:* Literally, now take it.

[2] *There is not a poet:* An allusion to the popular belief that every poet was inspired by a Jinn or Satan. Cf. the twenty-seventh Maqáma, p. 137, line 5. For a similar story, see Letters of Abu 'Alá al-Mu'arrí, translated by Professor Margoliouth, p. 74 and Yaqût, vi, 122.

[3] *Abú Múrrah:* Literally, the father of calamity. The most famous of the nicknames of Iblís. Said also to have been the nickname of Pharaoh. Ibn al-Athír, *Kunya Lexicon*, edited by Seybold, p. 197.

[4] *A fly-whisk:* Literally a small leathern bottle.

[5] فَقُلْتُ Literally, so I said.

on a young she-camel, and supply me with some provisions.'[1] I said: 'That is thine.' Then he recited and said:—

'My soul a ransom[2] for the man who gave me the choice.
I tasked him extremely, but he was generous.
He scratched not his beard, he wiped not his nose and he did not cough'

Then I told him the story of the old man, whereupon he pointed to his turban and said: 'This is the fruit of his benevolence.' I exclaimed: 'O Abú'l-Fatḥ, hast thou begged from the devil? Thou art indeed a mighty mendicant.'

XXXVI. THE MAQAMA OF ARMENIA

'ÍSÁ IBN HISHÁM related to us and said: When I was returning from trading with Armenia,[3] the desert guided us to its children and we stumbled on them upon the outskirts thereof. They made our camels kneel down in that land of the ostrich, while they cleared our provision bags, and eased our camels of their burdens, and we remained all day[4] in the hands of the band. The thong held us bound in groups and our horses were forcibly tied up, until night followed up with its darkness[5] and the Pleiades extended its rays.[6]

Then they went in the direction of the hinder part of the desert and we betook ourselves to the front thereof, and thus we continued till the beauty of the dawn arose from behind the veil of modesty, and the sword of the morning was drawn from the sheath of darkness. But the sun arose upon nought except hair and skin. We ceased not to be in perils, averting their

[1] *Supply me with some provisions:* Literally, pour some water into the wood.

[2] *My soul a ransom:* Metre, *kámil.*

[3] *Armenia:* The modern name of a district south of the Caucasus and the Black Sea which formed part of the ancient kingdom of Armenia which, according to Yaqút, comprised 118 provinces.

[4] بياض اليوم *All day:* Literally, the whiteness of the day, i.e. daylight, and hence the whole day as long as it is light.

[5] *Its darkness:* Literally, its tails; the dense darkness is compared to the thickness of a horse's tail.

[6] أطنابه *Its rays:* Literally, its ropes; the similarity is obvious.

hindrances, and in the wastes traversing their surface,[1] till we arrived at Merágha.[2] And each one of us attached himself to a companion and took a road.[3] There clave unto me a youth with wretchedness apparent upon him and an old worn-out garment over him, surnamed Abú'l-Fatḥ al-Iskanderí. We went in search of the Father of Strengthening,[4] and we found him appearing from a flame fed with the *ghada* wood. So al-Iskanderí went to a man, begged a handful of salt, and said to the baker: 'Allow me to use the top of the oven,[5] for I am smitten with the cold.' Now, when he had ascended its hump, he began to relate to the people his condition, to inform them of his loss, and to scatter about the oven salt from beneath his skirts, making the people think he had vermin in his clothes. So the baker said: 'What aileth thee? Perish thy father! Gather up thy skirts, for thou hast spoiled our bread.' And he proceeded to take the loaves and to throw them away. And al-Iskanderí began to pick them up and to put them under his arm. Now his cunning in what he did amused me. He next said: 'Wait for me till I scheme to get something to eat with it, for there is no device with destitution.' And he went to a man, who had arranged in rows clean vessels, in which were different kinds of milk, so he enquired the price and asked permission to taste it. The man said: 'Do so.' Then he moved his fingers about in the vessel as though he were seeking something he had lost, and said: 'I have not the price of it with me, but hast thou a desire for a shave?' The man exclaimed: 'God disfigure thee! Art thou a barber?'[7] He replied: 'Yes.' Then he made for his ancestry to revile it,

[1] نَقْطَعُ نُجُبَهَا *Traversing their surface:* Literally, stripping their bark, figuratively for traversing the surface.

[2] *Merágha:* A town in Azerbaijan the north-west province of Persia.

[3] *Took a road:* That is, each took a different way.

[4] *Abu Jábir: The Father of Strengthening:* Bread. Harírí calls haríseh 'ummu Jábir', The Mother of Strengthening. *Ḥariri*, p. 224.

[5] *Allow me to use the top of the oven*: Literally, lend me the head of the oven.

[6] أُدْمٌ *something to eat with it:* From أَدَمَ he mixed the bread with seasoning.

[7] *Art thou a barber?* An allusion to the contempt in which the calling of a barber was held. According to Jáḥiz the barber was taken as typical of the lowest class of society. Ḥaywán, iii, 46. Cf. *Ḥariri*, p. 629.

and the vessel to empty it. So al-Iskanderí said: 'Prefer me to Satan.' He said: 'Take it, and mayest thou not be blessed through it.' So he took it and we went to a secluded spot and consumed it all at once. Then we journeyed on till we came to a village, and we begged food of its inhabitants. So a young man from among the people hastened to his house and brought us a large bowl whose utmost capacity milk had filled.[1] We sipped it until we finished it. Then we asked them for bread, but they refused it except on payment of the price. Al-Iskanderí asked: 'What aileth ye that ye are generous with the milk but refuse the bread except on payment?' The boy answered: 'This milk was in a large vessel and a mouse fell into it. Therefore we give it as alms to travellers.' Al-Iskanderí exclaimed: 'Good God!'[2] and he seized the bowl and smashed it. Then the boy shouted: 'Alas the loss! Alas my spoilation!' Then did our flesh creep, our stomachs were turned and we got rid of what we had eaten. And I said: 'This is the reward for what we did yesterday.' And Abú'l-Fath al-Iskanderí indited saying:

> 'O soul be not squeamish,[3] for the hardy hath no qualms,
> He who associates with Time eats, the while, fat and lean.
> Therefore wear for one season the new, and put on for another the old.'

XXXVII. THE MAQAMA OF THE NAJIM

'ÍSÁ IBN HISHÁM related to us and said: I passed a night with a company[4] of clever men of my friends. We discussed chaste speech, and we had not bidden farewell to the conversation when our door was knocked at. So I asked: 'Who is the nocturnal visitor?' He answered: 'The envoy of night and its messenger.

[1] سَدَّ ٱللَّبَنُ أَنْفَاسَهُ *Whose capacity milk had filled:* Literally, the milk had stopped its breath.

[2] إِنَّا لِلّٰهِ Good *God!* The full formula is, 'verily we belong to God', so that He may do with us what He pleaseth 'and verily to Him do we return', in the ultimate state of existence. Said on an occasion of an affliction or calamity.

[3] *O soul be not squeamish:* Metre, *mujtath.*

[4] كَتِيبَة *A company:* Literally, a military force, a troop.

The defeated of hunger and its outcast, and an exile whose beast is lean and fatigued, whose life is hardship, and between whom and his two chicks are vast deserts. A guest whose shadow is light,[1] and whose stray is a loaf. Is there, therefore, among you a host?' So we hastened to open the door, we made his camel kneel down, concentrated his purpose, and said to him: 'To thine own house hast thou come, and thine own people hast thou reached, and come into the house.' We smiled upon him, welcomed him, and showed him his stray. We helped him till he was sated, and we talked to him until he became friendly, and then we asked: 'Who is this star rising from his orient, the bewitcher with his diction?' He answered, 'None knows the wood like the biter.[2] I am popularly known as the Nájim.[3] I have associated with Time that I might test it. I have extracted its essences, and milked all its teats.[4] I have tried the people that I might know them—and I know the lean and the fat among them—and exile that I might taste it. No country has looked at me whose eye I have not plucked out[5], and there is no gathering together of friends that I have not entered. Therefore I am talked of in the east and I am not repudiated in the west. There is not a king whose carpet I have not trodden upon, no serious situation whose flank[6] I have not penetrated, and no war has ceased in which I have not been an envoy. Time has tried me in its two phases, ease and distress, and it has met me with its two faces, the smiling and the frowning, but I exposed not myself to its hardship save in its own garb.[7]

1 ظِلُّهُ خَفِيفٌ *Whose shadow is light:* Contrast this with ثَقِيلُ ٱلظِّلِّ of oppressive shade, i.e. disagreeable, or inconvenient. Cf. *Hariri*, i. 250.

2 ٱلعَاجِمُ *The biter:* An Arab bites a piece of wood to test its soundness for making an arrow or a lance.

3 ٱلنَّاجِمُ *The Nájim:* Literally, the Rising Star.

4 حَلَبتُ أَشْطُرَهُ I *have milked all its teats:* Freytag, *Arab Proverbs*, i, 346. A figure for having experienced varieties of fortune, its straitness and its ampleness, as compared to one who has milked all the teats of the camel, that which yields plenty and that which does not.

5 فَقَأْتُ عَيْنَهَا *Plucked out its eye:* That is, trod its surface.

6 سَمَاطَهُ *Its flank:* Literally, its rank.

7 بِلَبُوسِهِ *In its garb:* Cf. the saying of Baihas. البَس لِكُلِّ حَالَةٍ لَبُوسَهَا 'Wear for every condition its proper dress,' also, Hamasa (edited by Freytag), p. 510.

And if the changing of Time[1] formerly injured me,
And loaded me with its evil-accidents what it loads with,
It verily brought benevolence when it set me down
In a good place from which there is no removal.’

We said: ‘May thy teeth not be broken![2] How excellent art thou and thy father! Silence is not unlawful except to thee, and speech is not lawful save to thee. Whence hast thou risen and where dost thou set? What is that which impels thy desire before thee and drives thy object in front of thee?’ He said: ‘As for the native land, it is Yemen; as regards the need it is the rain, and as for the motive it is distress and the bitter life.’ Said we: ‘If thou wouldst but stay in this place we would share our life with thee and all else. Thou wouldst get rain with which to cultivate, and heavy downpours from the rain-stars[3] deep enough to drink from, without using hand or vessel.’ He said: ‘I will not prefer any companions to you, for I have found your court spacious, but your rain is water and water quencheth not the thirsty.’ So we asked: ‘What rains will satisfy thee?’ He answered: ‘The rain of Khalaf.’ And he indited saying:—

‘O fleet camel! To Sijistan![4]
And to the ocean to whose shores desires repair.
If thou visit Arján,[5] thou wilt go to it,

[1] *And if the changing of Time:* Metre, *ṭawīl.*

[2] *May thy teeth* (literally mouth) *not be broken:* The phrase as used by the Prophet, is: لَا يَفْضُضِ اللّٰهُ فَاكَ May God not break thy mouth.

[3] ٱلأنواء *The rain-stars:* pl. of نَوْء The literal meaning of نَوْء is the setting in the early morning of one of the twenty-eight mansions of the moon, or نُجوم آلأخذ while the opposite constellation, called its رَقِيب or watcher, was rising. The auroral settings of these constellations served among the Arabs to denote the seasons of rain, wind, or heat. Just as among the Greeks and Latins the setting of the Hyads or the rising of Sirius indicated particular states of the weather. As the Arabs in their observations of the seasons thought chiefly of rain, which was to moisten their parched fields, the word نَوْ became equivalent with rain. *Ḥarīri,* i, 215. The belief of the Arabs of the Ignorance that the rain was produced by the settings of the stars was discouraged by Muslim teachers; and from an anecdote related of ‘Umar (See Lane, Article جدح) the Khalifa seems to have considered that the supply of rain was a sign that sins were pardoned, basing his opinion on Qur'án, lxxi, 10. Chenery's Translation of *Ḥarīri,* i, 443-5.

[4] O *fleet camel! To Sijistan:* Metre, *mutaqárib.*

[5] *Arjan* and *Arrajan:* a large town in Seistan, sixty parasangs from Shiraz, famous for its palm-trees, olive groves and fruits.

Desiring one and wilt return with a hundred complete,
And the superiority of the Amir over Ibn al-'Amíd.[1]
Is like that of the Quraish[2] over Báhila!'[3]

Said 'Ísá ibn Hishám: Then he went forth and we bade him farewell. After he had gone we continued a long while wishing for him, while his absence pained us. Now one cloudy day we were seated together like the string of the Pleiades, when suddenly mounts were driven, led horses were brought up, and lo! a man ran in upon us. We asked: 'Who is the intruder?' and behold it was our Shaikh, the Nájim, walking proudly in the guise of realized desires and in the skirts of wealth. We arose, and, embracing him, asked: 'What is behind thee, O 'Iṣám?'[4] He answered: 'Laden camels, loaded mules and locked bags.' And he indited saying:—

'O my master,[5] what base thing is there that Khalaf doth not disapprove of?[6]
And what good thing is there that he doth not attain to?
The seekers of largess hear no word save "Take it",
And he is not answered, save by "Give it".

[1] *Ibn al-'Amid* (ob. A.H. 359 or 360).

[2] *Is like that of the Quraish over Báhila.* This was praise indeed. Abû'l-Faḍl Muḥammad Ibn al-'Amid, Wazir of Rukn Al-Daula, the Buwayhid prince, was one of the great men of the fourth century of the Hijra. He was a versatile and an accomplished scholar and was called a second Jáḥiz. Tha'álibí says (*Yatíma*, iii, 3) that epistolary writing began with 'Abd al-Hamíd (d. A.H. 133) Kátib, or secretary, to Marwán the last of the Umayyad Khalífas, and ended with Ibn al-'Amíd. Among those who studied the epistolary art under him was the Ṣáḥib Ibn 'Abbád. As Wazir, his authority and influence were unbounded. (Ibn Khallikan, iii, 256; also *Der Islám*, iii, 323-5, were a full notice of the Wazir by H. F. Ahmedroz will be found.)

[3] *Báhila:* The meanest of the Arab tribes. The Arabs who were members of this tribe had an extreme repugnance to bearing this surname. A poet has said: 'If the words, "thou Bahilite" were addressed to a dog he would howl from the ignominy of such an appellation.' (Ibn Khallikan, ii, 518.) For a further example of this repugnance, see *Aghání*, vii, 12.

[4] ما وراءك يا عصام *What is behind thee, 'Iṣám:* Freytag, *Arab Proverbs*, ii, 589. Said to have been first used by Ḥárith ibn 'Amr king of Kindeh and addressed to 'Iṣám, a clever Kindite woman, whom he had sent to bring a description of the beautiful and gifted daughter of 'Owf ibn Muhallam, Al-Shaibání whom he wished to marry. This proverb is said to have another origin, see Chenery's Translation of *Ḥariri*, i, 519.

[5] O *my master:* Metre, *kamil.*

[6] D*oth not disapprove of:* Page 195, line 7 of Text, *for* بابها *read* يابها.

Verily noble deeds disclosed their faces fair,
And he was the mole on their cheeks.
May my father be a ransom for his qualities which manifest greatness,
And for the hand in whose movements thou seest blessings!
Whoever counts them the benefactions of the age, verily I
Am one of those that reckon the age to be one of their benefactions.’

Said ‘Ísá ibn Hishám: ‘We asked God to spare him and to bless us with his company. And the Nájim stayed for days restricting his tongue to expressing gratitude for his[1] kindness, and employing not his speech save in praising his days and talking of his gifts.’

XXXVIII. THE MAQAMA OF KHALAF[2]

‘ÍSÁ IBN HISHÁM related to us and said: When I was invested with authority over Basra, and was going down thither from the Presence,[3] there accompanied me on the boat a youth, as though he were health in the body. He said: ‘In the sides of the world and its directions I am lost, but I can be counted equal to a thousand and I can take the place of a line. Dost thou desire to take me as a favourite,[4] and not seek from me any recommendation?’ I said: ‘What recommendation stronger than thy excellence, and what means greater than thy wisdom?

[1] *His*, i.e. Khalaf's, *kindness*. The part of this Maqáma where the Nájim describes himself has much in common with the fourth Maqáma, pp. 16, 17.

[2] *Khalaf ibn Ahmed:* Amir of Sijistan (Seistan) (b. 326, died in prison A.H. 399). The date of his appointment by the Samanide ruler is not given but in 354 there is a reference to a revolt against his rule (Ibn al-Athir, viii, 416). In 393 Maḥmúd of Ghazna wrested Sijistan from him and sent him into honourable captivity to Juzján, but four years later he was detected in an attempt to incite Ilik Khan against the conqueror and was kept in close confinement in Jardiz till his death in A.H. 399. He was a great patron of letters and is said to have got together a number of learned men to make an exhaustive compilation of interpretations of the Qur'án. The result of their labours was a work of a hundred volumes! His cruel treatment of his sons and the treacherous way he compassed the death of the Qáḍi Abu Yúsuf have cast a stain upon his memory. (H. F. Ahmedroz in the *JRAS*, 1901, pp. 524-31, and Ibn al-Athír, ix, 113-123.)

[3] *From the Presence:* That is, from the presence of the Khalifa at Baghdad.

[4] صَنِيعَةٌ *A favourite:* Literally, a good action.

Nay, but I will render thee the service of a friend[1] and be partners with thee in easy and straitened circumstances.' So we travelled on. Now, when we reached Basra, he disappeared from me for days, and, because of his absence, my endurance was straitened[2] and I had no patience left, so I searched for him in the interior[3] of the country till I found him. Then I asked him: 'What didst thou disapprove of and why didst thou flee?' He said: 'Verily estrangement rankles in the breast as fire is kindled in the fire-stick. If it be extinguished, it will subside[4] and vanish, but, if it continue to exist, it will scatter and spread. And the vessel will fill and overflow, if the drops fall into it consecutively; and reproach, when it is left alone, will hatch and lay.[5] No snare catches the free-born like bounty, and no scourge repels him like rudeness. But, in any case, we look down from above, upon the generous with an amorous glance, and upon the ignoble with a contemptuous regard. Therefore he who meets us with a long nose,[6] we will meet him with an elephant's trunk, and him who regards us askance, we will dispose of for a paltry price. Now, thou didst not plant me for thy slave to uproot me, nor didst thou buy me for thy servants to sell me. A man is known by his servants, as a book is known by its superscription. Therefore, if their rudeness was something that thou didst command, what made it necessary? And, if thou wast not aware of it, that is most surprising.' Then he said·—

1 ٱلرَّفِيق *The friend:* Another, and more appropriate, reading ٱلرَّقِيق 'the slave'.

2 فَضَقْتُ ذَرْعًا *My endurance was straitened:* Literally, my arm, the symbol of power, was contracted.

3 جُيُوب *Interior:* Literally, the pockets; and also the approaches of a country.

4 نَارَت *Will subside:* (Literally, spread). Another reading and the one I have translated, بَادَت subsided. Cf. the expression نَارَت ٱلفِتْنَةُ sedition spread.

5 فَرَّخَ وَبَاضَ *Hatch and lay:* The natural order has been reversed for the sake of the rhyme. Probably an allusion to the tradition quoted by Lane (p. 2362) بَاضَ فِيهِم الشَّيْطَانُ وَ فَرَّخَ The Devil made his fixed abode among them like as a bird keeps to the place of its eggs and young ones.

6 بِأَنْفٍ طَوِيلٍ *With a long nose:* Figurative for great disdain.

'The two hands of Khalaf[1] ibn Ahmad have prospered, for he is
Easy of access, and his servants are respectful.
Hast thou not observed that generosity passes over mankind
And takes its abiding place in his hand?'

Said 'Ísá ibn Hishám: 'Then he turned away and I followed him to conciliate him, and I ceased not to soothe him till he turned back after he had sworn, "I will not go to one whose company is bad." So I gave him the respect due to him.'

XXXIX. THE MAQAMA OF NISHAPUR

'ÍSÁ IBN HISHÁM related to us and said: I was at Nishapur[2] on a Friday so I presented myself at the *obligatory*.[3] When I had performed it there passed by me a man who had donned a tall hat and turned a portion of his turban beneath his chin[4] like the Sunni's. So I asked the worshipper at my side, 'Who is this?' He said: 'This is a moth that attacks none but the woollen garment of the orphans, a locust that falls upon none but the forbidden crop, a burglar that breaks into[5] none but the treasury of pious bequests, a Kurd that raids upon none but the weak, a wolf that preys upon none but God's servants, between their kneeling and prostration, a warrior that plunders nothing but God's property, under cover of covenants and witnesses. He has donned his tall hat but doffed his piety; he has conventionally put on his cloak but perverted the use of his hand

1 *The two hands of Khalaf:* Metre, *kâmil*. Cf. Letters, pp. 264-5.

2 Nishapur (*Naisabur*): A well-known town, the capital of the province of the same name, situated forty-nine miles west of Meshed. It was captured by the Arabs in A.H. 31. Yaqút in his *Geographical Dictionary*, iv, 757, referring to this place says of all the cities he had visited Naisabur (Nishapur) was the finest. It was in this city, says Tha'alibi (*Yatima*, iv, 168) that Hamadhaní wrote his four hundred maqámát and vanquished his great literary rival the renowned Abú Bakr al-Khwárazmí.

3 *The obligatory:* See Qur'án, lxii, 9, which commands attendance at congregational worship on Fridays.

4 *Turned a portion of his turban beneath the chin:* Ibn al-Athir refers to a tradition of the prophet wherein the people were commanded to tie the extremity of the turban under the chin and were forbidden to do otherwise. (Niháyah under التَّلَحِّي.)

5 يَنْقُبُ *Breaks into:* Literally, bores.

and tongue; he has clipped short his moustache[1] but lengthened his snares; he has displayed his vehement eloquence,[2] but covered up his defects; he has whitened his beard,[3] but blackened his record; he has paraded his abstinence, but concealed his greed.' I said: 'May God curse the fellow! but who art thou?' He replied: 'I am a man known as al-Iskanderi.' I said: 'May God bless the land[4] that grew this excellence, and the father that left this progeny, and, where art thou going?' He answered, 'To the Ka'ba.' So I said: 'Excellent! Excellent! is its feast, though still unprepared! We are, in that case, fellow-travellers.' He said: 'How is that, when I am going up and thou art going down?' I asked: 'How canst thou go *up* to the Ka'ba?' He replied: 'But I am going to the Ka'ba of the needy, not to the Ka'ba of the pilgrims, to the station of generosity not the station of sanctity,[5] to the house of captives,[6] not to the house of sacrifices, to the source of gifts,[7] not the Qibla[8] of prayer, to the desire[9] of guests, not to the Mina of Khaif.'[10] I asked: 'And where are these excellences?' Then he indited saying:—

1 قصّ سَبَالَهُ *Clipped short his moustache:* Still regarded as an outward mark of piety.

2 شَقْشَقَة *His vehement eloquence:* From شَقْشَقَ he (a camel) brayed in his shiq-shiqa, or faucial bag. The primary meaning is loudness of voice and then vehement eloquence. Shiqshiqa is also the name of a sermon preached by 'Alí and interrupted by a member of the congregation, a man from 'Iráq, handing him a letter. When desired by Ibn 'Abbás to continue his address, 'Alí answered: 'Alas! Ibn 'Abbás, the Shiqshiqa has roared and subsided', meaning that the inspiration of the moment had gone. [*Nahaj al-Balágha*, p. 26 (Beyrut ed. A.H. 1308)]. The saying became proverbial. See Freytag, *Arab Proverbs*, i, 673.

3 *Whitened his beard:* To give himself a venerable appearance.

4 سَقَى ٱللّهُ أَرْضًا *God bless the land!:* Literally, may God water the land!

5 مَشْعَرُ ٱلْحَرَام *The station of sanctity:* That is, Muzdalifa.

6 بَيْتُ السَّبْى *The house of captives:* The spoils of his victorious campaigns.

7 ٱلصِّلَاتُ وَٱلصَّلَاة *Gifts and prayer:* See De Sacy, *Hariri*, i, 18 for a similar play on these words.

8 *Qibla:* That part of the horizon, or of a mosque, which is in the direction of Mecca towards which Muslims turn to say their prayers.

9 *Desire:* Text, p. 201, line 5, *for* مِنَى *read* مُنَى.

10 *Mina al-Khaif:* A small town near Mecca, to which the pilgrims descend on the morning of the 'Id.

'Where are the Faith and the king[1] strengthened with might,
Through whom the cheek of noble deeds is dyed rosy red.
In a land where hopes flourish,
For Khalaf ibn Ahmad is its rain-cloud.'

XL. THE MAQAMA OF KNOWLEDGE

'ÍSÁ IBN HISHÁM related to us and said: I was crossing one of those parts where exile had thrown me, when behold I met a man who was asking another, 'By what means hast thou acquired knowledge?' And the latter, answering him, said: 'I sought it and found it to be difficult of access.[2] It is not shot with a shaft, nor allotted by the divining arrows.[3] It is not seen in the dream nor controlled with the bridle.[4] It is neither inherited from paternal uncles, nor borrowed from the generous. Therefore I adopted, as a means of attainment thereto, the making of clods a bed, the taking of a stone for a pillow, repelling weariness, braving danger, prolonging vigils, making a companion of travel, much reading and meditation. And I found it to be a thing suitable only for planting, and it is not planted save in the mind. A quarry that is ensnared but rarely and is not caught, save in the breast. A bird that is deluded only by the snaring of the word, and nought catches it but the net of memory. Therefore I laid it upon my soul and confined it within my eye. I spent

1 *Where are the* Faith *and the king:* Metre, *wafir.* These expressions regarding the two Ka'bas will be found in No. 38, page 101, of Hamadhání's Letters. They are cited by Tha'álibí (*Yatíma* iv, 176) as a specimen of Hamadháni's elegant epistolary style. They are also quoted by Ibn Khallikan, 113. Their chief merit consists of a mere play on words impossible to preserve in a rendering into English. For similar and additional criticisms of the Qáḍi and a description of what a Qáḍí should be, see the Author's Letters, pp. 168-9.

2 بَعِيدُ ٱلْمَرَامِ *Difficult of access:* This and the succeeding five sentences will be found in No. 41, p. 165 of the Letters where almost the entire maqáma is reproduced verbatim.

3 بِٱلْأَزْلَامِ *By the divining arrows:* By means of which the Arabs in the time of the Ignorance. (Barbarism), sought to know what was allotted to them. This practice is forbidden in Qur'án, v, 4.

4 بِٱللِّجَامِ *With a bridle:* Literally, with a bit, i.e. the appurtenances of a bridle, by an extension of meaning, applied to this with its straps; arabicized from the Persian لگام *Lagám.*

my means, but stored my mind. I wrote elegantly by virtue of much reading, and passed on from reading to investigation, and from investigation to composition, and I relied therein on divine guidance.'

Now I heard language such as penetrated the ear, reached the heart, and quickly entered the breast, so I asked: 'O young man! Whence the orient of this sun?' Then he began to say:—

> 'Alexandria is my home,[1] if but in it my resting-place were fixed.
> But my night I pass in Syria, in 'Iráq my day.'

XLI. THE MAQAMA OF ADVICE

'Ísá ibn Hishám related to us and said: When Abú'l-Fath al-Iskanderí equipped his son for commerce, he made him sit down to admonish him. After he had praised God and re-praised Him, and blessed His Apostle—May God bless and save him!—he said: 'O my dear son, though I rely upon the soundness of thy wisdom and the purity of thy stock, still I am solicitous[2] and the solicitous augurs ill. And I am not free from fear for thee on account of desire and its power, and lust and its demon. Therefore seek aid against them, in the day by fasting, and in the night by sleeping. Verily it is a garb whose exterior is hunger and whose interior is sleep, and no lion has ever put it on whose fierceness has not been softened. Hast thou understood them both, O son of the vile woman?[3]

And, as I fear the consequences of that on thee, I am not reassured as to the effect upon thee of two thieves, one of them is generosity, and the name of the other is greediness.[4]

[1] *Alexandria is my home:* Metre, *mujtath.*

Cf. the fifteenth maqáma, p. 74. A very interesting disquisition on knowledge and the course to be followed in the acquisition thereof. We have doubtless in this maqáma a statement of the author's own methods of study. An amplification of the idea will be found on pp. 165–8 of the Letters. For a synopsis of both, see end of the Cambridge MS, 1066 (Badi' al- Zamán).

[2] إِنِّي شَفِيقٌ *Still I am solicitous:* An allusion to the proverbial saying: إِنَّ ٱلشَّفِيقَ بِسُوءِ ٱلظَّنِّ مُولَعٌ 'Verily the very solicitous, or affectionate, is addicted to evil opinion (Lane's Lexicon, p. 1573), i.e. he fears for his friend the accidents of time.

[3] يابْنَ ٱلْخَبِيثَةِ *O son of the vile woman:* An example of playful abuse.

[4] ٱلقَرَم *Greediness:* Literally, intense longing for meat.

'Beware of these two! Verily generosity is quicker in consuming wealth than the moth-worm[1] is in wool, and greediness is more unlucky than Basús.[2] Do not quote me their saying, "Verily God is generous", that is a ruse to wean the child. Yea, verily God is indeed generous, but God's generosity increases us but does not decrease Him; it benefits us, but does not injure Him. Now whoever is in this condition let him be generous. But a generosity that does not increase thee till it decreases me, that does not feather thee till it plucks me,[3] is an abandonment, I will not say[4] a fiendish one but a fatal one. Hast thou

[1] أَسْرَعُ مِنَ ٱلسُّوسِ *Quicker than the moth-worm:* The proverb is آكَلُ مِنَ ٱلسُّوسِ more voracious than the moth-worm. See *Arab Proverbs*, i. 133.

[2] أَشْأَمُ مِنَ ٱلْبَسُوسِ More *unlucky than al-Basús:* (Freytag, *Arab Proverbs*, i, 683). Al-Basús was the daughter of Munqaḍ the Temímite and aunt of Jessas ibn Múrrah. She had a neighbour named Sa'd, and his she-camel named Seráb (See *Arab Proverbs*, i, 704) having trespassed on the guarded domain of Kulayb Wail, the powerful chief of the stock Rabiah, Kulayb shot it. Jessas, incited by al-Basús, who was enraged at this outrage upon her neighbour, slew Kulayb and the feud began between the tribe of Taghlib, of which Kulayb's brother Muhalhil was now chief, and the tribe of Bakr. This war, which lasted forty years, ended in the utter defeat of the tribe of Taghlib. *Ḥariri*, i, 307 and *Aghání*, iv, 139-151.

[3] *That does not feather thee till it plucks* (Literally, pares) *me:* Cf. the proverbial expression. فُلَانٌ لَا يَرِيشُ وَلَا يَبْرِي such a one neither profits nor injures.

[4] لَا أَقُولُ عَبْقَرِيٌّ وَلَـٰكِن بَقَرِيٌّ *I will not say 'Abqari but Baqari':* This is one of the several indigestible morsels to be found in this maqáma. As regards the first word the legend is that عَبْقَر (Abqar) was a resident of the Jinn. So that whoever does a thing superlatively well is said to be a sprite of Abqarí. (See De Sacy, *Hariri*, i, 257), لَا يُبَارِي عَبْقَرِيَّهُ 'whose sprite is not to be vied with'. Hence it came to mean some one pre-eminent; e.g. the Prophet related in a dream mentioning 'Umar, وَلَمْ أَرَ عَبْقَرِيًّا يَفْرِي فَرِيَّهُ 'and I have not seen a chief of a people do his wonderful deed.' Literally, strike his stroke. It is applied as an epithet denoting superlativeness of any quality. As used by Zuheir:

بِخَيْلٍ عَلَيْهَا جِنَّةٌ عَبْقَرِيَّةٌ * جَدِيرُونَ يَوْمًا أَنْ يَنَالُوا فَيَسْتَعْلُوا

'With horses upon which were demons
Deserving to get what they sought and to conquer the foe.'

(Shu'ará Nasrániah, p. 570, edited by Sheikho, Beyrut).

Al-Sam'ání shows 'Abkar to have been a real person who was remarkable for his great strength (*Ansab*, p. 382, line 24). Cf. Herculean. It is, therefore, clear, when the Arabs wish to exaggerate the description of a thing, they call it 'Abqarí.

بُقْرِيٌّ or بَقَرِيٌّ *Baqari* is applied to those who dwell with a man and

understood them, O son of the unlucky woman? Verily merchandise brings water out of the stones.[1] And imagine between one meal and another an ocean gale, except that there is no danger, and the distance to China, except that there is no travel. Wilt thou abandon it when it is presented and then seek it where it is not to be had? Perish thy mother! Hast thou understood them both?

Verily it is wealth—May God bless thee!—therefore be sure not to spend except from the profits. Thou shouldest eat bread and salt, and thou hast permission in regard to vinegar and onions, as long as thou feelest no repugnance towards them and dost not unite them. And flesh is as valuable as thine own flesh and methinks thou eatest it not. And sweetmeat is the food of him who cares not on which side he falls.[2] And one meal a day[3] is the fare of the pious. And eating, when hungry, is a protection against loss, but, when sated, it invites death. Then be with people like the chess[4] player, take all they have and keep all thou hast. O my dear son, I have caused thee to hear and delivered the message, therefore, if thou accept it, God will be sufficient for thee, but, if thou reject it, God will be thy reckoner. God bless our Lord Muhammad, his family and his companions all.'

whose maintenance is incumbent upon him, and, therefore, *dependents*; or بَقَرِىٌّ Relating to the ox, ox disease or bulimy.

If 'I will not say', etc., be taken as qualifying 'abandonment' the interpretation will be as in the translation, but if regarded as qualifying 'generosity' the rendering would be: 'I will not call it (generosity), something superlatively good but a deadly evil.'

[1] إِنَّمَا ٱلتِّجَارَةُ تُنبِطُ ٱلْمَاءَ مِنَ ٱلْحِجَارَةِ *Merchandise brings water out of the stones*: Apparently a proverbial saying. Cf. maqáma, xxii.

[2] *Who cares not on which side he falls*: Said of one who deliberately does something which will ruin him.

[3] اَلْوَجَبَاتُ *One meal a day*: From وَجَبَ he ate once a day.

[4] اَلشِّطْرَنْجُ *Chess*: Arabicized from Old Persian Chatranj, Sanskrit Chaturanga, literally, the four angles, or members of an army (elephants, horses, chariots, foot-soldiers). See Letters, p. 393, where there is a composition almost identical with this maqáma. The conventional concluding lines are wanting. Cf. *Hariri*, ii, 654.

XLII. THE MAQAMA OF SAIMARA

'ÍSÁ IBN HISHÁM related to us and said: Said Muhammad ibn Isḥáq, popularly known as Abú'l-'Anbas of Ṣaimara:[1] 'Of the things that have come down to me from my brethren whom I chose, selected, and stored up against calamities, wherein was a matter which has in it admonition, warning and education for such persons as will take them, that it is to say, I was coming from Ṣaimara to the City of Peace and I had bags of dinars, furniture, equipment, etc., on account of which I needed no one. So I associated with people of great families, secretaries of state, merchants, leading men of fame, from among men of wealth, fortune, and opulence, and owners of estates; a company that I selected for social intercourse and treasured for adversity.'

And we ceased not indulging in the morning and the evening draughts, feeding on sucking-kids, Persian omelets[2] minced meat *a la Ibrahím*,[3] pungent fried meats, kabob[4] *a la Rashíd*,[5] and lamb. And our drink was mead, and our singing was by beautiful and skilled ladies of world renown. Our dessert was peeled almonds, sugar, and sugar-candy.[6] And our sweet-smelling flower was the rose and our perfume was *Nad*. And because of my liberality, my generosity and the squandering of my store, I was, in their opinion, wiser than 'Abd-Alláh ibn

1 *Ṣaimara:* A town near Baṣra. Muḥammad ibn Isḥáq ibn Ibrahim ibn 'Alí al-'Absi, generally known as Abú'l-'Anbas of Ṣaimara (d. A.H. 275) was a cultured poet, a celebrated wit, a famous raconteur, and the author of about thirty-four works on a variety of subjects, several of them of a humorous character. He held the office of Qáḍí of Ṣaimara and was the boon companion of the Khalifa Mutawakkil (assassinated A.H. 247). (Yaqút, vi, 401; iii, 443.)

2 ألطّبا هجات ألفارسيّة *Persian omelets:* A food of a species of flesh-meat, eggs, onions, and water, arabicized from the Persian تباهه or تباهچه

3 *A la Ibrahím:* That is, Ibrahim al-Mehdí, the brother of Hárún al-Rashíd, who is supposed to have been very fond of this dish, born A.H. 162, died A.H. 224. Ibn Khallikan, i, 16.

4 *Kabob:* A well-known word, applied to small morsels of meat generally roasted on skewers, said to be Persian.

5 *A la Rashid:* Relating to the Khalifa Hárún al-Rashid.

ألطّبرزد *Sugar-candy:* Literally, sugar chopped with an axe, or hatchet, arabicized from the Persian تبر an axe and زد *perf.* of زدن to strike.

'Abbás,[1] wittier than Ahú Núwás, more generous than Haṭim,[2] braver than 'Amr,[3] more eloquent than Sahbán Wá'il,[4] more artful than Qáṣir,[5] a greater poet than Jarir, sweeter than the water of the Euphrates, and more delightful than health.[6] But, when the cargo became light, the sails collapsed, and the bag was empty, the company hastened to the door, when they perceived the fact.

Disgust[7] entered their hearts and they called me Burṣeh,[8]

1 *Ibn 'Abbás:* Abd Alláh ibn 'Abbás, cousin to Muḥammad, was born at Mecca A.D. 619, three years before the Hijra. He was the ablest of the expounders of the Qur'án in his time and the most liberal of the early Muslims. He was remarkable for his great knowledge, acuteness and prodigious memory. It was due to his efforts that the study of pre-Islámic poetry became of such importance to the Muslims, for he frequently quoted verses of the ancient poets in proof of the explanations he gave of difficult passages of the Qur'án. He used to say: 'Whenever you meet with a difficulty in the Qur'án look for its solution in the poems of the Arabs, for these are the registers of the Arab nation.' He was for some time governor of Baṣra under the Khalifa 'Alí; died at al-Ṭaif A.H. 68. Ibn Khallikan, i, 89.

2 *More generous than Haṭim:* Of the tribe of Tai. The prototype of generosity throughout the Muslim world.

3 *'Amr:* 'Amr ibn Ma'dí Karaba. This chieftain and warrior was a contemporary of Muḥammad and the first four Khalifas. For his adventures, see Caussin de Percival, *Essaie sur l'histoire des Arabes.*

4 *More eloquent than Sahbán Wá'il:* A brilliant preacher of the early days of Islám, whose name became proverbial for eloquence like that of Qoss, Bishop of Najran. He was born in the time of Muḥammad and died in the year A.H. 54 (A.D. 673). One of the earliest extant specimens of an Arab Khutba, or sermon in rhymed prose, is by Saḥbán. This sermon contains the usual incentives to morality founded on the shortness of life and the certainty of future reward and punishment. Freytag, *Arab Proverbs*, i, 450. See De Sacy, *Ḥariri*, i, 49 and Chenery's Translation of *Ḥariri*, p. 309.

5 *More artful than Qáṣir:* Qáṣír was a freedman of Júdhíma al-Abrash, the king of 'Iráq. His master having been treacherously murdered by Queen Zebba (Zenobie) he determined to revenge his death on her. He cut off his nose with his own hand and complained to the Queen that 'Amr, the murdered Jadhíma's nephew, had done this, because he suspected him of complicity in the betrayal of his master. So plausible a story found ready acceptance with the queen. In this way he gained her confidence and was frequently sent to 'Iráq to bring her some of the rare products of that province until, eventually, he contrived to introduce in boxes, supposed to contain goods, a number of armed men who fell upon the queen and slew her. This act of self-mutilation gave rise to the proverb: 'For some purpose Qáṣír cut off his nose.' *Ḥariri*, i, 327.

6 أطيب من العافية *More delightful than health:* Cf. the proverb أطيب من الحياة—More delightful than life. Meidaní, i, 388. Bulak edition.

7 غصّة *Disgust:* Literally, choking.

8 برصة *Burṣeh: Barren spot:* White places in sand where nothing grows,

and they arose with alacrity to flee, like shooting sparks of fire. Vexation took possession of them and they slipped away drop by drop,[1] and they dispersed right and left and I remained on the floor.[2] They bequeathed to me regret, and, because of them, tears overwhelmed me. I was not worth a piece of dung, alone, solitary, like the owl branded with ill-luck, sitting down and standing up as if the state in which I had been had never been.

And I repented when repentance availed me not. Therefore was my comeliness changed to wildness. A deafness came over me worse than that of Rahta the crier. As though I were a monk of the people of al-Hira.[3] The property had gone and derision was left, and there was in my hand only the she-goat's tail.[4] I found myself in my house alone, with my liver crushed, because of the fall of my fortune. My tears had furrowed my cheek. I dwelt in an abode whose ruins had been obliterated and whose traces the torrents had effaced, and where the wild beasts roamed and strayed morning and evening. My position had gone, my substance was exhausted and my comfort[5] was diminished. My boon-companions and my old friends deserted me. No head was raised for me and I was not reckoned among the people. More contemptible than Baz'i the pottage-maker and Warzín the rope-maker. I wandered to and fro on the river bank as if I were a keeper of ducks.[6] I walked barefoot,

also an alighting-place of the Jinn. The commentator thinks it means a lizard of the species called *gecko*. كَيكَق (Malay), an imitation of the animal's cry, of a leprous hue as its name (بُرَمَة) indicates, but in that case it would have to be vocalized بَرَص I have, therefore, rendered it by 'barren spot' as being more consistent with 'Abú'l-'Anbas' circumstances.

1 *Drop by drop*: That is, quickly as drops fall away from the cloud.

2 الآجُرَّة *The floor*: Literally, the bricks, arabicized from the Persian آكور baked clay. A loan word from Aramaic.

3 عُبَّادِى *The people of al-Ḥira*: The term applied to the Christian Arabs of Ḥira. The religion and culture of the 'Ibbád were conveyed by various channels to the utmost recesses of the peninsula. See Nicholson, *Lit. History of the Arabs*, pp. 38-9.

4 *The she-goat's tail*: Figurative for something mean and worthless.

5 مَرَاحِى *My comfort*: Gives a better sense than مُرَاحى 'my nightly resting-place' according to the vocalization of the text.

6 بَطّ *Ducks*: Arabicized from the Persian بت.

scouring the deserts.[1] My eye was inflamed and my life was in pledge, as though I were a madman escaped from a cell, or an ass going around the enclosure.

I was sadder than al-Khansa[2] over Ṣakhr, and Hind[3] over 'Amr. My reason was lost, my health was good for nothing, my purse was empty and my slave had fled. My evil dreams multiplied and in evil suggestions I exceeded the limit. I became like the Jinn that inhabit houses and the evil spirit of the dwelling. I appeared in the night and hid in the day. I was unluckier than the grave-digger, more burdensome than the rent of the house, more stupid that Tiṭi the bleacher, and more foolish than Dáúd the oil-presser. Scantiness had become my ally and abjectness had encompassed me. And I was outside the pale of the community and hated for the sake of God. I had been Abú'l-'Anbas[4] and I became Abú 'Afllas[5] and Abú Faq'as. I had lost the road, and argument was against me.

I found no helper and I saw destitution before me. Now, when I perceived the affair had become difficult and that Time had the rabies, I solicited money and behold it was with the two vultures[6] and at the parting of the two seas,[7] and more remote

1 أتبعُ ٱلْفَيَافِى *Socuring* (literally, chasing) *the deserts.*

2 *Al-Khansa:* The most celebrated Arab poetess, especially noted for her elegies on her brother Ṣakhr. She was a contemporary of Muḥammad by whom she was received with great respect and to whom she recited her poetry. *Hariri*, ii, 516 and Chenery's translation, pp. 387-91.

3 *Hind:* The mother of 'Amr son of Mundhir III, King of al-Ḥíra, commonly called 'Amr son of Hind after his mother who was the aunt of Imr al-Qais. 'Amr ibn Hind was slain by the poet 'Amr ibn Kúlthúm, author of one of the Mu'allaqát, for an insult offered to his mother, Layla, by Hind. See *Aghání*, ix, 175.

4 أبو ٱلْعَنْبَس *Abú'l-'Anbas:* Literally, father of the frowning lion. There is a play here on the real and the nicknames. See *Harírì*, i, 380, where other such fanciful names are introduced.

5 أبو عَفْلَس *Abu 'Aflas:* I have not been able to trace, but أبو أفلس father of bankruptcy, a bankrupt, would give a suitable meaning.

6 ألنَّسرَين *The two vultures:* That is (1) ألنَّسرُ ٱلْوَاقِع The falling vulture. (2) ألنَّسر ٱلطَّائر The flying vulture.

The former is a bright star in the constellation Lyra, and the latter consists of three well-known stars in the constellation Aquila.

7 مُنقطَع ٱلْبَحرَين *The parting of the two seas:* That is of the salt water and the fresh. Cf. Qur'án, xxv, 55.

than the two pointers. So I started wandering, as though I was the Messiah,[1] and I journeyed over Khurasan, its deserted and populous parts, to Kirman, Sijistan, Jilan, Tabaristan, 'Oman, to Sind and India, to Nubia and Egypt, Yemen, Ḥijáz, Mecca and al-Ṭa'if. I roamed over deserts and wastes, seeking warmth at the fire and taking shelter with the ass, till both my cheeks were blackened. And thus I collected of anecdotes and fables,[2] witticisms and traditions, poems of the humourists, the diversions of the frivolous, the fabrications of the lovesick, the saws of the pseudo-philosophers, the tricks of the conjurors,[3] the artifices of the artful, the rare sayings of convivial companions, the fraud of the astrologers, the finesse of quacks, the deception of the effeminate, the guile of the cheats,[4] the devilry of the fiends, such that the legal decisions of al-Sh'abí,[5] the memory of al-Dabbi[6] and the learning of al-Kalbi[7] would have fallen short of.

And I solicited gifts and asked for presents. I had recourse to influence and I begged. I eulogized and satirized, till I acquired much property, got possession of Indian swords and Yemen blades, fine coats of mail of Sábur[8] and leathern shields

[1] *The Messiah :* This is a play on the word ٱلْمَسِيح one who travels much, as a devotee or otherwise, and the well-known name the Messiah, the Anointed.

[2] أسمار *Fables :* Literally, night-talkings.

[3] ٱلْمُشَعْوِذِين *The conjurors :* From شَعْوَذَة legerdemain. According to the lexicons it is not a word of the language of the people of the desert. Cf. Gaubari, *Endeckte Geheimnisse* (de Goeje. Z.D.M.G.) xx, 500.

[4] ٱلْجَرَابِزَة *Cheats :* Plural of جُرْبُز arabicized from the Persian گربز or گرپز

[5] *The decisions of al-Sh'abi :* Abú 'Amr (A.H. 19-104) was an eminent jurisconsult distinguished for his profound learning. al-Zuhrí (A.H. 51-124) says that the really learned men were four in number. (1) Ibn al-Musaiyab at Madína, (2) al-Sh'abi at Kufa, (3) Ḥasan al-Baṣri at Baṣra, and (4) Makhul in Syria. See Freytag, *Arab Proverbs*, i, 413 and Ibn Khallikan De Slane's translation, ii, 4.

[6] *The memory of Al-Dabbi :* Muḥammad ibn al-Mufaḍḍal (ob. A.H. 308) a native of Baghdad, was one of the most eminent doctors of the Sháfi'ite sect and an author of a number of works. Ibn Khallikan, ii, 610.

[7] *The learning of al-Kalbi :* Hishám ibn al-Kalbi was remarkable for his extensive knowledge of the science of genealogy, the battle days and the history of the Arabs on which subjects he wrote upwards of a hundred and fifty works. He died A.H. 204 or 206. Ibn Khallikan, iii, 608.

[8] ٱلسَّابِرِيَّة *Of Sábur :* Relating to King Shahpur, or to the town or province of that name situated twenty-five parasangs from Shiráz.

of Tibet, spears of al-Khaṭṭ[1] and javelins of Barbary, excellent fleet horses with short coats, Armenian mules, and Mirris[2] asses, silk brocades of Rúm and woollen stuffs[3] of Sús.[4] Various kinds of curios, presents, offerings, and gifts, with prosperity and opulence.

Now, when I arrived at Baghdad and the people got news of me, and of how I had been prospered in my travels, they were delighted at my arrival, and they all came to me complaining of what loneliness they had experienced on account of my being away, and what had happened to them because of my absence, and they complained of the intensity of longing and the pain of yearning. And each of them began to apologize for what he had done and to manifest regret for what he had committed. So I made them think I had forgiven them and I did not exhibit to them a sign of vindictiveness because of their conduct. Therefore they were pleased, their limbs ceased trembling, and they went away in that belief.

The next day they returned to me and I detained them with me. Then I dispatched my agent to the market and he did not omit a thing of all that I had charged him to buy. We had a skilful female cook, and I got prepared twenty sorts of pungent fried-meats, divers kinds of omelets, and rare preparations. We ate and then adjourned to the drinking-saloon, and there were presented before them bright and clear old wine[5] and fair and expert singers.

1 *Al-Khaṭṭ:* A place on the coast of 'Omán to which lances and spears were exported and where they were straightened and then sold to the Arabs.

2 مِرِّيس مِرِّيسة *Mirrisah:* The name of a village, or province, in Egypt famous for the excellence of its mules. Yaqût, iv, 515.

3 خز *Khaz, A woollen stuff.* A cloth woven of wool and silk said to be arabicized from the Persian قز *Qaz*, raw silk.

4 السُّوس *Sús:* A district in Ahwáz. There are several places of this name given in Yaqût, iii, 189.

5 خَنْدَرِيسَة *Old wine:* Dozy calls it *Vin Grec.* It may therefore be arabicized from the Greek χόνδρος, groats of wheat, a mucilaginous drink made of groats of wheat. The expressions حِنْطَة خَنْدَرِيسَة old wheat and تَمْر خَنْدَرِيس old dates are suggestive as referring, by an extension of meaning, to the kind of wheat and date suitable for making wine. See Gawálíkí, *Almu'arrab*, p. 55.

They betook themselves to their task and we drank, and there passed for us the pleasantest day. Now I had prepared, according to their number, fifteen brinjal baskets, each basket with four handles.[1] And my slave had hired for each one of them a porter, each porter at two dirhems, and he had informed the porters of the houses of the company, and charged them to present themselves the next evening. And I commanded my slave, who was a crafty one, to give the company to drink by the pint and by the quart,[2] and to serve them while I fumigated before them with nad, aloes and ambergris. Before an hour had passed they[3] were all dead drunk and unconscious. Their slaves came to us at sunset each one with a horse, or an ass, or a mule, but I told them their masters were passing the night with me and so they went away. Then I sent for Bilál, the barber, and I brought him in. I placed food before him and he ate. I gave him wine of Quṭrubbul and he drank till he became intoxicated. Then I placed in his mouth two yellow[4] dinars and said, 'Do your duty to the company.' And in a single hour he shaved off fifteen beards, and the company became as smooth-faced as the denizens of Paradise.[5]

I placed the beard of each one of them pursed in his clothes and with it a letter wherein was written, 'Whoever harbours perfidy against his friend and forsakes faithfulness, this is his recompense and reward,' and I put it in his pocket. Then we tied them up in the baskets. The porters came the next evening and carried them off with a losing return and they reached their homes. But, when they arose in the morning, they perceived in themselves great grief. Not a merchant from among them went forth to his shop, not a clerk to his office, nor could he appear before his brethren. And every day a large crowd of their

1 آذَان *Handles*: Literally, ears.

2 ٱلْمَنَ وَٱلرِّطْل *By the pint and by the quart*: A *mann* equals 2 lbs. troy and a *ratl* 1 lb. avoirdupois.

3 هُم *They*: That is, the company.

4 أحْمَرَين *Yellow*: Literally, red.

5 كَأَهْلِ ٱلْجَنَّة *As the denizens of Paradise*: An allusion to the tradition which says the people of Paradise are جُرْدٌ مُرْدٌ having no hair upon their bodies and beardless (Lane. p. 407).

dependents, women, boys and men, came and reviled and reproached me, and invoked upon me divine judgement, but I remained silent and did not return them an answer, nor did I heed their words. The news of my treatment of them spread over the City of Peace, and the matter ceased not to magnify until it reached the Wazir al-Qasim ibn 'Ubeid-Alláh,[1] in this wise. He wanted his clerk but failed to find him and it was reported: 'He is at home and unable to go out.' He asked: 'Why?' And it was said: 'Because of what Abú'l-'Anbas has done to him for he had the misfortune of being associated with and tried by him.' He laughed heartily and said: 'By Heavens he was perfectly right to do what he did,[2] let him alone, for he understands them best.' Then he sent me a splendid robe of honour, had led to me a horse with a carriage and forwarded to me fifty thousand dirhems as a mark of his admiration of my action. I stayed at home for two months, spending, eating and drinking and then I appeared in public, after concealment, and some of them reconciled themselves to me because of what the Wazir had done; and another swore by the triple divorce[3] and by the emancipation of his slaves, male and female, that he would never again speak directly to me. By God, whose dignity is great, and whose evidence is exalted! I did not make much of that, nor did I care, nor was the lobe of my ear scratched, nor did my stomach ache. Neither did it injure me, rather did it delight me, and 'it was a need in Jacob's soul which he

[1] *Al-Qasim ibn 'Ubeid-Alláh:* If we accept Yaqút's statement (*Geographical Dictionary*, iii, 443; *Dictionary of Learned Men*, vi, 401) that Abú'l-'Anbas died A.H. 275, this is chronologically impossible. Al-Qasim ibn 'Ubeid-Alláh ibn Suleiman ibn Wahb was appointed Wazír in A.H. 288, so that the Wazír referred to in the narrative must have been al-Qasim's father 'Ubeid-Alláh ibn Suleiman ibn Wahb the Wazir of Mu'tamid and Mu'taḍid.

It was this al-Qasim 'Ubeid-Alláh who poisoned Ibn al-Rúmí (see note on p. 116), because he dreaded the poet's satirical attacks. Here again there is some confusion of dates. Ibn Khallikan, ii, 299, gives the date of Ibn al-Rúmí's death as 284 or 276, whereas al-Qasim ibn 'Ubeid-Alláh was not appointed Wazir until his father's death which took place in A.H. 288. See al-Fakhrí (edited by Ahlwardt), pp. 301-3.

[2] لقد أصاب وما أخطأ فيما فعل *He was perfectly right to do what he did:* Literally, he hit and did not miss in what he did.

[3] بالطّلاق الثّلاث *By the triple divorce:* 'Ye may divorce your wives twice, but, if the husband divorce her a third time she shall not be lawful for him again until she marry another husband.' Qur'án, ii, 229, 230.

performed.' [1] And verily I have only called attention to this that people may be on their guard against the sons of the time, and give up depending on sordid and base brethren, and upon so-and-so, the copyist, the calumniator, the great deceiver who repudiates the claims of the cultured, makes light of them and borrows their books and does not return them. And we implore God's aid and we rely upon Him.

XLIII. THE MAQAMA OF THE DINAR

'ÍSÁ IBN HISHÁM related to us and said: I happened to have made a vow to give a dinar in charity to the greatest mendicant in Baghdad. I enquired for him and I was directed to Abú'l Fatḥ al-Iskanderí. So I went to him to bestow it upon him, and I found him amongst some companions who had gathered in a circle around him. So I said: 'O sons of Sásán, which of you knows his stock-in-trade best and is the sharpest in his art so that I may give him this dinar?' Said al-Iskanderí: 'I am.' Another of the company said: 'Nay, but I am.' Then they wrangled and disputed till I said: 'Let each of you revile his fellow, then whoever gains the mastery carries off the booty, and whoever overcomes takes the spoil.' [2] So al-Iskanderí said: 'O cold of the old woman! [3] O sultriness of Tammuz! [4] O

[1] *It was a need in Jacob's soul which he performed:* Qur'án, xii, 67, 68. When Jacob's sons went the second time down into Egypt taking Benjamin with them, their father commanded them not to enter all at the same gate but at several. This is explained to mean that, because of their personal beauty and the favour shown them by the governor, if they all entered by the snme gate, they might be smitten with the evil eye. This they did and, though they could not have changed God's will concerning them, still it satisfied a desire in Jacob's mind. Baiḍáwí's commentary (Fleischer), i, 466.

Abú'l-'Anbas died eighty-three years before Hamadhání was born. It is evident, therefore, that this maqáma is founded on a popular story, handed down from the former, or extracted from one of the numerous works of a humourous character he is said to have composed.

This lengthy maqáma contains no poetry.

Cf. Shakespeare, *Timon of Athens*; the themes are identical.

[2] مَن عزّ بزّ *Whoever overcomes takes the spoil:* Freytag, *Arab Proverbs*, i, 677, Cf. Hebrew בַּז spoil.

[3] *Cold of the old woman:* That is, the four last days of February and three first days of March, thus called because they are the latter part (عَجُز) of winter.

[4] *Tammuz:* The Syrian month sacred in ancient times to the god of that name, corresponding to July. This god is mentioned in *Ezekiel*, viii, 14.

filth of the goglet![1] O non-current dirhem! O conversation of the singers![2] O unfortunate year! O unlucky star! O oppression of the nightmare![3] O sick headache! O Ummú Hubein![4] O ophthalmia! O morning of separation! O estrangement of friends! O hour of death! O scene of the martyrdom of al-Husain! O burden of debt! O mark of infamy! O ill-starred messenger! O banished for his meanness! O porridge of garlic! O desert of the *Zaqqum*![5] O refuser to lend the things of the house! O year of the bubonic plague! O rebellious slave! O damnatory clause! O oft-repeated speech! O worse than حَتّى (*till*) in various constructions! O worm of the privy! O furred garment in the summer-quarters! O coughing of the host, when the bread is broken! O belch of the intoxicated! O fetid breath of the hawks! O peg of the tent![6] O prop[7] of the pot! O non-recurring Wednesday![8] O avarice of the vanquished at dice! O grumbling of the tongue! O *lotium spadonis!* O eating of the blind! O intercession of the naked![9] O Saturday of the children![10] O letter of condolence![11] O pool of impurities! O

1 الكُوز *Al-Kúz:* A water-bottle, a goglet, arabicized from the Persian كوزه.

2 *Conversation of the singers:* Obviously it is the singing of the singers and not their conversation that people want to hear.

3 وَطْأُ الكابوس *Oppression of the nightmare:* Some think this is not an Arabic word and that the proper word is نَيدُلان (Lane, p. 2588). I see no difficulty, however, in evolving this meaning from the root كَبَسَ he pressed or squeezed.

4 *Ummu Hubein:* A species of stinking lizard.

5 *Zaqqum:* A certain kind of tree having small leaves, evil-smelling and bitter, found in Tehameh, also the name of the infernal tree whose fruit is the food of the people of hell. See Baiḍáwí, ii, 172.

6 O *peg of the tent:* Cf. more dishevelled than a tent peg. Freytag, *Arab Proverbs*, i, 706.

7 خُذْرُوفَة *Prop:* Literally, the handle of the upper millstone.

8 أَرْبِعاءُ لا تَدُور *Non-recurring Wednesday:* The unlucky Wednesdays of the month, to which this is an allusion, are those which have the number four, e.g. the fourth or the fourteenth of the month; the fourteenth or twenty-fourth, or the fourth before the end of the month. Mas'údí, *Les Prairies D'or*, iii, 422. Freytag, *Arab Proverbs*, i, 276 and Meidání (Bulak edition), i, 139, when it comes at the end of the month.

9 O *intercession of the naked:* That is, one who is so utterly destitute that he needs to ask for himself, not for others. For the opposite sentiment, see *Aghání*, viii, 182.

10 O *Saturday of the children:* Succeeding the holiday on Friday. Cf. English school slang, Black Monday.

11 O *letter of condolence!* Because it is supposed to be a very difficult thing

stinginess of the man of Ahwaz![1] O garrulousness of the man of Rayy![2] By Heavens! if thou wert to place one of thy feet on Arwand[3] and the other on Demawand,[4] take in thy hand the rainbow and card the clouds in the garments of the angels, thou wouldst only be a wool-carder!'

Then said the other: 'O trainer of monkeys! O felt of the Jews! O fetid breath of the lions! O non-entity in existence! O dog in strife! O monkey on the carpet! O pumpkin with pulse![5] O less than nothing! O fumes of naphtha![6] O stench of the armpit! O decline of power! O halo of death! O viler than one to whom clings the disgrace of divorce and refuses to return the marriage dowry! O mud of the road! O water taken in the state of fasting![7] O shaker of the bone![8] O accelerator of digestion! O tartar of the teeth! O filth of the ears! O tougher than the rope of cocoanut fibre! O less than a *fals!*[9] O more traitorous than a tear! O more rebellious than a needle! O direction of the boot! O landing-place of the palms! O the word 'would that'! O leaking of the house! O such and

to write if the deceased is not a near relative, or because it is a painful thing for one who is bereaved to read.

1 *Stinginess of the man of Ahwaz:* The people of Ahwaz were notorious for their avarice, stupidity and the vileness of their inclinations. Yaqút, i, 411, 12.

2 *Garrulousness of the man of Rayy:* The word فُضُول also means meddlesomeness, or immoderation of any kind, but I have not been able to find any evidence that the people of Rayy were notorious for any of these things.

3 *Arwand:* or Elwand, the Orontes of the ancients, at the foot of which lies the town of Hamadhán.

4 *Demawand:* A mountain north of Teheran. His feet would thus be more than two hundred miles apart!

5 ماش *Pulse:* Arabicized from the Persian ماش Sanskrit másha, peas.

6 *O fumes of naphtha!:* Apparently a genuine Arabic word from نَبَطَ. It (water) welled or issued forth, and نَبَطٌ what oozes or exudes from a mountain as though it were sweat from the sides of the rock. (Lane's Lexicon art. نَبَطَ p. 2759) Cf. Greek ναφθα which is probably a loan word from Arabic.

7 عَلَى آلرِّيق *In a state of fasting:* Anything eaten or drunk in a state of fasting. The text is wrongly vocalized, *for* آلرِّيقَ *read* آلرِّيق.

8 *Shaker of the bone:* That is, ague.

9 فَلْسٌ *A fals:* A small copper coin, the forty-eighth part of a dirhem, i.e. about half a farthing. A loan word from Aramaic.

such![1] By Heavens! wert thou to place thy *seant* on the stars and extend thy feet to the limits of the world, take Sirius as a boot and the Pleiades as a raiment, and wert to make the sky a loom, weave the air into a coat, make its woof with the Flying Vulture and weave it with the revolving sphere, thou wouldest be but a weaver!' [2]

Said 'Ísá ibn Hishám: 'By Heavens! I did not know which of the two I should prefer, for nought proceeded from them save marvellous language, wonderful aptness, and intense enmity. So I left the dinar before them undivided and I know not what Time did with them.'

XLIV. THE MAQAMA OF POETRY

'Ísá ibn Hishám related to us and said: I was in the region of Syria and there joined me a party of travelling companions. Now one day we were assembled together in a circle and we began to discuss poetry and to quote verses difficult in meaning, and to propound enigmas. And there stood near us a youth who listened, as though he understood, and remained silent as if he regretted doing so. So I said: 'O young man, thy standing up annoys us, therefore either sit down or go away.' He replied: 'It is impossible for me to sit down, but I will go away and return, so keep your places.' We said: 'We will do that with pleasure.' Then he withdrew his presence, but he delayed not to return immediately. And he asked: 'Where are ye with those verses and what have ye done with the puzzles? Ask me concerning them.' And we asked him not a verse but he answered, nor a meaning but he correctly explained it. Now, when we had emptied the quivers, and made an end of the stores, he turned upon us interrogatively, renewed the discussion

[1] *O such and such*: Or 'so and so', referring to something too gross to mention. Cf. *Harírí*, p. 235, line 3., and see Wright's Grammar, i, 268

[2] حائك *A weaver*: The vocation of the weaver appears to have been regarded by the Arabs as a degrading one. Cf. Letters, p. 273, 'Verily shaving is learnt on the heads of the weavers', also Yaqút, *Geographical Dictionary*, iv, 1036. Cf. *Harírí*, p. 31, on the subject of the dinar, and p. 628 for an example of similar mutual abuse; also see Horace, *Satires*, Book I, Satire 7.

This maqáma contains no poetry.

and said: 'Tell me what verse is that, half of which elevates and half repels? And what verse is it the whole of which slaps? And what verse is that half of which is angry and half jests? And what verse is it the whole of which is mangy? And what verse is that the last foot of whose first half fights, and the final foot of whose second half conciliates? What verse is that whose whole is scorpions? What verse is that which is unseemly in original intent but can be made proper by punctuation.[1] What verse is that whose tears cease not to flow?[2] What verse is that all of which runs away except its foot? What verse is that whose subject is not known?[3] What verse is that which is longer than its fellow, as though it were not of its kind?[4]

What verse is that which cannot be dissolved, and whose soil cannot be dug? What verse is that half of which is perfect and half clothes? What verse is that whose number cannot be counted? What verse is that which shows thee what pleases? What verse is that which the world cannot contain? What verse is that half of which laughs and half feels pain? What verse is that if its branch be shaken, its beauty departs? What verse is that if we collect it together, its meaning is gone? What verse is that if we set it at liberty, we cause it to go astray? What verse is that whose honey is poison? What verse is that whose praise is censure? What verse is that whose expression is sweet, but underlying it there is grief? What verse is that whose dissolving is binding up, and the whole of it is paid down? What verse is that half of which is prolongation and half rejection? What verse is that half of which is elevation and its elevation is a slap? What verse is that whose expulsion is eulogy, but whose converse is censure? What verse is that which, in a visitation, is a prayer for the time of peril?[5] What verse is that which the sheep eat when they please?

[1] *Proper by punctuation:* Cf. Maqáma xxviii.

[2] *Whose tears cease not to flow:* Cf. Maqáma xxviii.

[3] *Whose subject is not known:* Cf. Maqáma xxviii.

[4] *Of its kind:* Cf. Maqáma xxviii.

[5] صَلَاةُ ٱلْخَوف *A prayer for the time of peril:* In cases of extreme danger in lieu of the rak'as or genuflexions, the bowing of the head is sufficient. See *Minháj al-Ṭálibín*, par Van Den Berg, 181-5.

What verse is that which when it hits the head, smashes the teeth? What verse is that which extends till it reaches six pounds? What verse is it that stood up, then fell down and went to sleep? What verse is it that wished to decrease, but increased? What verse is it that was about to go and then returned? What verse destroyed 'Iráq[1]? What verse conquered Baṣra? What verse is it that melted under torture?

What verse grew old before adolescence? What verse is it that returned before the appointed time? What verse is it that alighted and then passed away? What verse is it that was tightly twisted and then became strong? What verse is that, which was adjusted till it became rectified? What verse is that which is swifter than Tirimmaḥ's arrow?[2] What verse is it that issued from their eyes? What verse is it that contracted, and then sufficed to fill the world? What verse is it that returned and excited pain? What verse is that half of which is gold and the remainder tail? What verse is that some of which is darkness and some of which is wine? What verse is that whose subject is converted into the object, and whose understanding is made to be understood? What verse is that the whole of which is inviolate? What two verses are like a string of camels? What verse is it that descends from above? What verse is that whose prognostication is ominous? What verse is that whose end flees but whose beginning seeks? What verse is that whose beginning gives, but whose end plunders?'

Said 'Ísá ibn Hishám: 'Thus did we hear something which we had never heard before. So we asked for the explanation, but he denied it to us, and, therefore, we considered them to be words finely hewn, but with no ideas underlying them. Then he said: 'Choose five of these problems so that I may explain them, and do ye exert yourselves a few days in finding out the rest. It may be that your vessel will sweat, and your minds be generous. Then, if ye fail, let us have a fresh reunion in order that I may explain the remainder.'

And among those we selected was the verse which is

[1] *Destroyed Iráq*, Text, p. 224, line 3 *for* حَرَبَ *read* خَرَّبَ.

[2] *Ṭirimmáḥ's arrow*: Ṭirimmáḥ ibn Ḥakím ibn al-Ḥakam, the name of a famous poet, a contemporary of Dhú al-Rumma (ob. 117 A.H.) I have not been able to find anything to connect the poet with archery.

unseemly in original intent but can be made proper by punctuation. So we asked him concerning it, and he said: 'It is the verse of Abú Núwás:—

> And we passed the night,[1] God regarding us as the vilest company, trailing the skirts of wickedness, and no boast.'

We asked: 'And the verse whose dissolving is binding up and the whole of it is paid down?' He replied: 'It is the verse of Al 'Aasha,—

> All our dirhems are good,[2] so delay us not by testing them.'

And the paraphrase of that would be to say: 'Our dirhems are good, all of them, so delay us not by testing them.' Now the metre is not destroyed by this paraphrase. We asked: 'And the verse half of which is prolongation and half rejection?' He replied: 'It is the verse of al-Bakri,[3]

> A genuine dinar came to thee[4] short of sixty fals,
> From the most generous of men, except as regards origin, development and personality.

We asked: 'And the verse that the sheep eat when they please?' He said: 'It is the verse of the poet:

> "May separation be cut off![5] May separation be severed!
> I perceive separation[6] to be a great severer of friends."'

We asked: 'And the verse which extends till it reaches six pounds?' He replied: 'It is the verse of Ibn al-Rúmí,

> "When he gives,[7] he makes not his gift an obligation and he says to my soul, O soul respite me."'

1 *And we passed the night.* Metre *ṭawíl.*

2 *All our dirhems are good:* Metre, *mutaqárib.*

3 *Al-Bakri:* For further specimens of this early poet's verses, see *Aghání*, iv, 143, 146, and 147.

4 *A genuine dinar came to thee:* Metre, *mujtath.*

5 *May separation be cut off:* Metre, *ṭawíl.*

6 النّوى *Separation:* The point here is the double meaning of نوى 'separation' and the plural of نواة a date stone. I am unable to say, however, whether sheep eat these stones.

7 *When he gives:* Metre *ṭawíl.* اذا منّ *When he gives*—The play is on منّ which means, 'he bestowed', and a certain weight which is generally considered as equal to two pounds troy weight. The repetition of this word four times works out exactly six ratls or pounds.

Said 'Ísá ibn Hishám: Then we knew that the problems were not destitute of beauty.[1] So we tried hard and we found out some, and obtained information about the others. Then I recited after him, while he was running quickly away:—

'Men differ in excellence[2] and some resemble others,
But for him I should have been like Raḍwá[3] in length, depth and breadth.'

[1] لَيْسَتْ عَوَاطِل *Not destitute of beauty.* From عَاطِل applied to a woman who is unadorned with a necklace, the emblem of female dignity.

[2] *Men differ in excellence:* Metre, *mujtath.*

[3] كَرَضْوَى *Like Raḍwá:* There are several mountains of this name in Arabia. The one alluded to is probably that near Madina which the Arabs quote as synonymous with something weighty and responsible. Cf. the line by Mú'arrí cited by the Commentator, Text, p. 226: 'And the weight of Raḍwá is less than that which I bear'.

SOLUTIONS BY THE COMMENTATOR:

The verse half of which elevates and half repels:
'And I have one side of my life for God which I do not waste,
'And I have another side for discussion and depravity.'

The verse half of which is angry and half jests: 'Amr ibn Kúlthúm's lines:
'As if our swords, ours and theirs, were wooden blades in the hands of players.'

The verse whose beginning gives, but whose end plunders, 'Amr ibn Kúlthúm's lines:—

'We entertained you and we hastened your entertainment,
A little before the morning, with the grinding of the millstone of war.'

The verse that cannot be dissolved: 'And verily He who hath raised the heavens hath built for us a house whose supports are most substantial and lofty.'

For an illustration of the meaning of سَمَكَ he raised, or elevated, see Qur'án, lxxix, 28.

The verse, if we set it at liberty, we cause it to go astray:
'Am I not in sorrow upon a worn-out camel,
Conducted by an experimenting guide followed by my heart?'

The verse that stood, then fell down and went to sleep:
'O ye sleepers! awake from your sleep!
I will ask you, does love kill a man?'

The verse, when its branch is shaken, its beauty departs:

'Thou hast such a form, that were it not for the hawks of thine eyes, the grey pigeon would surely sing upon it.'

The verse whose beginning seeks, but whose end flees

'With ignorance like the ignorance of the sword, when it is drawn.
And clemency like the clemency of the sword, when it is sheathed.'

The verse that was about to go away and then returned:

'And I am not one of those happy in enjoyment among them,
But I am a mine of glittering gold.'

XLV. THE MAQAMA OF KINGS

'ÍSÁ IBN HISHÁM related to us and said: I was on my way back from Yemen and making for my native land. I was journeying in a night when nothing auspicious save the hyena passed from the left, and nothing inauspicious from the right save a lion. Now when the blade of the morning was drawn, and the brow of the orb of day came forth, there appeared before me on the bare plain a rider fully armed. There seized me because of him, what seizes an unarmed person from the like of him when he advances. But I put on a bold front, stood and said: 'Perish thy mother! Stand! Before thou canst attain thy object thou wilt have to endure wounds of steel, strip the tragacanth of its leaves, and face the pride of an Azdite.[1] I am for peace[2] if thou wilt, but who art thou?' He answered: 'Peace hast thou found and a travelling companion according to thy desire.' I then said: 'Thou hast answered well.' So we travelled on and, when we had become mutually intimate and exchanged confidences, the story revealed Abú'l Fatḥ al-Iskanderí, and he asked me concerning the most generous of kings I had met. So I mentioned the kings of Syria and the generous ones among them, the kings of 'Iráq and the noble ones of them, and the Amirs of

The verse whose praise is blame:

'And verily my tribe, numerous though they be,
Are worthless in war, though it be an insignificant affair.' Freytag, *Ḥamasa*, p. 7.

The verse that contracted and then filled the world: 'It is not a hard thing for God to collect the world in a single individual'

The verse that was adjusted till it was rectified:

'Say not one piece of good news, but two—
The dignity of the host and the feast of Mehraján.

يوم ٱلمهرجان The feast (day) of Mehraján. The autumnal equinox, the name of a festival celebrated in Persia in the month of September. For the origin of this word see Mas'údí iii, 404. These lines were recited in praise of al-Ḥasan ibn Zaid the ruler of Tabaristán, died A.H. 270. (Ibn al-Athir, vii, 286.) The text is wrongly vocalized, *for* غُرَّة *Whiteness or blaze; read* عِزَّة dignity or puissance.

This maqáma is identical in theme with and largely a reproduction of No. xxviii. Cf. *Ḥariri*, ii, 453–70.

1 *An Azdite:* Azd the name of a famous Arab tribe to which the typical Arab heroes, Shanfara and Taabbata Sharrn, and the accomplished scholar and poet Ibn Duraid belonged.

2 *I am for peace:* Literally, I am peace.

the provinces, and I extended[1] the enumeration to the kings of Egypt. I narrated what I had seen and I recounted to him the benevolent acts of the kings of Yemen and the favours of the kings of Ṭá'if, and I concluded the praise of all by mentioning Saif al-Daula. Then he recited saying:—

'O nocturnal traveller[2] by the stars of the night, praising them,
Had he but seen the sun, he would not have considered them to be of any importance,
And, O praiser of the streams, I grant thou hast not visited the encircling ocean, but dost thou know nothing of it?
He who has seen the pearl will not compare a stone with it,
And whoever has seen a Khalaf will not think of any other man.
Visit him and thou wilt visit a king who has been given four,[3]
That no one has acquired, so observe him and thou wilt see,
His days are bright and his countenance is as the moon,
His determination is like Fate and his gifts like rain;
I ceased not to praise people whom I thought
To be the purity of the age but, compared with him, they were turbid.'

Said 'Ísá ibn Hishám: So I asked: 'Who is this compassionate and generous king?' He replied: 'How can that be which the imagination cannot grasp, and how can I express that which reason will not accept? Now, when was there a king who disdained noble men when they gave silver[4] while gold, a thousand pieces of it, is the easiest thing for him to give and nothing vexes him but evil words?'[5] And a mountain of collyrium is

[1] سُقْتُ *I extended:* Literally, I drove.

[2] *O nocturnal traveller:* Metre, *basit.*

[3] بِأَرْبَعَةٍ *Four:* That is, four things.

[4] الدَّرَاهِمُ *Silver:* Literally, dirhems.

To obtain the required sense in line 11, p. 229 (Text) *for* يَعُمُّهُ *read* يَغُمُّهُ.

[5] الخَلْفُ *Evil words:* For this meaning of the word cf. سَكَتَ أَلْفًا وَنَطَقَ خَلْفًا.

decreased by the style, then how is it this bountiful giving does not affect his fortune? And can there be a king, who, in the matter of bounty, is referable to squandering, and, in the matter of character, to sublimity, and, in the matter of religion, to devotion, and, in the matter of royalty, to universal empire, and, in the matter of origin, to the most ancient, and, in the matter of descendants, to the most recent?

> 'Would that I knew[1] what he, whose gracious qualities these are, expects to get more by reaching the Pleiades.'

XLVI. THE MAQAMA OF THE YELLOW

'ÍSÁ IBN HISHÁM related to us and said: When I desired to return from the Pilgrimage there came into my presence a youth and he said: 'I have a young man of yellow origin who invites to unbelief and dances upon the finger. Exile has disciplined him. The desire for recompense has brought me to thee that I might represent his case before thee. He has demanded of thee in marriage a yellow damsel[2] that pleaseth the company and rejoiceth the beholders. Now, if thou dost assent, there will be begotten of them both an offspring[3] that will fill the regions and men's ears. And when thou hast folded this robe[4] and rolled up this thread[5] it will have preceded thee into thy country. Therefore now decide regarding the unfolding of what is in thine hand.'

He held his tongue from a thousand words and then uttered the wrong thing. Cf. Letters, p. 339, and

ومن هتمنى خلفًا فجزاه مائة ألف

'He who reviles me with evil words, his reward will be a hundred thousand (of them).'

For another extraordinary eulogy on Khalaf see p. 433 of the Letters and p. 58 of the *Diwán*. Khalaf's cruel treatment of his sons, his treachery towards the governor of Kirman, and the murder of the Qáḍi Abú Yúsuf show that he was not the paragon of excellence Hamadhání makes him appear to be. See Ibn al-Athír, ix, 58-9.

1 *Would that I knew:* Metre, *basit*.

2 *A yellow damsel:* An allusion to Qur'án, ii, 64.

3 *An offspring:* That is, praise.

4 *When thou hast folded this robe:* Cf. the third Maqáma, p. 33.

5 قد سبقك It (i.e. praise) will have preceded thee.

Said 'Ísá ibn Hishám: I was astonished at his narration and his witticism in his solicitation, so I complied with his request. Then he recited saying:—

'By the lower hand,[1] glory is duped,
But the hand of the generous man and his judgement are supreme.'[2]

XLVII. THE MAQAMA OF SARIAH

'ÍSÁ IBN HISHÁM related to us and said: While we were at Sariah[3] with the governor thereof there came before him a youth with the fragrance of saffron upon him. So the assembly stood up for him and, out of respect, he was seated in the chief place; but awe of him hindered me from asking him his name. Then he began and said to the governor: 'What hast thou done with yesterday's discussion, perhaps thou hast relegated it to oblivion?'[4] He said: 'God forbid! but there has hindered me from attaining to it a reason which it is impossible to explain, and one whose wounds[5] cannot be healed?' Said the intruder: 'Sirrah, the delay in the fulfilment of this promise has been long, and I shall not find thy morrow regarding it other than thy to-day, or

[1] *By the lower hand:* Metre, *kamil.* يَدُ ٱلسُّفْلَى *The lower hand:* The receiving or begging hand. *As opposed to the supreme or superior*, i.e. the giving hand. A tradition of the Prophet ٱلْيَدُ ٱلْعُلْيَا خَيْرٌ مِنَ ٱلْيَدِ ٱلسُّفْلَى supports the explanation given in the note. See Musnad of Imam Ibn Hanbal. (Ob. 241 A.H.) vol. ii, p. 524, line 13, vol. iii, page 402, line 14, and p. 503, line 10. Also al-Jamá al-Saghīr with commentary by al-Zubeidī, part i, pp. 97-98, lines 20-23 and line 1 respectively. Cf. English Bible: 'It is more blessed to give than to receive' (Acts xx. 35.). Also the line of the poet:

فَانَّكَ لَا تَدرِى اِذَا جَا سَائِلٌ * أأَنتَ بِمَا تُعطِيهِ أم هُوَ اَسعَدُ

For verily thou knowest not when a suppliant comes whether he or thou art more blessed through what thou givest him. (Al-Jamá al-Ṣaghīr, part i, p. 97.) See note on page 40.

[2] *But the hand of the generous man and his judgement are supreme:* The fact of the generous man being beguiled into giving is not to be attributed to the weakness of his intellect. Cf. *Ḥariri*, i, 31, on the subject of the dinar.

[3] *Sariah:* A town in Tabaristan (Mazandaran) and the seat of the governor during the rule of the Ṭáhirides.

[4] اَلْمَنسِى *Oblivion:* Probably an allusion to Qur'án, xix, 23.

[5] *Whose wounds:* That is, the effects of his inability to perform what he had promised.

thy to-day concerning it other than thy yesterday. In promise breaking, I can only compare thee to the Salix Aegyptia tree whose blossoms fill the eye, but there is no fruit there.'

Said 'Ísá ibn Hishám: When he had reached this point,[1] I cut him short and said: 'God guard thee, art thou not al-Iskanderí?' He answered: 'And perpetual may thy preservation be, how excellent is thy sagacity!' Then I said: 'Welcome to the commander of speech and to the stray of the generous.[2] I have searched for it till I found it, and sought it till I obtained it.' Then we became mutually friendly till the highland attracted me and the lowland swallowed him. I ascended and he descended, and I fared eastwards and he westwards. After his departure, I said:—

'O would that I knew of a brother[3] whose hands were straitened, but whose fame was extensive·
Last night he passed with me, but where will he pass this our night?
May poverty not prosper,[4] for he is its exile, and, owing to poverty, I have been deprived of him.
I will surely place over it, in Khalaf ibn Ahmad, one who will destroy it.'

XLVIII. MAQAMA OF TAMIN

'ÍSÁ IBN HISHÁM related to us and said: I was appointed to the governorship of a province in Syria. There arrived there Sa'd ibn Badr[5] of the tribe of Fazára, and he was made wazir. Ahmad ibn Walid[6] was placed over the postal department,

[1] هذا المكان *This point*: Literally, this place.

[2] ضالة الكرام *The stray of the generous*—That is the stray *camel* of the generous to which 'Ísá ibn Hishám here compares al-Iskanderí.

[3] *O would that I knew of a brother*: Metre, *kamil*.

[4] لا درّ درّ الفقر *May poverty not prosper*: Literally, may the milk of poverty not flow copiously!

[5] *Sa'd ibn Badr. The Fazárite*; I have not been able to identify this individual with any of the important persons of this tribe mentioned in the Ansáb of al-Sam'ání, pp. 427-8.

[6] *Aḥmad ibn al-Walid*: I have not been able to identify this person and the name is probably fictitious.

Khalaf ibn Sálim[1] was posted to the court of appeal, one of the Banú Thowába[2] was appointed to the secretariat, and the assessment office was given to a Syrian. Therefore the country became the delight of the intellectuals and their alighting-place. And they ceased not to arrive, one after the other, until they filled the eyes of the townsfolk and oppressed their minds. And among those that came, there arrived Abú'l-Nadá, the Temímite,[3] but eyes rested not upon him and hearts were not sincere towards him.

One day he came into my presence, and I appreciated him at his true worth, I seated him in the chief place of the assembly and I said: 'What hope has the Master in life and how does he find his affairs?' He looked right and left and then he said: 'Between loss and meanness, between baseness and contempt, and a people like donkey's dung. Prosperity smells them[4] but they are evil-smelling. They are treated with kindness, but show none, By Heavens! I have come to find them to be a people who resemble human beings only in head and dress.' And he began to recite:

'O land of Sijistán[5] may the countries be a ransom for thee!
And for the noble king the people!
And even if the days will help me,
And if mount and provisions take me there,
Still who will compensate me for what has perished of it,
And for the life which cannot be restored?'[6]

[1] *Khalaf ibn Sálim*: This name is probably fictitious.

[2] *Banú Thowába*: The name of a family, originally Christians, not of a tribe as stated by the commentator, distinguished as official writers or secretaries of state. The most accomplished member of the family was Abú 'Abd Alláh ibn Aḥmad ibn Thowába, secretary to the Khalifa Mu'taḍid (A.H. 279–89). See Fehrist, p. 130.

[3] *Abú'l-Nadá, the Temímite*: This is probably another fictitious name. There is no trace of any such person in the Ansab of al-Sam'áni, p. 109.

[4] يَشَمُّهُم *It smells them*: The commentator says it means 'to regard with favour or consideration.' It seems to signify to test by experiment which, perhaps, by an extension of meaning, may be said to connote to pay attention to, to take notice of and the like.

[5] *O land of Sijistán*: Metre, *wafir*.

[6] *Still who will compensate me for what has perished of it (time), And for the life which cannot be restored*: That is, what will make up for the time I have

XLIX. THE MAQAMA OF WINE

'ÍSÁ IBN HISHÁM related to us and said: In my early youth I happened to have an equable temperament and accurate judgement, and so I held the balances of my reason even and counterbalanced my seriousness with my jesting. And I adopted some friends for love and others for pleasure. I set apart the day for the people and the night for the wine-cup. He said: 'Now one night there assembled with me some familiar friends, masters of pleasant ideas, and we ceased not to hand one another the stars of the drinking-bowls [1] until the wine we had was exhausted.'

He said: 'The boon-companions were unanimous in their decision to broach the wine vats, and we drew forth their contents [2] and they remained like the shell without the pearl, or a country without a free-born man.' He said: 'When we felt the effect of that our predicament, mischievous inclinations led us to the inn of the female vintner. The brocade of night was green and its waves were tumultuous. Now when we had begun to wade along, the crier of the morning [3] chanted the summons to prayer and so the fiend of youthful lust shrank back,[4] and we hastened

lost, when absent, and for that portion of my life spent away from Sijistán, which cannot be recalled? This is a somewhat obscure passage and the commentator has understood it to refer to the death of the ruler, Khalaf ibn Aḥmad, but this cannot be as Khalaf died in A.H. 399 the year following the death of al-Hamadhání (A.H. 398). It is evident this maqáma was composed before A.H. 393, the year in which Sijistán was wrested from Khalaf by Maḥmúd of Ghazna. See note on page 148, *supra*. Cf. the following parallel lines by 'Alí Ḥusain, Governor of Ahwaz, brother of Sharaf al-Daula imprisoned and put to death by his uncle in A.H. 375.

هَبِ ٱلدَّهرُ أرضَانِى وَأعتبَ صَرفُهُ * وَأعقبَ بِٱلحُسنَى وَفَكَّ مِنَ ٱلأَسرِ
فَمَن لِى بِأيَّامِ ٱلشَّبَابِ ٱلَّتِى مَضَتْ * وَمَن لِى بِمَا قَدفَاتَ فِى ٱلحَبسِ مِن عُمْرِى

Grant that time may conciliate me, and its vicissitudes regard me with favour,
That it recompense me with kindness and release (me) from captivity,
Still, who will compensate me for the days of youth that have gone,
And who will make up for me for what has been lost of my life in prison?

Ibn al-Athir, ix, 31.

1 *The stars of the drinking-bowls*: That is the cups of sparkling wine.

2 نَفْسَهَا *Their contents*: Literally, their soul.

3 مُنَادِى ٱلصُّبحِ *The crier of the morning*: That is, the Mu'adhin (muezzin).

4 خَنَسَ *Shrank back*: Cf. ٱلخَنَّاسُ the epithet applied to the devil because he shrinks at the mention of God. See Qur'án, cxiv, 4 and Baiḍáwí, *Commentary*

forward to obey the call, and stood behind the Imám with the standing of the noble pious, with dignity, sedateness, and measured movements. For every commodity hath its time and every craft its place.

Now our Imám was energetic in his bending and rising, and by his delay was inviting us to slap him, till he came to his senses and raised his voice to pronounce the final salutation. Then he sat cross-legged at a side of the niche, turned his face towards his audience,[1] looking down for a long time and snuffed the air continually. Then he said: ' O people, he who has rendered his conduct unseemly, and is afflicted with his foul behaviour, should remain at home,[2] instead of polluting us with his breath, for verily all this day I have perceived the fumes[3] of the mother of enormities[4] from some of the people. Now what is the desert of him who has passed the night prostrated by the influence of Ṭaghút[5] and then comes betimes to these houses[6] which God hath commanded to be raised, and hath purposed

---

(Fleischer ed,) ii, 424. A similar idea is suggested in Faust by Mephistopheles shrinking at the sight of the cross or the sound of sacred music.

[1] أَصْحَابَهُ *His audience :* Literally, his companions.

[2] دِيمَاسَهُ *At home :* Literally, at his house ; Dozy's opinion is that the word دِيمَاس is arabicized from the Greek. Cf. δομος a house. δημος, people, δημοσιος a public place belonging to the public, a state prison. The name of Hajjaj's dungeon at Wasıt, half way between Baṣra and Kufa (Yaqut, ii, 712). The word is found in Rabinnical Hebrew דימוס

[3] *The fumes :* According to the law of Abú Ḥanífa a man does not render himself liable to scourging (حَد) because he smells of wine, unless witnesses give evidence, or he himself admits, that he has actually drunk wine. The mere smell, adds the same authority, is not sufficient, for the odour consequent upon eating a quince would be precisely the same. *Mabsút,* xxiv, 31.

[4] أُمّ ٱلْكَبَائِرُ *The mother of enormities :* Cf. the more popular term أُمّ ٱلْخَبَائِث mother of vices, wine.

[5] ٱلطَّاغُوتُ *Ṭaghút :* According to Baiḍáwí, *Commentary,* i, 213, it means any vain thing which is worshipped. It signifies an idol or whatever is worshipped besides God, and particularly the two goddesses of the Meccans, al-Lát and al-'Uzzá, and also the devil and any seducer (Sale's translation of the Qur'án, p. 28 note). See Qur'án, iv, 54, and liii, 19.

[6] *To these houses :* An allusion to Qur'án, xxiv, 36. The term houses quoted from the Qur'án is applied to those edifices set apart for divine worship, particularly the principal temples of Mecca, Madína and Jerusalem. Baiḍáwí, *Commentary,* ii, 25.

that the last of these should be cut off?'[1]—and he pointed to us. Then was the congregation incited against us, and they fell upon us till our outer-wrapper garments were torn to tatters, the napes of our necks were covered with blood, and we vowed to them we would not revert to it. Then we escaped from among them with difficulty, but, owing to our escaping safely,[2] we all forgave such a calamity.[3] We enquired of the children that passed by us concerning the Imám of that village and they said: 'It is the godly man Abú'l Fatḥ, al-Iskanderí.' So we exclaimed: 'Good gracious, occasionally a blind man receives his sight and a demon believes! And praise God! he has hastened in turning to Him and may God not deprive us of repentance like his.' And we passed the remainder of our day marvelling at his devotion in spite of what we knew of his immorality. He said: 'Now when the day was, or almost was, in its death throes, we beheld and lo! there were the banners of the wine-shops[4] like stars in a pitch-dark night. At the sight of them we exchanged gifts of gladness, announced to one another the glad tidings of a brilliant night, and arrived at the one with the biggest door and the stoutest dogs. And we made the dinar our leader and recklessness a thing inseparable from us. We were conducted to the possessor of a beautiful form, dalliance, and a slender waist,—when her glances killed, her words made alive again. She received us well and hastened to kiss our heads and hands while her aliens[5] hurried to unsaddle the camels and the horses.' Then we asked her concerning her wine and she said:—

'Wine, in sweetness,[6] deliciousness and pleasantness, like
the dew of my mouth,

1 *Should be cut off:* An allusion to Qur'án, viii, 7.

2 لِلسَّلَامَةِ *Escaping safely:* Another reading لِلسُّلَافَةِ For the sake of the old wine.

3 *We forgave such a calamity:* That is, we were glad to get away at all.

4 رَايَاتُ ٱلْحَانَاتِ *The banners of the wine shops:* Evidently in the time of the author the sale of intoxicants in Muslim lands was not prohibited and it was permitted to display flags to distinguish those institutions.

5 ٱلْعُلُوجُ *Aliens:* Plural of عِلْجٌ the term was applied first to foreigners, especially Persians, then to Christians who had become Muslims and to Muslims who had become Christians and, finally, to renegade foreigners in the service of Muslim princes.

6 *Wine in sweetness, like the dew of my mouth:* Metre, *kámil.*

> It leaves the clement one without the smallest quantity of
> the grace of his clemency.'

It is as if my grandfather's ancestors had pressed it from my cheek and coated it with pitch[1] like unto my separation and aversion; the trust of the ages, the hidden thing in the bosom of happiness. The righteous have not ceased to inherit it and the nights and the days to take away from it, until nought remaineth save aroma, rays, and a pungent flavour. It is the fragrance of the soul, the fellow-spouse of the sun,[2] the damsel of the lightning, a coaxing old dame. It is like the heat in the veins and the coolness of the gentle breeze in the throats, the illumination of thought and the antidote[3] to the poison of the age. With the like of it the dead is strengthened and raised to life again, and the one born blind is treated so that he sees. So we said: 'By thy father this is the stray! And who is the minstrel at thy court? Perhaps it is diluted for the drinkers with the sweet dew of thy mouth?' She said: 'Verily, I have an old man of pleasant disposition and rare humour. He met me on Sunday at the convent of Mirbad. He spoke to me confidentially till he pleased me, and so a friendship sprang up and joy recurred. He told me of his great honour, and of the nobility of his people in his own country that which directed my love to him, and made him a favourite, and you will soon make friends with, and have a longing for him.' He said: 'Then she called her old man, and lo! it was our Iskanderí, Abú'l-Fatḥ!' So I said: 'O Abú'l-Fatḥ! By heavens, it is as though he who recited *these lines* had looked upon thee and spoken with thy tongue:—

> 'In times gone by,[4] I had wisdom, religion and uprightness,
> Then praise God! we sold jurisprudence for the craft
> of the cupper.
> And, if we live but a little longer, God save us.'

[1] سَرْبَلُوهَا مِنَ ٱلْقَار *Coated it with pitch:* An allusion to the practice of besmearing the winevat with pitch.

[2] *The fellow spouse of the sun:* That is, something calculated to excite jealousy.

[3] تِرْيَاق *An antidote*; Probably arabicized from the Greek *θηριακα, φαρμακα,* antidotes against poisonous bites.

[4] *In times gone by:* Metre, *ramal.*

He said: 'Then he snorted as snorts the vain, he shouted, he grinned and laughed immoderately and then he said: "Is it said of the likes of me, is one like me proverbially spoken of?"'

'Cease from blaming,[1] but what a deceiver[2] thou perceivest me to be!
I am he whom every Tahamite and every Yemenite knows,
I am of every kind of dust, I am of every place.
At one time I cleave to the niche, at another to the location of the wine-shop.
And thus acts whoever is wise in this time.'

Said 'Isá ibn Hishám: 'I sought refuge with God from the like of his condition, and I marvelled at the holding back[3] of subsistence from men of his ilk. We enjoyed that week of ours with him and then we departed from him.'

L. THE MAQAMA OF THE QUEST

'Ísá ibn Hishám related to us and said: One day I joined a company like unto the flowers of spring, or the stars of night after the third watch, with bright countenances and agreeable dispositions. They resembled one another in appearance and were alike in good circumstances. And we began to pull the skirts of conversation and to open the doors of debate. Now there was in our midst a youth, short of stature among men, with clipped mustachios, who uttered not a word, nor entered with us into a description, until, finally, the discussion led us to the praise of wealth and its possessors, to the mention of property and its excellence and to the assertion that it is the adornment of men and the goal of perfection. Then, as if he had awoke from a sleep, or presented himself after an absence, he opened his diwán,[4] loosed his tongue, and said: 'Silence! Verily ye have failed in a thing that ye lack; ye have come short in the search of it and

[1] *Cease from blaming:* Metre, *ramal.*

[2] دَكَّاكٌ *A deceiver:* Literally, a demolisher, from دَكَّ he crushed or demolished, also one who mixes one substance with another, a cheat.

[3] قُعُود *Holding back:* Literally, sitting down. Cf. *Ḥariri*, p. 140.

[4] *His diwán:* Figuratively for his store of prose and poetry, his repertoire.

then despised it. Ye have been cheated out of the eternal by
the temporal, and the near[1] has preoccupied you to the exclusion
of the remote.[2] Is the world other than the camping-ground of
a camel-rider, or the hasty meal of the wayfarer? Is wealth
aught but a loan to be returned, or a trust to be given up? It is
transferred from one people to another, and those who come
first hoard it for those who come after. Do ye see wealth with
any but the niggards, to the exclusion of the generous? or with
the ignorant, to the exclusion of the learned? Beware of delusion,
for there is no glory except in one of two directions, and no
precedence save in one of two lots, noble pedigree or eminent
learning. And how excellent a thing is that whose bearer is
borne on people's heads, and whose aspirant despaireth not! By
heavens! were it not for the preservation of life and honour, I
should have been the richest man on earth. For I know of two
treasures, one of them is in the region of Tarsus[3] and men's
minds crave for it. It belongs to the treasures of the Amalekites
and to the stores of the Patricians.[4] There are in it a hundred
thousand pounds weight. As for the other, it is between
Sora[5] and Hilleh.[6] It contains of the treasures of the Persian

---

[1] الدَّانِي‎ The near: That is, the present life.

[2] النَّائِي‎ The remote: That is, the future life.

[3] غَرسُوس‎ Ṭarsus: A well-known ancient city in the fertile plain of Cilicia.
It was captured by the Arabs shortly after A.D. 660. For more than a century after
its conquest it was in ruins. But Hárún al-Rashíd rebuilt its wall in A.D. 787 and
made it the north-western capital of the Arab power in the long wars against the
Byzantine empire. The Khalífa Mamúm died and was buried here in A.H. 218
(August A.D. 833). The ruins of the ancient city are extensive but are deeply buried.
(Encyclopædia Britannica, xxvi, 433). The assertion that a treasure lay buried
here was, therefore, not inappropriate.

[4] بَطَارِقَة‎ Patricians: Plural of بِطْرِيق‎ a leader of an army, one who is over
ten thousand men. It is arabicized from the Latin patricius. From the time of
Constantine (A.D. 288-337) patrician became the title of a person high in office at
court.

[5] Sora: In Babylonia quite close to Hilleh and Waqf, the seat of a famous
Jewish academy founded in the third century A.D. by the renowned scholar Abba
Arika, which played a dominant rôle in Babylonian Judaism for several centuries.
It was noted for wine. Jewish Encyclopædia, i, 145, and Yaqút, iii, 184.

[6] الجَامِعَين‎ Hilleh: of Banú Mazyad, a town of Asiatic Turkey between Kúfa
and Baghdad and sixty miles south of the latter city. It is situated on both banks
of the Euphrates. Many of the houses of the town are built of bricks, not a few

kings[1] and of the hoards of the Tyrants sufficient for mankind and Jinn. Most of it consists of red rubies, pearls and gems, bejewelled crowns and ten thousand talents amassed.' Now when we heard that, we came before him, leaned towards him, and began to consider his judgement weak in being content with a scanty livelihood in spite of his being aware of these stores. Then he hinted that he was afraid of the Sulṭán and relied upon none of his brethren. So we said: 'We have heard thy argument and we accept thy excuse. Now, if thou wouldst see fit to do us a kindness, to oblige us, and to acquaint us with one of these treasures, on condition that two-thirds shall be thine, do so.' Then he extended his hand towards us and said: 'He who sends something in advance will find it again, and to him who knows what is obtainable the bountiful giving of money is easy.' So each one of us gave him what was ready to hand and was eager for what he had mentioned. Now, when we had filled his palm, he raised his eyes towards us and said: 'We must get a bare sufficiency[2] of the means of subsistence and obtain what will maintain strength.[3] Our time is short and, if God will, exalted be He! the meeting-place will be here to-morrow.'

Said 'Isá ibn Hishám: When that company dispersed, I sat after them for a while. Then I advanced towards him and seated myself before him and said—and verily I desired to make his acquaintance and my soul longed to converse with him: 'It is as though I knew thy pedigree and had met thee.' He said: 'Yes, a road united us and thou wast my travelling-companion.' So I said: 'Time hath changed thee to me and none made me forget thee except Satan.'[4]

of them bearing an inscription of Nebuchadnezzar, obtained from the ruins of Babylon which lie less than an hour away to the north. *Encyclopaedia Britannica*, xiii, 467; and Yaqút, ii, 10 and 322.

1 كُنُوزُ ٱلأكاسِرَة *The treasures of the Persian Kings:* The royal treasures which fell into the hands of the Arabs on the overthrow of the Persian monarchy in the Khalifate of 'Umar (A.D. 634–44) were enormous; see al-Fakhrí, p. 101. The term, consequently, came to be synonymous with immense wealth. Cf. Persian كنج.

2 عَلَقًا *A bare sufficiency:* Literally, that suffices the cattle of what they obtain from trees or plants; hence food sufficient to maintain life.

3 ما يُمسِك رَمَقًا *What will maintain strength:* Literally, what will arrest the remains (رَمَق) of life.

4 *None made me forget thee except Satan:* An allusion to Qur'án, xviii, 62.

Then he recited saying :—

'I am the tyrant of the time,[1] of folly I have many ideas
And, when money faileth, I spend from the purse of desires.
Whoever desires greedy feeding and deep drinking, to the sound[2] of the lute,[3]
And prefers the smooth-faced, oblivious of so and so, and so and so,
Thou wilt see him secure against wealth and prosperity.'

LI. THE MAQAMA OF BISHR

'ÍSÁ IBN HISHÁM related to us and said : Bishr ibn 'Awánah, the 'Abdite, was a robber, and he made a raid upon some riders on camels among whom was a beautiful woman whom he married. And he said : 'I have never seen the like of to-day.'[4] So she recited :—

'The intense blackness in my eye,[5] and a fore-arm white as silver have delighted Bishr,
Whilst there is near him, within view, one of slender waist walking proudly in a pair of anklets,
The most beautiful of those that walk on two feet.[6]
If Bishr were to bring her and me together,
My exile would be lasting and my separation prolonged :
And, if he were to measure her beauty with mine,
The morning would manifest itself to the possessor of two eyes.'[7]

[1] *I am the tyrant of the time :* Metre, *ramal.*

[2] عَزْفٌ *The sound :* Literally, a humming, or rumbling sound.

[3] المَثَانِى *The lute :* Literally, the chord (of a lute) composed of two strings, or, as some say, the second chord. See *Hariri*, i. 244.

[4] *I have never seen the like of to-day :* Cf. the saying (1) of al-Farazdaq, Ibn Qutaiba, *Sh'ir wa Shu'ará*, p. 49, and (2) of 'Amr ibn-Hind, when he heard 'Amr ibn Kúlthúm recite his qaṣida, *Mu'allaqát*, (edition by Lyall), p. 107.

[5] *The intense blackness in my eye :* Metre, *rejez.*

[6] *That walk on two feet :* Cf. Qur'án, xxiv, 44.

[7] *The morning would manifest itself to the possessor of two eyes :* Cf. a similar phrase quoted by Lane, p. 2647. Art. التَّبَسّ.

Said Bishr: 'Fie on thee! [1] Whom dost thou mean?' She replied: 'Thy paternal uncle's daughter, Fátima.' He asked: 'Is she as beautiful as thou hast described?' She answered: 'More so, and much more so.' Then he recited saying:—

'Fie on thee! O possessor of white front teeth, I did not think I would exchange thee;
But now thou hast signified by allusion, the valley is open to thee, so sing and lay thine eggs.[2]
Mine eyelids shall not close in slumber until I raise mine honour from base degrees.'

So she said:—

'Many a wooer [3] has importunately pressed his suit for her,
While she is cousin to thee, the daughter of a paternal uncle, closely related.' [4]

Then he sent to his uncle asking for his daughter in marriage, but the uncle denied him his request.[5] Therefore he swore not to show any of them any consideration, if he would not marry his daughter to him. So he inflicted many injuries upon them, and continuously vexed them. Therefore the men of the tribe assembled before his uncle and said: 'Save us from thy madman.' He replied: 'Clothe me not with infamy, [6] but respite me that I may destroy him by stratagem.' They said: 'Do so.' Then his uncle said to him: 'I have sworn not to marry this my

1 *Fie on thee!* Metre, *rejez.*

2 *So sing and lay thine eggs:* A variation of Tarafa's line. See Freytag, *Arab Proverbs*, i, 432.

3 *Many a wooer:* Metre, *rejez.*

4 لَبِحًّا *Closely related:* That is, his first cousin.

5 *The uncle denied him his request:* Cf. *Aghâni*, xii, 10. This refusal was a breach of Bedawin law 'which acknowledges a right in first cousins to the hands of marriageable daughters. At the present day the consent of all first cousins on the father's side must be obtained to a girl's marriage with a stranger.' Blunt's translation of the romance, *The Stealing of the Mare*, pp. 8 and 122.

6 لَا تُلبِسُونِى عَارًا *Clothe me not with infamy:* By asking him to save them from his madman because (1) he was unable to put a stop to his ravages by force, and (2) if he were now to give his consent to the marriage, he would expose himself to the charge of having submitted to *force majeure* himself.

daughter, save to him who will drive to her a thousand she-camels as a dowry, and I will be satisfied with none but the she-camels of the Khuzá'ah.'[1] Now the object of the uncle was that Bishr should traverse the road between him and the Khuzá'ah so that a lion might tear him to pieces; for the Arabs used to avoid that way in which there was a lion named Dadh and a serpent called Shuja'. One of them says concerning her:—

'Swifter to slay[2] than Dadh[3] and Shuja'.
If Dadh is the king of beasts, she is the queen of serpents.'

Then did Bishr travel that road, but he had not traversed half of it when he met the lion. His colt reared and beat the ground with its hind-feet. So he alighted and hamstrung it. Then he drew his sword on the lion, attacked it and cut it in two, breadthwise. Then he wrote with the blood of the lion on his shirt to his cousin:—

'O Fáṭima,[4] if thou hadst been present in the valley of Khabt,[5] when the lion met thy brother Bishr,
Then thou wouldst have seen a lion[6] visiting a lion, the lion victorious meeting another.
"He advanced proudly,[7] and my colt timidly drew back and I exclaimed, "Mayest thou be slaughtered for a colt!
Let both my feet reach the surface of the ground, for I perceive the earth has a surer back than thou."

[1] *Khuzá'ah:* The name of an Arab tribe.

[2] *Swifter to slay than* Dadh: Metre, *rejez.*

[3] ذَاذ D*adh:* According to Dozy the people of North-West Africa call the white chameleon اَلذَّاذ اَلْوَحِيد, The unique dadh.

[4] أَفَاطِمُ O *Fáṭima:* Metre, *wafir.* An example of apocopation. These verses are attributed to 'Amr ibn M'adí Kariba, but the commentator considers it merely a coincidence of ideas and that the lines refer to two distinct episodes. See *Hamasa,* i, 73. Cf. al-Wasáṭa, pp. 109-111.

[5] *Khabt:* There are four places of this name: (1) the desert of al-Jamísh, between Mecca and Madina. (2) The oases of Kalb. (3) Bazwá, between Mecca and Madina. (4) A village in Yemen. Yaqút, ii, 397.

[6] هِزَبْر *A (fierce sturdy) lion:* According to Dozy it is the name of an animal which resembles the wild cat found in Abyssinia.

[7] تَبَهْنَس *He advanced proudly:* Literally, he played the lion (بَهْنَسَ). Freytag says the word also means an obsequious camel. Cf. *Hariri,* p. 376, line 5.

And I said to him[1]—and he had displayed sharpened fangs and a frowning face;
In treachery one of his paws gripped the ground while he stretched forth the other to pounce upon me,
Indicating his strength of claw, sharpness of fang and glances thou wouldst reckon to be live coals;
And in my right hand was a keen edge, upon whose blade the trace of deadly blows remains—
Hath it not reached thee what its keen edges did .at Káẕima,[2] the morning I met ‘Amr?
And my heart is like thine, it dreads not the attack, then how should it fear intimidation?
And thou desirest for the cubs food, and I seek for the paternal uncle's daughter a dowry.
Therefore in respect of what dost thou induce one like me to turn his back, and, perforce, to place his life in thy hands?
I have admonished thee, O lion, therefore seek other than me as food, for verily my flesh is bitter.
But when he thought my counsel insincere and he disagreed with me, as though I had spoken vainly,
He moved and I moved, like two lions desiring one object, which, when they sought it, they found to be difficult of attainment.
I shook the sword at him and I thought verily I had with it drawn forth the dawn in the darkness.
And I bestowed upon him a deadly blow, which showed him that it told him false when it promised him it would betray me.
I let the Indian sword in my right hand go, and it slashed ten of his ribs.
So he fell on the ground covered with blood, and it was as though in him I had demolished a lofty edifice.
And I said to him; "It is to me a hard thing[3] that I have slain my like in courage and glory.

1 لَهُ *To him:* That is, to the lion.

2 *Kaẕima:* A desert in the direction of the coast between Baṣra and Baḥrein.

3 *It is to me a hard thing:* Cf. Letters, p. 80.

But thou didst desire a thing that none beside thee desired, therefore, O lion, I could not endure it.
Thou didst endeavour to instruct me to flee; by the life of thy father! thou didst attempt a difficult thing.
But grieve not, for thou didst meet an ingenuous one who is careful not to be blamed, therefore, thou hast died honourably.
For, if thou art slain, there is no disgrace, for thou didst meet one freeborn on both sides?" '

Now, when these lines reached his uncle, he repented of his forbidding him to marry her, and he feared lest the serpent might suddenly attack him. So he arose, went in his track, and came up with him when the fierceness of the serpent had taken possession of him, but, when he saw his uncle, rage of the days of savagery[1] seized him, so that he put his hand into the serpent's mouth, thrust his sword into her and said :—

'A Bishr, whose ambition[2] for greatness is far-reaching; when his uncle saw him in the open plain,
It was as though he were bereft of himself, and his mother were bereft of him;
She attacked with an attack that caused him concern.
Then he arose against the offspring of the desert and his hand and sleeve disappeared in its mouth.
And its life is my life, and my venom is its venom.'

Now when he had slain the serpent, his uncle said: 'Verily I exposed thee to danger in a matter from which God hath diverted me. So return, that I may marry thee to my daughter.' Now when he turned back, Bishr filled his mouth with boasting, until there appeared on his horse a beardless youth, like unto the crescent moon, enveloped in his weapons. So he said: 'O Uncle, I hear the sound of a quarry.' And he went forth and behold, a spear's length off, a young man who said: 'May thy mother be bereft of thee! O Bishr, if thou hast slain a worm and a beast, dost thou fill thy jaws with boasting? Thou art safe if thou

[1] الْجَاهِلِيَّة *The days of savagery:* Generally called the 'Days of the Ignorance,' or period of paganism, in Arabia before Islám.

[2] *A Bishr, whose ambition:* Metre, *rejez.*

surrender thy uncle.' Said Bishr: 'Perish thy mother! Who art thou?' He answered: 'The black day and the red death.'[1] Said Bishr: 'May she, who excreted thee, be bereft of thee.' He retorted: 'O Bishr and she that excreted thee.' Then each one attacked the other, but Bishr could do nothing to him, while the youth was able to inflict upon him twenty thrusts in the region of the kidneys,[2] but, as often as the point of the spear touched him, he prevented it from wounding his body, in order to spare him. He said: 'O Bishr, what thinkest thou? Could I not, if I wished, have given thee as food to the point of the spear?'[3]

He then threw down the spear, drew his sword, and struck Bishr twenty blows with the flat of the blade, but Bishr could not deal him one. Then he said: 'O Bishr, surrender thy uncle and go in safety.' He replied: 'Yes, on condition that thou tell me who thou art.' He said: 'I am thy son.' He[4] exclaimed: 'Good gracious! I have never approached a worthy woman, whence then this gift?' He answered: 'I am the son of the woman who directed thee to thy uncle's daughter.' Then said Bishr:—

'That staff is from this stave.[5]
Does the serpent bring forth other than the serpent?'[6]

And he swore never to ride a noble steed or wed a fair lady. Then he married his uncle's daughter to his son.

[1] أَلْمَوتُ الأَحْمَر *Red death:* Death by the sword.

[2] *In the region of the kidneys:* Literally, in his kidneys.

[3] أَنْيَابُ ٱلرُّمح *The point of the spear:* Literally, the fangs of the spear.

[4] قَالَ *He* (Bishr) *exclaimed.*

[5] تلكَ ٱلعَصَا من هَذه ٱلعُصَيَّة *That staff is from this stave:* Metre, *rejez.* Freytag, *Arab Proverbs*, i, 17 and Meidání (Bulak), i, 12. Al-'Asá is said to have been the name of a famous horse belonging to Jadhima'l-Abrash and 'Auṣayyah' that of its mother. See *Journal Asiatique, Mars*, 1838, pp. 245-51. Cf. English, 'A chip of the old block'.

[6] *Does the serpent bring forth other than the serpent:* Cf. Letters, p. 165.

17602438R10115

Printed in Great Britain
by Amazon